WORLD HEALTH ORGANIZATION

INTERNATIONAL AGENCY FOR RESEARCH ON CANCER
AND
INTERNATIONAL ASSOCIATION OF CANCER REGISTRIES

CANCER REGISTRATION

AND ITS TECHNIQUES

ROBERT MACLENNAN   CALUM MUIR   RUTH STEINITZ
ALI WINKLER

TECHNICAL EDITOR FOR IARC
W. DAVIS

IARC Scientific Publications No. 21

INTERNATIONAL AGENCY FOR RESEARCH ON CANCER
LYON
1978

The International Agency for Research on Cancer (IARC) was
established in 1965 by the World Health Assembly as an independently
financed organization within the framework of the World Health Organization.   The headquarters of the Agency are at Lyon, France, and it
has Research Centres in Iran, Kenya and Singapore.

The Agency conducts a programme of research concentrating particularly on the epidemiology of cancer and the study of potential
carcinogens in the human environment.   Its field studies are supplemented by biological and chemical research carried out in the Agency's
laboratories in Lyon and, through collaborative research agreements,
in national research institutions in many countries.   The Agency
also conducts a programme for the education and training of personnel
for cancer research.

The publications of the Agency are intended to contribute to the
dissemination of authoritative information on different aspects of
cancer research.

ISBN 92832 11219

PRINTED IN SWITZERLAND

WHO-IARC CANCER PATIENT INFORMATION SYSTEM

In 1976 the WHO Handbook for Standardized
Cancer Registries (Hospital-Based) was
published (WHO Offset Publications No. 25,
World Health Organization, Geneva).

This present publication has incorporated
the items of information from the WHO Handbook, and is intended for all types of
cancer registries.

The main aim of the WHO-IARC Cancer Patient
Information System as presented here and in
the above-mentioned publications is to
facilitate the international exchange of
comparable information derived from cancer
registration.

The information system could serve as a
base-line for inter-institutional and international evaluative studies or even clinical
trials in cancer, serving thus not only cancer
services but also cancer research.

CONTENTS

A cancer registry can serve many purposes: assessment of cancer incidence; centralizing patient records; systematic collection of clinical data; assessment of present and future needs for cancer services. The registry is also one of the more useful epidemiological research tools available for assessing the causes of cancer in man, providing not only data on geographical and temporal differences in cancer risk on which to build etiological hypotheses, but also an economical mechanism for the follow-up of industrial and other groups with specific exposures.

In recent years it has been realized that it would be advantageous if cancer registries could collect their data in as comparable a manner as possible. Developing countries are becoming aware of the need to have more accurate information about their cancer problems, problems which will become more prominent as infectious diseases are controlled. These considerations suggested the need for an authoritative text dealing with all aspects of cancer registration, whether hospital- or population-based. While all registries are unlikely to wish to collect the same data, the definitions of items and codes used should be uniform to permit comparisons. It is thus hoped that this monograph will become a standard work of reference.

Those about to start a cancer registry should examine critically the purposes for which the registry is being established. Registration for its own sake is not a sufficient reason to begin an undertaking that requires a long-term investment of effort and funds. There is a great deal to be said for starting simply, with limited aims. If necessary, the scope of registration can later be expanded along the lines suggested in the monograph.

The present publication is the result of collaboration between the International Agency for Research on Cancer, the Cancer Unit of the World Health Organization and the International Association of Cancer Registries. A major contribution, especially on techniques of registration, came from Dr Ruth Steinitz of the Israel Cancer Registry; Dr C.S. Muir of IARC took a special interest in the sections dealing with the classification and coding of neoplasms; Dr A. Winkler of the WHO Cancer Unit developed the WHO Handbook for Standardized Cancer Registries (Hospital-Based) which has been incorporated into Chapter 4. Dr R. MacLennan of IARC, responsible for the project since 1975, reorganized and wrote much of the text.

John HIGGINSON, M.D.

Director

International Agency
for Research on Cancer,
Lyon, France

PREFACE

The attack on the group of diseases we call cancer is being
conducted throughout the world and on many fronts. Methods of
diagnosis, forms of therapy, means of prevention, are continually
being improved, but advances are often slow and hesitant, and
genuine breakthroughs are rare.

The role of the cancer registry

The cancer registry plays the central role in the systematic
collection, recording and analysis of data relating to individual
cases of cancer in a specific area. Its aim is to include on its
register details of every case that occurs within its defined boundaries
or, more precisely, that occurs among people who are normally resident
within those boundaries. For each such case it is the function of the
registry to record, as fully and as accurately as may be possible, both
a clinical description of the extent of the disease and also information
which will identify the patient, the tumour, the hospital and the
clinicians involved with the case. When these data are combined with
additional information describing treatment and subsequent progress
(routine follow-up), in which recurrences, metastases and further treatment are included, terminating with the date and cause of death
(whether from cancer or not), a very full and invaluable data bank can
be created, which will in the course of time yield a unique fund of
material concerning the natural history of the disease in the registry's
area. With time, trends of incidence may be used to identify possible
etiological factors, and changes in the pattern of development of the
disease, perhaps in relation to methods of treatment, will be reflected
in the rates of survival.

Not every registry will be able to include all of the ramifications
outlined above, although the majority will aspire to do so, as time and
opportunity permit. Many begin as hospital-based registries, or as
outgrowths based on the records of a laboratory of histopathology, but
the advantages of a population base for the construction of incidence
rates provides a strong motivation for a more extensive collection of
cases. This monograph describes not only the many varieties of cancer
registry which can exist, but it also provides guidelines which help to
maximize the usefulness of the data collected in each type; furthermore, it describes the necessary transitions for upgrading to a more
comprehensive version. Although it cannot adequately cover every
situation, it is derived from a broad base of experience, and its
recommendations are therefore practicable and tested.

The value of good relations

The cancer registry, in the collection of all the data referable to each case of cancer, must seek its information from a variety of sources; the importance of good liaison with those who supply such information quickly becomes apparent. These already have problems and difficulties of their own, and it may often appear that the registry is adding to that load, with little immediate benefit to show in return. It is thus essential to emphasize the *raison d'être* of the registry and the services it can provide, even after the lapse of a relatively short time, if its data are reasonably complete. The multidisciplinary nature of its information can foster the exchange of ideas, techniques and knowledge among all the participants, and particularly so if the registry plays an active and dynamic role in coordinating their interests. Physicians, surgeons, radiotherapists, chemotherapists, epidemiologists - all are finding a new unity of purpose and mutual respect in the science of oncology.

The importance of morbidity rates

Death is a clearcut event in time to which one or more causes can be assigned; the accuracy of these is likely to be improved if the death is medically certified, and is again improved if there is a necropsy report. Mortality statistics based on death certificates, related proportionately to the population at risk, have been available generally for a very long time, although their quality shows some variation. Morbidity statistics, on the other hand, are usually very much more difficult to obtain, except in the case of malignant disease in a region where there is a good cancer registry. For those cancers where survival is brief, mortality and morbidity show little difference; but as survival improves, so they diverge. In particular, non-melano-matous skin cancers are not often fatal, and thus appear only infrequent-ly in mortality statistics; yet these cancers can be sensitive indica-tors of changing exposure to a number of carcinogenic agents, such as are found in industry or from sunlight or sources of ultraviolet radiation, and only morbidity statistics can reflect these changes.

In short, cancer registries have an important contribution to make to the monitoring and control of malignant disease and to the detection of new carcinogenic agents. If this monograph succeeds, as I very much hope it will, in promoting the establishment of more and better cancer registries, and if it also succeeds in setting and maintaining common standards of classification and presentation so that their data will be directly comparable from one part of the world to another, it will have achieved a most valuable objective.

J.A.H. Waterhouse

President
International Association
Birmingham   of Cancer Registries
January 1978

ACKNOWLEDGEMENTS

This monograph on cancer registration has evolved over a number of years, and many persons contributed significantly to its conception and development. Although the original intention was to limit the scope to population-based registries, their close relationship with hospital registries led to the decision to include these as well.

The first publication in what it is hoped will be a WHO-IARC series providing a standard framework for the collection and use of information about cancer patients was the *WHO Handbook for Standardized Cancer Registries (Hospital-Based)* which appeared in 1976 and to which Drs N. Gray, A. Miller, J.A.H. Waterhouse and A. Winkler contributed substantially. Essentially all of that material has been incorporated in the present work, but with additions and changes in emphasis appropriate to population-based cancer registries. We are indebted to a considerable number of persons and organizations for permission to use and adapt their material, especially the American College of Surgeons for their *Cancer Registry Manual, 1974* and the late Mr P.M. Payne for his unpublished manuscript on cancer registration.

Among individuals who contributed, we are especially grateful to members of IARC staff, notably, Dr N. Breslow for material on data processing, Dr A. Tuyns who was closely involved in the early development of the project and Mrs J. Nectoux for assistance with the references. Dr J. Staszewski helped with the index and Dr K. Tanahashi of WHO, Geneva, advised on the organization of material relating to input and output operations.

Many cancer registries generously gave us copies of their procedure manuals and offered helpful advice, especially those in Detroit, New Mexico, New Orleans, New Zealand and Seattle. Detailed comments have recently been made by Drs J. Berlie, N. Racoveanu, K. Shanmugaratnam, J. Staszewski, M. Thangavelu, J.L. Young and J.A.H. Waterhouse. Many others commented on earlier drafts.

Nevertheless, the authors accept full responsibility
for the present content and emphasis of the work.
Despite the expert editing of Mrs Elisabeth
Heseltine, the grammatical structure of some of the
text still reveals the varied linguistic backgrounds
of the authors, but we do not wish to further delay
publication in a search for stylistic perfection.

It is realized that a first edition will have many
faults, and the authors would welcome criticism and
comment together with further examples of registration
problems and their solutions.

INTRODUCTION

1. INTRODUCTION

Cancer is regarded universally as a dreaded disease and an important health problem. Thus, 'cancer is the number one health concern of the American people. A poll conducted in 1966 showed 62% of the US public feared cancer more than any other disease' (US Senate, 1971). In a survey in Cali, Colombia, cancer was considered to be the most important unsolved health problem (MacLennan[1]). There is considerable international variation in the incidence of all cancers and much greater contrasts in the incidence at different sites. Even within a country, certain classes of people and certain geographical areas may be shown by cancer registration to have distinct patterns of cancer incidence.

Cancer registries are now in operation in many countries throughout the world, and many more are now considering their formation. Common to all is the desire to improve efforts towards cancer control by indicating the size of the cancer problem, its distribution in various segments of the population (age, sex, occupation, etc.), the organs most commonly attacked and, often, the survival of those affected. In the initial stages, most registries have benefited from the experience of established ones; however the majority have had considerable difficulties, both initially and subsequently. In the face of diverse local conditions, levels of competence and purposes of data collection, comparability has suffered most.

This monograph aims

(a) to promote the development of cancer registries, especially in those areas in which cancer occurrence is as yet poorly described, by indicating how a registry can be established and operated, and

(b) to facilitate international comparability of cancer data by providing common nomenclature and definitions of various aspects of cancer registration.

Great care has been taken to ensure compatibility with the *WHO Handbook for Standardized Cancer Registries (Hospital-based)* (WHO, 1976a).

Although the bias of the authors is towards population-based registries, the respective functions of and interrelationships between population-based and hospital cancer registries will be delineated and stressed throughout this monograph. Since conditions vary so widely,

---

[1] Unpublished data

the details of registration cannot always be the same in all countries. The general principles discussed are, however, universal, and examples are given to illustrate how local practices may differ.   Individual chapters are not intended to stand alone, and cross-references are made to other chapters.   Use should also be made of the index.

During the last few years several publications have appeared on cancer registration: *The Hospital Cancer Registry* (American Cancer Society, 1964); *The Registry in Cancer Control* (Knowelden et al., 1970); and manuals for use in the US SEER (Surveillance, Epidemiology and End Results) programme (NCI, 1974, 1975a) and by the American College of Surgeons (1974a).   The latter two publications help to ensure comparability of national data, and their programmes include some very extensive cancer registration systems.   Although they are compatible with a standard set in the *WHO Handbook* (WHO, 1976a), some of these publications go into such depth and detail that those who wish to begin cancer registration in a different situation may be discouraged. We believe that much can be done with simpler methods.   Various aspects of registration can be expanded, if necessary, to meet local needs while maintaining general comparability.

Since all cancer registries modify their procedures from time to time, even established registries may find some points of interest in this book, particularly with regard to the discussion of the new *International Classification of Diseases for Oncology* (WHO, 1976b).

A number of aspects of cancer registration are examined systematically.   The chapter on 'purposes' discusses the traditional concerns of hospital and population-based registries and how registries might be used in the future.   The planning of a registry is outlined next, and this is followed by a discussion of those items of patient information which should be collected.   It cannot be stressed too strongly that one should think small in order to maintain quality rather than volume.   The next chapters concern the collection of information and its processing by the registry; here, the underlying principles are outlined, and the details of data processing, which vary greatly and are undergoing rapid change, are discussed separately.   A chapter is devoted to special aspects of cancer registration in developing countries.   As mentioned previously, the chapters of the monograph do not stand on their own, and each must be considered in conjunction with others; e.g., items of information (Chap. 4), sources of information (Chap. 5), case finding and collection of documents (Chap. 6) and input operations (Chap. 7) are very closely related.

2. PURPOSE OF CANCER REGISTRATION

2. PURPOSE OF CANCER REGISTRATION

2.1 *Overview*

The broad purpose of cancer registration is to help assess and control the impact of malignancies on the community. Hospital registries are primarily concerned with improving the care of cancer patients seen in hospitals, and with the evaluation of treatment. Population-based registries are mainly concerned with assessing the impact of cancer on the community. Most cancer registries are multi-purpose, and what is done in a particular registry will depend on its size, resources and orientation. Hospital and population-based registries have much in common but differ in emphasis and, consequently, in organization and operation and in possible areas of research. The characteristics of these two main types of cancer registry are summarized in Table 2.1. Some registries may be 'mixed' in function, and there is no absolute demarcation between the two main types. The term 'hospital registry' is used in the text rather than 'hospital-based registry' to distinguish the reference group of cancer patients (here, patients in a hospital) from the physical location of the registry (a population-based registry could be situated or 'based' in a hospital).

Table 2.1   Summary of characteristics of cancer registries

Characteristic	Hospital cancer registry	Population-based cancer registry
Primary concern	The cancer patient in hospital	Cancer in the community
Assessment of dimensions of the cancer problem	Number of diagnoses per year; relative frequencies of cancer by site	Cancer incidence and prevalence; trends in cancer incidence and survival
Contributions to:		
(a) Patient care	Active follow-up; contact with patient or physician	Indirect follow-up, e.g., *via* hospital and other sources of notification, including death certificates; useful for 'mobile' patients
	Shows time trends in ratio of early to late stages at time of diagnosis	Can assess 'state of the art', e.g., investigations by cancer centres compared with general patient care
	Describes length and quality of survival in relation to site, stage and treatment	Evaluates overall survival by site
(b) Research - treatment	Participates in clinical research to evaluate therapy	Provides background for clinical research
- prevention	Assists case-control studies by rapid notification	Assists case-control and prospective studies
	Develops and evaluates classification	
	Identifies groups with high and low relative frequencies of certain cancers	Identifies high and low incidence groups
(c) Health services	Helps assess quality of hospital care and cancer services in covered area	Helps assess effectiveness of preventive measures and community care
	Helps plan hospital facilities	Helps plan services for geographical areas
	Contributes to professional education	Contributes to professional and public education

Interest in a particular form of neoplasm may lead to the setting up of special (or *ad hoc*) tumour registries, e.g., those for uterine cervical cancer, bone tumours, etc.   Unlike comprehensive cancer registries, these are generally conceived for only a short-term existence.

2.2 *Definitions*

Cancer registration is the process of continuing, systematic collection of data on the occurrence and characteristics of reportable neoplasms.

A *population-based cancer registry* attempts to record information on reportable neoplasms that occur in a given, geographically-defined population.   A *hospital cancer registry* is limited to persons attending a given hospital, and generally neither the size of the population in the geographical area, nor the proportion of cases registered from it, are precisely known.   Special registries may be set up for other well-defined groups, such as persons employed in certain occupations or those with suspected carcinogenic exposure.

The '*continuing collection*' of data is the main feature that distinguishes cancer registration from a cancer survey, which is a time-limited, systematic collection of cases of cancer in a given population.

'*Systematic*' implies complete coverage of the various sources of cancer cases in a given population.

The term '*reportable neoplasms*' generally includes cancers at all sites (including *in situ*) and may include certain benign tumours or other neoplasms of uncertain behaviour, e.g., thyroid adenomas.   Due to differences in the availability of information, the lists of reportable neoplasms frequently differ in hospital and population-based registries.   Depending on local interests and conditions, certain malignant neoplasms e.g., basal-cell and squamous-cell carcinomas of the skin, may not be registered.

A *cancer registry* is an organization to which cases of reportable neoplasms are notified and by which this information is checked and processed.   Since benign neoplasms may also be reported, it is frequently referred to as a 'tumour registry'.   In practice, the terms 'cancer registry' and 'tumour registry' may be regarded as synonymous. In the United States, the functioning of such registries in hospitals is an important part of their cancer programme (American College of Surgeons, 1974b).

A cancer registry should not be confused with a *cancer centre*, which is a facility for the diagnosis, treatment and follow-up of cancer patients, and where laboratory and clinical research, including clinical trials, are normally undertaken.   Such a centre will often have its own tumour registry.   Non-cancer patients may also be examined because of the special diagnostic facilities available at such a centre, and persons at high risk may be examined regularly.

A *central cancer registry* is a coordinating facility of cooperating hospital registries in a specified geographic area, which collects, combines, compares and evaluates uniformly defined information on cancer patients (Ringel, 1970); it may or may not cover a geographically defined population.

A *cancer register* is simply a list of cases of reportable neoplasms.

2.3 *Assessment of the dimensions of the cancer problem*

Hospital registries. Hospital registries provide data on the relative frequency of cancer by site and, in some areas, can provide minimum incidence figures[1]. The number of diagnoses per year indicates the demand for cancer diagnosis and treatment but may seriously underestimate need.

One must always keep in mind, however, that material thus obtained may refer to a selected group of cancer patients: i.e., those who attend a certain hospital. They are rarely representative of all the cancer cases in a geographical region, and it is not unusual for patients seen at renowned cancer centres to represent only a fraction of the total. An estimate made in Belgium has placed this figure at approximately 25 per cent for that country.

Some hospitals claim to see the majority of cancer patients within a region; however, it is wise to confirm that this is so, for even under the most favourable circumstances there are certain categories of patients who, for one reason or another, do not attend. It is possible that cancers amenable to easy treatment, such as skin cancers and cancers of the cervix, are treated elsewhere, in dermatology and gynaecology services, respectively. Forms of cancer relevant to specialities that may not be represented in the hospital (for example, neurosurgery or endocrinology) may not be seen.

On the other hand, it frequently happens that famous cancer hospitals attract a clientèle not only from the region but also from other parts of the country, or even from foreign countries. Should the items of identity and residence not have been taken with desirable precision, these patients may subsequently be notified to the population-based cancer registry as residents of the region covered by the registration system, whereas in fact they are not. The population-based cancer registry is nevertheless well advised to register these persons, with a special indication for 'non-resident', for identification in case of readmission and to keep such cases out of incidence tabulations.

---

[1] A large hospital, especially in a developing country, may provide all diagnostic and treatment services for cancer in a city. Thus, for the population of that city the hospital registry can provide minimum incidence figures, termed as such because there is likely to be underreporting. Alternatively, the term 'reporting rate' may be used.

Population-based registries.   The extent of the cancer problem, and other aspects of epidemiology, can best be assessed by a population-based cancer registry.   Information concerning the incidence of cancer by site, sex, age and geographical region is needed in order to plan diagnostic and treatment facilities.   The prevalence of cancer by site, including the number of existing cases and the number that need medical care of different kinds, is also important information for planning: estimates are needed of the number of patients with breast cancer who require hospitalization as opposed to outpatient treatment and of the number of patients with 'benign' bladder papillomas who may need frequent admission for cystoscopy.   Although it is unlikely that population-based registries will have this information, data on the prevalence of cases enables them to extrapolate information from hospital registries to the community.

Other information needed for planning treatment services includes the anatomical site and geographical distribution of cases - useful for siting radiotherapy centres.   Data on time trends, which are provided by continuing cancer registration, can assist in longer-term planning, including projections of the number of hospital beds that will be required for cancer patients in the future.   It should be noted that the health services themselves can affect the quality of cancer registry data;   for instance, the location of a service and the mode of patient referral can affect its utilization and, in turn, the accuracy of diagnosis of cancer.

2.4 *Follow-up of cancer patients*

Hospital registries.   An important service to physicians and a contribution to patient care is the active participation of the hospital registry in follow-up, carried out by contacts with the patient and/or the physician.

The hospital registry needs very detailed, standardized information from follow-up examinations in order to assess treatment in its institution or group of institutions.   This has been done on a large scale by the French Enquête Permanente Cancer since 1943 and is currently done by the US National Cancer Institute (NCI, 1974, 1975a). Collaboration among oncologists, including follow-up according to a strict protocol, is of primary importance in clinical trials.

Hospital registries aim at a thorough documentation of the findings at follow-up examinations, of therapeutic methods and also of the quality of survival of the patient.   The end-point of follow-up is the death of the patient.   Data concerning causes of death, etc. are recorded for survival analyses and evaluation of treatment.

Whereas the US End Results programme attempted 95% follow-up, it is obvious that this may not be possible in other situations; e.g., benign and *in situ* lesions may be followed only for a limited period, or not at all;   relative absence of telephonic communications can be a severe handicap in developing countries. The knowledge that an organized follow-up will not be possible, however, should not prevent the giving of the best possible treatment.

Population-based registries. Follow-up by population-based registries is commonly indirect. The best method is to arrange that oncological clinics and treating physicians send regular follow-up reports to the registry. When hospital registries also exist in the same area, follow-up information should be readily available.

Some population-based registries (e.g., the South Metropolitan in the UK) provide a service to hospital oncologists by reminding them of the anniversary date and sending letters to the hospital for mailing to patients asking them to attend. However, it is almost impossible for the population-based registry, except under very favourable conditions, to obtain exact and complete follow-up information comparable to that collected by a hospital registry. To do so would involve an unnecessary duplication of effort; it is sufficient for the population-based registry to know where and how to find the detailed information if it should be requested.

Date and cause of death. The search for information on deaths among cancer patients is an important function of the population-based registry, and this information (including cause if possible) is passed on to the hospital registry, which may not have information on all deaths. The South Metropolitan Cancer Registry in the UK sends extracts of death certificates to the treating physician to complete the case record for the deceased patient.

Follow-up of all registered cases from a geographical area is desirable for the following reasons:

(a) Many hospital registries may lose sight of patients and have no information on their date of death.

(b) Survival rates based on population data may be different from those based on hospital data.

(c) Diagnoses coded in the registry can be validated. Follow-up information may lead to a change in diagnosis of malignancy or even to cancellation in a proportion of cases; cancellation of a diagnosis of cancer is rarely reported spontaneously to the registry.

Direct contact with patients. It cannot be emphasized too strongly that the population-based registry must not contact the patient or his family. The registry must be on guard to avoid being accused of interfering with the personal patient-physician relationship, for this would mean the end of cooperation with the medical profession. This may not always be fully understood by a student or physician who might be using registry data.

2.5 *General contribution to patient care and management*

'The effectiveness of (secondary) cancer control is best measured
by the survival rates attained.   However, such results can be brought
to light only through careful compilation of adequate clinical records,
covering the diagnosis, treatment and follow-up of patients with the
disease' (American Cancer Society, 1964).   By identifying patients,
the cancer registry could also assist social services to care for
socially handicapped persons (e.g., through provision of home care
and transportation).

Hospital registries.   Within the hospital context, the existence
of a cancer registry fosters the keeping of good records, ensuring
that a basic minimum of information is available for each patient in
no matter which service of the hospital he may be treated.   In addition
to the keeping of basic records, the registry may be charged with the
initiation of follow-up, inviting patients to attend on a given day
according to a predetermined scheme, or by reminding the treating
physician to do so.   Record keeping for controlled clinical trials
may be entrusted to the hospital registry.

The hospital registry can thus not only help the treating physician
to improve patient care by good standard record keeping and standard
follow-up procedures but can also potentially provide a considerable
amount of information about patient characteristics, such as age,
sex, socio-economic level, whether or not the case was seen at an
early stage and related factors, such as delays between symptoms and
diagnosis and between diagnosis and treatment.   Further, statistics
of a more administrative nature, such as facilities used, length of
time used, bed occupancy, etc., can be provided.   By furnishing exact
figures about the demands made by cancer patients on the facilities,
personnel and resources of the institution, including changes in these
demands with time, the hospital cancer registry can provide a sound
basis for hospital administration, planning, and evaluation of different
aspects of cancer control activities.

By meticulous follow-up, the hospital registry can, if it has
access to information on deaths, provide the basic material for
computations of survival.   A major contribution is the transmission
to the regional population-based registry, should one exist, of
accurate, 'clean', standard notification data.   Hospital registries
may also stimulate the improvement of medical records in general.

Population-based registries.   The population-based registry
usually contributes only indirectly to patient care and management.
It can be used to describe patient pathways and referral patterns,
e.g., patterns of hospitalization for patients with cancers at certain
sites.   Information from death certificates, collected whenever
possible, enables the evaluation of overall survival by site, thus
supplementing the more detailed information collected by hospital
registries.

2.6 *Cancer registries and medical research*

Hospital registries can assist the evaluation of therapy and, by rapid identification of cases, can assist case-control studies designed to elucidate etiological factors.   In a case-control study it is frequently very difficult to trace all the clinical and pathological records necessary for establishing the final diagnosis in the cases of cancer or to confirm that the controls were not cancer cases. For this task, a population-based cancer registry can be of great assistance;   it can also determine the proportion and other characteristics of the samples of cancer cases studied in relation to all cancer cases occurring in the same population during the relevant period.

Population-based registries can assist epidemiological research, the aim of which is the prevention of cancer, by elucidating causal factors, identifying high-risk groups, towards which preventive measures can be focused, and assessing the effects of preventive programmes.

2.6.1 *Elucidating the causes of cancer*

A description of the distribution of cancers, described in section 2.2 above, also contributes to an understanding of the causes of cancer by providing clues to etiology.   The population-based registry can further contribute by participating in and assisting epidemiological research and by monitoring the environment for new carcinogenic risks.   This potential has not been exploited by many registries, and the following is concerned more with the future than with the past.

Detecting associations with cancer.   Associations may be found between cancer and other data notified to the registry, e.g., between cancer at a specific site and an ethnic group, geographical region or occupation.   Although not necessarily causal (Berkson, 1946), such associations may lead to etiological hypotheses and to studies to test such hypotheses.   Linkage of cancer registers and registers of other diseases may also reveal associations.   Disease registers for specific conditions, e.g., congenital malformations, diabetes mellitus, tuberculosis, epilepsy, organ transplants, etc., already exist.   Programmes such as Hospital Activity Analysis (in the UK) have been in operation for a shorter period than have the specific disease registers, but as these collate information on all diagnoses, hitherto unsuspected associations might be discovered.

The linkage of personal data with the cancer registry may present many difficulties, the most important of which concerns confidentiality (section 3.4).   The technical problems of linkage vary according to the type and accuracy of the identifying information.

Surveillance and monitoring.   The purpose of surveillance and monitoring is to provide early warning of the presence of new carcinogens in the environment so that these may be investigated as soon as possible.   Cancer registries have a key role in discerning when

significant changes in incidence may have occurred by continuing
observation of populations (Muir et al., 1976).

Total population data as reported to the registry could be
monitored for changes over time: thus, an increase in lung cancer
and a decrease in gastric cancer have been detected by many registries.
Subdivisions of populations, such as by sex, age or occupation, or
different ethnic groups, could be identified within the registry and
analysed separately. However, the sensitivity of this type of surveillance would be relatively low, and a new carcinogen would be
unlikely to be detected unless there were a very high relative risk.
This would imply a large number of cases of a common cancer or the
occurrence of an unusual histological type, and even this may first
be detected clinically, as in the cases of the recently described
vaginal adenocarcinoma (Herbst et al., 1974) and hepatic angiosarcoma
(Creech, 1974).

A potentially more sensitive method of monitoring is to link the
cancer registry with other records that contain information on the
actual or potential exposure of individuals to environmental agents,
for instance, the proposed international registry of vinyl chloride
workers, or a sample of occupations as stated on census returns.
The long latent period of cancer implies that records from the past
would be used, at least initially. Groups of individuals for whom
a record indicates an actual or possible exposure would be observed by
means of the cancer registry, e.g., children treated with irradiation
as part of treatment for ringworm on the scalp were shown to have a
higher incidence of brain tumour (Modan et al., 1974). Persons
receiving drugs in either high or prolonged dosages should also be
monitored by means of cancer registries. However, much caution is
needed before publishing incriminating studies: the recently reported
increased risk of breast cancer in women treated for hypertension
with reserpine (Armstrong et al., 1974; Jick, 1975) has not been
confirmed.

Prospective epidemiological studies. The major distinguishing
feature of prospective studies associated with cancer registries, as
opposed to surveillance and monitoring, is hypothesis testing, although
similar methodology may be used for both purposes. Cancer registries
can be used in prospective studies to follow persons exposed and not
exposed to suspected etiological factors. The exposed persons are
notified to the cancer registry, which reports which members of the
cohort in question develop cancer. The non-exposed persons may be
a specific group of individuals, or the experience of the total population may be considered to represent non-exposure to the substance
in question. Since persons frequently migrate from one part of a
country to another such studies are facilitated by the existence of
linked regional registries.

Cancer in families.   The study of cancer in families may provide leads to the relative roles of genetic and environmental factors in cancer etiology.   For example, an increased incidence of large-bowel cancer in the spouses of patients with this cancer would suggest common environmental factors in its etiology.   In studies among genetically related individuals, it is difficult to separate the possible effects of genetic and of environmental factors.

2.6.2 *Identification of high- and low-risk groups*

Differences in the distribution of a cancer in a population may provide leads to its etiology;   e.g., differences in incidence among various ethnic groups may be due to differences in environment, including diet and occupation, or in genetic susceptibility.   The cancer patterns in many populations throughout the world are unknown, and it is likely that many important differences have yet to be discovered (Doll, 1967).   This is illustrated by the recently described differences in cancer incidence among Singapore Chinese;   in this group, there is a much higher incidence of nasopharyngeal carcinoma in the Cantonese than in the Hokkien and Teochew dialect groups, but cancers of the oesophagus and stomach are fewer (Shanmugaratnam & Wee, 1973).   In Bombay, female breast cancer is found in higher incidence in Parsis than in other groups (Jussawalla & Jain, 1976).

Groups at high risk should be given priority in prevention programmes;   these may include elimination of exposure (e.g., smoking), reduction in susceptibility (if such factors can be identified) or early detection (e.g., in relatives of patients with certain types of cancer).

2.6.3 *Assessment of preventive measures*

Assessing primary prevention.   The primary prevention of cancer, that is, prevention by removal of causal factors such as cigarette smoking, is measured in intervention studies as (hopefully) reduced incidence rates, which are best assessed by means of population-based registries.   For many sites, population-based cancer registries provide a more sensitive assessment and, consequently, an earlier answer than is obtainable from mortality data.

Assessing early detection and screening (secondary prevention).
Early detection programmes need the help of population-based registries from the planning stage through to evaluation.   Registry data may indicate whether patients referred from the detection programme at an early stage of the disease are different from the rest of the population.   Mortality analysis is the best assessment of the efficacy of early detection programmes.   Survival of patients referred from the early detection programmes is most probably longer than that of other patients;   this may be explained in part by the definition of survival, which is estimated from the date of diagnosis. Thus, patients in these detection programmes are known for a longer period, while the natural history of the disease might not be different

from that of cases seen at a later stage.   Nevertheless, encouraging
results have been obtained from sound studies in Finland (Hakama &
Pukkala, 1977) and Iceland (Johannesson et al., 1978).

2.7 *Other aspects of cancer registration*

2.7.1 *Health services research*

In addition to providing data needed for planning, many population-
based cancer registries could do special surveys to answer questions
such as, 'What kind of hospital?' 'For how long?' 'How frequently?'
'How many episodes of hospitalization?' and, not less important,
'What is the percentage of patients that die at home after hospitalization?' 'How long did they stay at home?' and 'What is the experience
of patients who were never hospitalized?'.   Hospital registries can
give information on the waiting time between diagnosis and treatment
(or admission to hospital).

2.7.2 *Expert evidence in litigation*

This function is likely to be of increasing importance in the
future, due to growing awareness of environmental factors.   The cancer
registry might be asked to provide background information on risks and
probability in cases of industrial or other occupational litigation;
for instance:

(a) A chest physician who worked for more than 30 years on tuberculosis control and was thus exposed to large doses of radiation from
his fluoroscopic studies of patients, at a time when no tagging was
used, developed a malignant bone tumour of the mandible (Steinitz[1]).

(b) In a chlorine plant in a chemical factory there were three cases
of laryngeal cancer.   All three patients were heavy smokers and
belonged to an ethnic group known to be highly affected by this sort of
cancer.   The latent period between exposure and development of the
cancer was too short for chlorine to have been a likely cause.   The
observed number of cases, when adjusted for origin, age and smoking,
did not exceed the expected number (Steinitz[1]).

2.7.3 *The registry as a teaching resource*

Medical students, epidemiologists, statisticians and sociologists
may come to the registry to learn more not only about cancer epidemiology but also about the methodology of research into chronic diseases.
They have access there to qualified advice and study material.
Unpublished registry data can be used as the basis for an MD thesis,
with a member of the registry staff appointed by the medical school as
a tutor (see section 2.4).

---

[1] Unpublished data

2.7.4 *Comparison of cancer registration with other information systems*

If there were no cancer registration, the information would need to be acquired in other ways, for example, by reference to mortality statistics, information in the records of individual hospitals, hospital activities analysis, hospitalization statistics or special surveys (Payne, 1973).

Mortality statistics have been invaluable for studying the changing impact of diseases on the population, but their use is restricted by the relatively small amount of information contained in death certificates and by the limited accuracy of this information. Since mortality depends on both incidence and survival, caution must be exercised in estimating incidence from mortality. Where cancer incidence data are not available, estimates of incidence may be derived from mortality rates using appropriate conversion factors (Doll, 1972).

2.7.5 *Collaboration with research workers*

A cancer registry must avoid suspicion that it is monopolizing its information; contributing physicians and institutions must be encouraged to use it. In the course of doing so, they may detect inaccuracies which should be reported to the registry; these may be real or only apparent, due to some feature of the data. For this reason, registries may insist that one of the staff be a coauthor of such studies, since registry workers are more likely to know the data. This step avoids situations in which the outside research worker publishes 'better' data and castigates the registry as being unreliable.

3. PLANNING A REGISTRY

3. PLANNING A REGISTRY

3.1 *Decision to establish a registry*

In many countries cancer is so obviously a major problem that
there is ready acceptance of the importance of studying all of its
aspects.   In other, developing countries the importance of cancer may
be masked by the large incidence of communicable diseases.   However,
if causes of mortality are studied by age, cancer ranks much higher
in adults: in some Latin American countries cancer is the leading
cause of death in persons aged 15-74 years (Puffer & Griffith, 1967).
The well-off in many developing countries may be at high risk for
cancers of the lung, colon and breast;   the poor may have high risks
for other types of cancer, e.g., primary carcinoma of the liver and
carcinoma of the uterine cervix in parts of Asia, Africa and Latin
America.

The proposed registry should be discussed with members of the
medical profession and medical agencies.   Possible benefits for the
management of cancer patients should be pointed out, together with
possible future gains through prevention.   The priority given to
cancer registration relative to other medical activities will be
decided on the basis of a variety of local factors, which, ideally,
would include a rational assessment of need, although political and
other considerations are usually more important.   It is often not
feasible to have continuing comprehensive registration throughout
a country, and registration of limited duration may be used in some
regions.

Some registries in the developing world have been established in
universities and associated hospitals;   many have become centres of
excellence.   In practice a registry is often run by a core of full-
time staff, with others part-time.   It is essential to begin simply,
and to consider first the basic needs of a cancer patient information
system.   Much can be done with minimal information (section 4.2).

3.2 *Optimal size*

Hospital registry.   Does the number of expected new cases justify
a special set-up in a hospital? There is no easy answer.   What is
the expected number of new cases for a hospital registry serving one
or more general hospitals? A very rough estimate, arrived at under
US conditions, is an average of 3.0% of all admissions, in hospitals of
various sizes (American Cancer Society, 1964).   It would be unrealistic
to establish a hospital cancer registry for less than 400 new cancer
patients a year.

Population-based registry.   Is the population to be covered large
enough to provide meaningful computations in a reasonable time (e.g.,
by site, sex and age group for the total population at least)?   Or,
is it too large, in terms of manageability and quality control?
A population of 3-5 million is considered to be optimal: with larger
populations it might be difficult to maintain completeness or quality
of data; with smaller populations it takes longer to obtain meaningful figures.   There are, however, registries operating with populations of 17 million (German Democratic Republic) and of 200 000
(Iceland).   In countries with large populations, autonomous but linked
regional registries may be more effective.

In Poland, the government has decided to institute nation-wide
registration but has at the same time created several centres for
high quality registration designed to cover selected urban, rural and
industrial areas (Koszarowski et al., 1972).   This is a situation
which may appeal to other countries.

3.3 *Preliminary steps*

Hospital registry.   The flow of information within the institution,
the kind of information routinely available and its form in each institution can have a bearing on the availability and completeness of
information required by cancer registries.   Is there a diagnostic
index for all hospital departments?   Is there one in the pathology
department?   A system whereby there is compulsory reporting of
health statistics, including all hospital discharges (e.g., hospital
activities analysis), with indication of diagnosis, can be a very
efficient tool for checking completeness of reporting.   Most hospitals
keep a record by date of all discharges, including deaths.   These may
be helpful in tracing cases known only from death certificates.

Population-based registry.   Visits to the various institutions
that will be asked to supply the basic information - hospitals,
cancer centres, pathological institutes, etc.- are important (see
section 3.7).

3.4 *Confidentiality*

Modern cancer care is increasingly becoming the responsibility of
a large number of physicians, nurses, laboratory technicians and
medical record librarians.   Thus, although confidentiality has been
a basic concept in medical care from ancient times and is expressed in
the Hippocratic oath, traditional concepts of professional secrecy are
in a state of transition.   Confidentiality has been modified by legislation in the case of certain diseases in which the patient, due to
his illness, constitutes a danger to the public, e.g., those with
tuberculosis and venereal diseases.   In the US some diseases are
classified as 'reportable', i.e., they must, by law, be reported;
whereas others are 'notifiable', i.e., reporting is voluntary, but there
is a legal sanction to report to the appropriate body.

Confidentiality generally poses no problem for a hospital cancer registry, where the information stays within the precincts of the organization responsible for the medical care.   The question of how the principle of medical confidentiality can be upheld in notification to and use of information by a population-based cancer registry may constitute a major obstacle to registration.   This point must, therefore, be discussed and settled during the planning stage.

Medical confidentiality is limited not only to medical information about individual patients held by physicians and medical institutions but also to that contained in death certificates and submitted to the vital statistics bureau.   In some countries (e.g., France, The Netherlands), the identity of the deceased may be separated from the medical information (cause of death) in order to guarantee confidentiality, and only the latter is processed for mortality statistics. For the population-based registry, the identifying information is a *sine qua non* for follow-up and for checking the completeness of coverage.   In several countries, population-based cancer registries have been unsuccessful due to this difficulty.

The cancer registry must take all precautions to ensure confidentiality.   Registry work, like that in all medical agencies and vital statistics bureaux, implies that non-medical personnel deal with names of patients and their diagnoses.   Every new registry worker has to be introduced to, and the staff reminded frequently of, the need for the strictest confidentiality.   This is by no means easy: friends, relatives or persons known in public life may be notified as having cancer.   On meeting these people, or hearing them mentioned, the cancer registry worker must avoid showing any sign of knowing about such an illness.   It should be made clear that the registry staff must divulge neither the fact that a certain individual is known to the registry nor, obviously, his diagnosis or state of health.   Such information should not be given even to medical colleagues for other than strictly professional reasons.

Medical confidentiality may also be a problem for research workers wishing to use cancer registry data.   This can be done only if written permission from the physician or agency treating the patient is obtained, and it is obligatory that the researcher not contact the patient or his family directly, unless permission to do so has been given by the treating physician (see sections 2.4, 2.6).

3.5 *Legal aspects*

In planning a population-based registry, a legal basis may first have to be established.   In many countries, legislation is needed that will facilitate cancer control while protecting individual privacy; thus, the hurdle of confidentiality can be overcome by adequate legislation in the interests of public health and cancer prevention.

Legislation will free those concerned - the vital statistics bureaux, medical agencies and, most important, general physicians - from the fear of litigation for breach of medical secrecy.   Thus, the New South Wales (Australia) Cancer Registry was established by amendment of existing legislation for tuberculosis control.

Although a legal basis may exist and reporting be compulsory, persuasion and the provision of a service (see Chap. 9) are much more effective in ensuring reporting of cases than are threats of legal action (which seems rarely to be taken).

3.6 Background data for population-based registries

3.6.1 Population denominators

When planning a population-based cancer registry, one must investigate the available population data: accuracy, frequency of statistical estimates and reports and the degree of detail published routinely, since all these have a bearing on the denominator to be used for calculations of incidence and mortality rates.   The cancer registry needs population figures by sex and five-year age group for its registration area or for any subdivisions which the registry might wish to examine; individual presentation is desirable for each year of age under five years.   The cancer registry must use the definitions of population groups, geographical areas, etc., exactly as they are presented in the official vital statistics of that country.   The registry needs to know: When was the last census?   How are intercensus estimates arrived at?   In what detail is the population distribution published or available?

If there is a distinction between urban and rural areas, the registry must know the criteria for making this division.   The registry must also keep itself informed well in advance of any changes in the definitions of denominators.

Previously rural areas may become urban as towns increase in size. Such changes, which are often made for political reasons, can create great difficulties for cancer registries: a change in the definition of ethnic origin in the Hawaiian census in 1970 has been described as a demographic disaster.

3.6.2 Vital and medical care statistics

Statistics covering births, morbidity and general mortality may be useful to a population-based cancer registry.   Figures that indicate the level of medical care in the country are also important, e.g., the doctor: patient ratio, the number of nurses and statistics of hospitalization.   However, these are not essential, and cancer registration has been established in many areas where no such figures are available.

3.6.3 *Geographical data*

An exact description of the geographical area covered by the registry, its longitude and latitude, its physical properties and climate are relevant to planning and to subsequent publication of results, so that data may be compared with those from other registries.

3.7 *Cancer registry advisory committee*

An advisory committee, representing sponsors, sources of information and users of the registry, is needed for all registries, although its membership will usually differ in hospital and population-based registries.   The advisory committee is important during the planning stage in order to facilitate establishment of a registry;   later, it will help the registry to function and to relate to other cancer control activities.   With regard to the functioning of the registry, the advisory committee will help to:

   (a) ensure an adequate budget;

   (b) facilitate access to pertinent data, e.g., medical records, death certificates;

   (c) facilitate the reporting of cases;

   (d) generally supervise the registry;

   (e) improve and approve access to registry data by the medical profession and appropriate research workers; and

   (f) approve reports of the cancer registry prior to their publication.

Membership of cancer registry advisory committees varies from country to country.   Organizations that may sponsor a cancer registry include health departments, cancer societies, medical schools and universities, health insurance companies and cancer institutes. Sources of information (see Chap. 5) must be represented (directly or indirectly) on the committee;   these could include a medical association or society, a hospital administration, specialized services, such as pathology and radiotherapy, a death registry and a government census department.   Persons employed by the latter have experience in data collection and processing and may be able to assist in training registry staff.   Users of the registry represented on the committee could include a clinical oncologist and an epidemiologist.   A representative of cancer patients might also be included.   The advisory committee for the registry must be distinguished from a 'cancer committee', which may exist to coordinate all cancer control activities.

3.8 *Administration and finance*

3.8.1 *Hospital registries*

When the registry serves a single hospital, the administration
of the hospital will usually be responsible for finance and administration.   However, the advisory committee of the registry will have
to justify staff requirements and the budget.   When the registry
serves several hospitals (a central cancer registry), it is desirable
for it to be autonomous.

3.8.2 *Population-based registries*

A cancer registry is a long-term project.   It needs not only a
competent staff, an adequate budget and independence in order to
secure and sustain efficient operation, but must also have sufficient
standing to be able to request and obtain detailed demographic and
medical information from all medical services in the region.   The
registry must thus be linked in some way with the governmental health
services (if they exist) or with professional groups.   There are
registries which are part of the health services; however, they should
be as autonomous as possible, since, under some circumstances, being
part of the established health services may pose certain problems:

(a) The increasing budgetary needs of the ever-growing registry
may not find the necessary understanding, since such growth will probably
be out of proportion to that of other services in the respective department.

(b) The public service rules regarding the creation of new jobs
may be a severe handicap to the registry.

(c) Bureaucratic hierarchy may interfere with the direct contact
that the registry might wish to establish on both national and international levels.

Some cancer registries are set up and administered by voluntary
agencies (a cancer association, welfare fund, research fund, etc.).
In such cases, the cancer registry may find itself lacking in authority,
and cooperation with various health agencies may be difficult to obtain.

A solution to such problems might be to set up the population-based
cancer registry as an autonomous incorporated society; this has been
done for a number of registries, according to the laws and customs of
the country.   In this way, official channels can be by-passed when
necessary, and financing may be more flexible; furthermore, the registry is free to hire the staff it wishes and has autonomy in establishing
links with national and international agencies.

One serious problem may arise, however: the cancer registry, as a
new employer, may not be considered an attractive prospect, and positions may be considered to be of doubtful permanence.   People may be
hesitant to accept jobs and suspicious about their social benefits;

a tendency to leave a job as soon as a more 'secure' one appears is
a well-known phenomenon.   The paying of salaries higher than are
usual for similar job descriptions is economically justified in
these conditions, considering the gravity of the loss of a specific-
ally trained worker.

With regard to senior positions, an arrangement may be made
whereby a physician is allowed, for instance, to stay on with the
government service and be 'on loan' to the cancer registry.

3.8.3 *Finance*

Whatever salaries are conventional in any country for the positions
described above and whatever the fees are for services, costs of equipment and supply and overheads (office, mail, telephone, etc.), one
thing is certain: a cancer registry will need an increasing budget.
After the first two years, a well-founded budget should be drawn up,
taking into account the increasing load, refinement of techniques,
additional staff and publications.   As soon as the registry is able to
show a product, outside funds can be sought for specific projects if
considered desirable.

3.9 *Personnel: number, qualifications, training*

Although most cancer registries begin with only one or two
persons, who carry out all of the various activities described in
chapters 6 to 9, longer-term needs should be considered during planning.
These will include consideration of the type of registry, the population
and geographical area covered and the methods used for case finding and
for the collection of patient information.

Complete staffing, with people who have the necessary qualifications,
will not be obtained right from the start of a new registry.   It is
better to begin with a reduced team, in which a smaller number of
persons share the various tasks.   There are basic, specific personnel
requirements common to all registries (apart from the usual office
staff, e.g., typists, administrators, etc.).   When registration
includes the follow-up of patients, which is the main function of a
hospital registry, the amount of work and the need for personnel
increase.   One estimate states that a hospital registry needs one
person for the follow-up for five years of 350 new cases a year.
Ringel (American Cancer Society, 1964) estimates that the increase in
patient load of a hospital cancer registry is as follows: if the
number of new cases is considered to be constant, then the live case
load to be followed will be three times in the 5th year, 4.5 times in
the 7th year and 5.5 times in the 15th year.

Population-based registries, which collect many items of patient
information, need a large staff; e.g., in the current US SEER programme
only four cases are abstracted per hour by experienced clerks.

The personnel of a registry can be divided into two groups, medical
and technical, each of which may have full-time or part-time staff.

The medical staff include the medical director and various consultants.
The technical staff include the registrar, records clerks and statistical clerks.   In practice, there may be considerable overlap, e.g.,
the medical director may also act as the registrar.

3.9.1 *Medical director*

In hospital registries, this position may be filled by an oncologist on a part-time basis.   In a population-based registry, the
director should preferably be a physician trained in epidemiology,
pathology, surgery, oncology or public health.

Personal qualities are of great importance; these include genuine
interest in the various aspects of cancer registration and ability to
be a leader, to get along with the staff and to establish and sustain
good relations with other agencies.   Finding a physician who will act
as the first director of a population-based registry or, later, as his
successor may be difficult, since 'desk jobs' that have no direct
contact with patients - in contrast to those in hospital registries -
are not appealing, especially to young physicians.   It may be useful
to make the position more attractive by linking it with another activity
of high standing, e.g., an academic appointment at a medical school.
Such a solution is also desirable in that it is a means of securing
more esteem and a better reputation for the cancer registry and also
of spurring interest and understanding among the medical profession.
Retired doctors may also be used, e.g., military doctors often retire
early.

The work of the director will shift in emphasis during the first
years of operation.   At first, he will have to become familiar with
the demands of his position and will have to establish rapport with
various medical agencies and other institutions through visits and
discussion of the programme.   He will need periodically to assess
procedures, although later he will delegate most of the practical
work to the technical staff.   Subsequently he will be concerned with
the first reports of registry data and with collaborative research.
Last but not least, he has to learn by trial and error.

3.9.2 *Consultants*

No matter what the discipline of the medical director, the
registry should have access to advice on pathology, clinical oncology,
epidemiology, public health, data processing and statistics.

When a cancer registry covers a population served by a large
number of pathology institutes, there may be conflicting diagnoses,
requiring the advice of a consultant pathologist or specialist panel,
e.g., for lymphatic malignancies, bone tumours, etc.   Requests of
this kind are likely to receive a positive response, in recognition
of the registry's desire for well-founded diagnoses.

Statisticians or data-processing experts must be associated with the registry from the beginning in order to plan data storage and retrieval.   Whether a statistician will be needed subsequently on the regular staff will depend on the scope of the research and other activities.   A trained statistician is not needed for simple tabulations and calculations of rates, which can be carried out by a statistical (or record) clerk.

3.9.3 *Registrar*

The registrar is responsible for the operation of the registry, including the supervision of staff, the preparation of reports and, with the medical director, the evaluation of results.   He is routinely responsible for coding medical terms, in close consultation with the medical director.   He should preferably be a trained medical record librarian.   After secondary education, his training should have included a special course (usually one academic year) covering relevant aspects of hospital procedures, medical records, diagnostic indexing and coding of medical terms.

3.9.4 *Record clerks*

The record clerks are the backbone of the day-to-day work in the registry.   They must be acquainted with the activities and requirements of registration, even if they are not actually performing each of them. They are needed for case-finding and abstracting (see Chap. 6) and for many of the input operation of the registry (Chap. 7).   Good record clerks are in some way 'detectives'.   They must be familiar with all the procedures and codes used in the registry.   Preferably, they should have had secondary education, but many registries may find it possible to make use of persons of good but less formal education. They may be trained on the job or, preferably, in a training course (see section 3.10).

For population-based registries and central cancer registries, record clerks will frequently work outside the registry.   Such field clerks travel to find cases and to abstract information at its source (Chap. 6).   Local conditions and geographical factors will influence the decision on whether it is worthwhile investing in a number of such persons.   In New Mexico, for example, 'registry abstractors, based in Albequerque, travel to hospitals and clinics throughout the state to obtain information.   This concept of ".circuit-riding" seems particularly suited to low density areas like New Mexico (3.2 persons per square kilometre), since many small, rural hospitals find it difficult to attract and keep trained registry personnel.   This method also provides completeness and uniformity of case registration and follow-up, facilitating computerization and quality control' (Key, 1976). In Birmingham (UK) and in Recife (Brazil), some hospitals, but not others, are visited by such persons.   In Iowa, part-time field clerks are being used on a trial basis in various regions.   The wives of medical students are a good source of abstractors.

Such methods are costly, especially if the hospitals cover a vast geographical area.   Although it is difficult to supervise the comparability of abstracted material provided by part-time field clerks in various regions, the quality of information is likely to be much higher than that which is notified spontaneously.

3.9.5 *Statistical clerks*

Statistical clerks are concerned with coding most patient information and with processing tumour records (Chap. 7).   They assist in file maintenance and in the routine analysis of data, e.g., using simple cards (section 9.2.2) or standard computer programmes. There may be some overlap with the work of record clerks.   In many registries, record clerks also do coding, which tends to be tedious; this means that their duties are varied and results in fewer errors. Secondary education is a desirable prerequisite for statistical clerks.

With mechanical and electronic data processing (Chap. 10), specially trained statistical clerks are needed for data entry. There should be at least two such clerks, one for data entry and the other for verification, even if each works only part-time.   Whether this is done at the registry itself depends on local conditions.   Data entry clerks who are on the staff understand the registry's operations and may thus detect problems; however, one must also take into consideration the extra space and equipment needed for data entry plus the time of the registry director for hiring and supervising the clerks, since this is a job with a high turnover.   Some registries relieve the monotony of the job by adding other duties such as data analysis.

3.10 *Training and motivation of staff*

It must be emphasized that work in a cancer registry, in no matter what capacity, is tedious and repetitive and, at the same time, demands great concentration.   It asks for specific training, mostly on the job, for all types of personnel.   Training courses for hospital registry staff are given regularly by the University of California in San Francisco (Zippin[1]), and self-instruction manuals for tumour registrars are issued by the SEER Programme in the USA (Shambaugh, 1975) and for cancer registry personnel in Canada (Miller, 1975). Special training courses are not feasible in many other countries but could be practical and useful on a regional basis.   A distinction should be made between courses intended for directors of registries, such as the Pan American Health Organization course in Cali in 1969, and courses on the various internal operations of a registry.   The training material used in the USA could be adapted for use elsewhere.

Officially accredited, trained registry staff will have greater job satisfaction and may belong to a professional organization. Associations of tumour registrars have been formed in the USA, and they hold meetings that assist in their continuing education.

[1] Paper presented to DepCa Symposium, New York, 1975

Keeping registry staff is often very difficult.   Therefore,
everything possible should be done to explain to the staff the aims
and purposes of cancer registration and their important role in the
registry.   In addition, there should be frequent promotion, thus
forestalling possible resignations of experienced personnel, which
are usually a severe loss to the registry.

3.11 *Physical location of the cancer registry*

Hospital cancer registries should be situated near oncological
services.   Although not in the medical records department, they must
have easy access to medical records.   Population-based registries can
be part of a department in a ministry of health, a district health
office or a department of preventive medicine in a medical school.
The location within an existing facility avoids unnecessary overhead
costs or, at least, should allow sharing of services, such as tele-
phones, mailing, cleaning, etc.   At the same time, future space needs
of a cancer registry must be considered.

3.12 *Equipment and office space*

Very little equipment is necessary to begin a hospital registry,
but planning must take future needs into account.   The division below
into basic and optional needs depends on the size and functions of the
registry and on local conditions such as the cost of manual data
processing.

3.12.1 *Basic needs*

Office.   A room with normal office equipment, such as a desk,
telephone, chair, typewriter, etc.

Storage of documents.   Secure, lockable storage facilities and
space for the basic documents (individual folders or boxes containing
up to 500 documents (see section 7.5.2).   Even when microfilming has
been adopted as a space-saving measure, the problem of storage will
come up at some stage of the registry's existence.

Space for files.   If files are on cards, the number of file
cabinets needed may take up a considerable amount of floor space,
which, in turn, contributes to the distance covered by the staff
each day.   On the other hand, for a computerized registry of, say,
100 000 names, not more than 1.50 m of shelf space are required for
each 'file'; even less is needed in a microfilmed registry.

Desk calculator.   Preferably with printout, to permit checking
of corrections of data entry.

3.12.2 *Optional needs*

Electronic data processing.   This is a rapidly changing field in
which costs and size of computers are being reduced.   It is not
necessary for a cancer registry to own or rent a computer installation:
only a few can afford to do so, and many have had to accept outside

work in order to make full use of this costly equipment.   If it is
decided to use electronic data processing, it is essential that a
conveniently located installation be found and that the registry have
guarantees of long-term access.   There is no point in developing a system
on a 'cheap' or 'free' university computer, only to find the facility
withdrawn or restricted in a few months or years.   No less important is
finding an automatic data processing consultant ready and able to understand the cancer registry's problems.   Both parties - the registry
staff (professional and clerical) and the computer consultant - must
learn to communicate and to know what is required of each other.
A member of the registry staff may be given some training in electronic
data processing and the use of package programmes.

     If in a computerized registry data entry services are also bought,
staff space, equipment and maintenance costs can be kept to a minimum.
In addition, the efficiency, the time saved and the versatility of output fully justify the apparently high cost of computer services.
Computer costs may further be reduced by using standard programmes.

     Photocopying machine.   For some registries, the acquisition of
portable photocopying machines may be a great help, especially when
data are collected at source by field clerks.   The registry might try
to share more costly models with other offices.

     Equipment for margin hand-punched cards (see section 10.2.2)
Expenses are minimal, since only card perforators and sorting needles
are required.

     Punching equipment for 80-column cards.   If the registry decides
to have punching done on the premises, a card-punch machine and a
card verifier are required.   Cards may be sorted on a mechanical
sorter.   More modern equipment enters data directly onto magnetic
tape, but the advantages of having rapid preliminary analysis with
a sorter in the registry are thereby lost.

4. ITEMS OF PATIENT INFORMATION WHICH MAY BE COLLECTED BY REGISTRIES

4. ITEMS OF PATIENT INFORMATION WHICH MAY BE COLLECTED BY REGISTRIES

4.1 *Overview*

The information needed by a cancer registry is directly related to its functions. Hospital registries are primarily concerned with the cancer patient in hospital, whereas population-based registries are primarily concerned with cancer in the community. This chapter first covers the concepts of minimal, core and optional data in relation to both hospital and population-based registries. There is then a general description of selected groups of items, and, finally, each item is described in more detail. Although the latter has also been done in the *WHO Handbook* (WHO, 1976a), the opportunity is taken here to clarify some of the descriptions.

At the national level, the definitions of items and codes used by a cancer registry should accord with those used in other systems. Thus, for instance, demographic codes (population groups, residence, etc.) should be identical with those of the census and statistics bureaux that supply denominators for epidemiological analysis. These may not be the same throughout the world (e.g., 'race' and 'country of origin' for immigrants may be defined differently in the USA than in other countries). Here, international comparability can be assured in the methods of collection of data and calculation of rates, and not necessarily in the nomenclature of the items. The degree of international comparibility will thus vary. It can and must be greatest for the description and coding of tumours. This is discussed at length in Chapter 8.

4.2 *Minimal, core and optional information*

The *minimal* information for any cancer registry is listed in Table 4.1. This list is relevant especially for those in developing countries (see Chap. 11) who wish to begin registration but have limited resources. The number of items of information can subsequently be enlarged by adding further items from the core and optional lists of the *WHO Handbook*. Alternatively, the minimal information may be added to in a modular fashion according to the interests of users of the registry. For instance, Laszlo et al. (1976) propose a minimal data hospital registry supplemented in a modular fashion for individual tumour types by specialized research registries whose maintenance is the responsibility of physician users. It must be remembered, however, that each additional item of information collected increases the cost of registration. Thus, for each item the registry should ask, 'Do we need it?' rather than 'Would we like to have it?'

Table 4.1 Minimal data for any cancer registry

Item no.	Item	Comments
	The Person	
	Personal identification[a]	
4	Name	According to local usage
5	Sex	
6	Date of birth	
or		
11	Age	Estimate if not known
	Demographic	
8	Address	Usual residence
54	Ethnic group	When population consists of two or more groups
	The Tumour	
18	Topography (site)	Primary if possible
19	Morphology (histology)	Whenever possible
13	Incidence date	Month and year
17	Most valid basis of diagnosis	
-	Source of information (e.g., hospital record no., name of physician, etc.)	To facilitate subsequent search for additional information

[a] The minimum collected is that which ensures that if the same individual is reported again to the registry, he will be recognized as being the same person.

Core items, as defined in the *WHO Handbook* (WHO, 1976a), are listed in Table 4.2, and optional items in Table 4.3.   Suggested priorities are also given, and these vary for hospital registries compared with population-based registries.   Optional items are generally given lower priority, although in most developing countries ethnic group is a high-priority item.

Core items have been assigned the numbers 1 to 28, and optional items 51 to 76 in the *WHO Handbook*;   these have been given to facilitate international exchange of information, since numbers do not change in translation as may the meaning of words.   Additional optional items for population-based registries are numbered 77 to 85.   If items are modified by registries they should be given new optional numbers.

Table 4.2   Core items for hospital and population-based registries

Item no.	Item	Suggested priority[a]		Comments
		HR	PBR	
1	Identification of the cancer registry	1	1	May not need specific collection
2	Patient registration number	1	1	See discussion of this item
3	Personal identification number	1	1	
4	Names	1	1	
5	Sex	1	1	
6	Date of birth	1	1	
7	Place of birth	1	1	
8	Address	1	1	
9	Marital status	2	2	
10	Telephone number	2	3	
11	Age at incidence date	1	1	
12	Date of first diagnosis by a physician	2	3	
13	Incidence date	1	1	
14	Hospital record number	1	2	
15	Previous diagnosis and/or treatment elsewhere	1	1	
16	Investigations used for planning initial treatment	2	3	
17	Most valid basis of diagnosis of cancer	1	1	
18	Anatomical site: topography (ICD-O)	1	1	
19	Histological site: morphology (ICD-O)	1	1	
20	Multiple primaries	1	1	
21	Clinical extent of disease before treatment	1	3	
22	Initial treatment	1	2	
23	Surgical-cum-pathological extent of disease before treatment	1	1	
24	Status at annual follow-up	1	2	Limited information for PBR
25	Date of death	1	1	
26	Cause of death (ICD)	1	2	
27	Result of autopsy	1	1	
28	Survival in months	1	3	Can be calculated and need not be collected

[a] A suggested priority for collection of each item by hospital (HR) and population-based (PBR) registries is assigned on a scale ranging from 1 (highest) to 3 (lowest).   Local factors may modify the priority of some items.

Table 4.3 Optional items for hospital and population-based registries

Item no.	Item	Suggested priority[a]		Comments
		HR	PBR	
51	Department of hospital	1	3	
52	Nationality	1	1	
53	Religion	1	1	One or more depending on local circumstances
54	Ethnic group	1	1	
55	Occupation	2	2	
56	Industry	2	2	
57	Reason for presentation of patient	2	3	
58	Staging of lymphomas (including Hodgkin's disease) and leukaemias	1	2	
59	TNM system	1	3	
60	Site(s) of distant metastases	2	3	
61	Co-morbidity	1	3	
62	Conditions affecting treatment	1	3	
63	Reasons for non-curative treatment	1	2	
64	Laterality	2	2	
65	Surgery	1	2	
66	Radiotherapy	1	2	
67	Chemotherapy	1	2	
68	Hormonal therapy	1	2	
69	Other therapy	1	2	
70	Summary of treatment delivered	2	2	
71	Chronology of treatment	2	3	
72	Disease status at discharge from hospital	2	3	
73	Duration of hospitalization in days	2	3	
74	Patient status (i) before and (ii) after first treatment and at anniversaries	1	3	
75	Additional causes of death	2	2	
76	Cancer entered on death certificate	2	2	
77	Year of immigration	3	2	
78	Country of birth of father	3	2	
79	Name of first hospital or institution where definitive diagnosis was made	3	2	
80	Documentation	3	2	
81	Certainty of diagnosis	3	2	
82	Other pathology at site of cancer	2	2	
83	Place of death	2	1	
84	Relation of cause of death to cancer	3	2	
85	Date of last discharge from hospital	3	2	

[a] A suggested priority for collection of each item by hospital (HR) and population-based (PBR) registries is assigned on a scale ranging from 1 (highest) to 3 (lowest). Local factors may modify the priority of some items.

Both core and optional lists contain fixed and up-datable items. Fixed items are those which *cannot* be modified in the light of subsequent information, e.g., item 21, clinical extent of disease before treatment. This is not applicable to errors, e.g., in diagnosis, names, date of birth, etc. or in data abstracted from sources; such errors must, of course, be corrected.

Up-datable items are those which can be modified, e.g., item 17, most valid basis of diagnosis of cancer; item 20, multiple primaries; item 24, status at annual follow-up; item 74, patient status after first treatment and at anniversaries.

4.3 *Selected groups of items*

The items of minimal information in Table 4.1 comprise two groups, concerning the patient and the tumour.   The first consists of unambiguous personal identification together with some demographic information, while the second consists of topography (item 18), morphology (item 19), incidence date (item 13) and most valid basis of diagnosis of cancer (item 17).   Diagnostic procedures, pretreatment extent of disease, treatment given, and response to treatment are collected mainly by hospital registries.   However, the least ambiguous measure of response to treatment, total survival assessed by date of death can be collected more comprehensively by population-based registries. Further comments are given immediately below and with the description of each item.

Personal identification (items 3-8)

Unambiguous personal identification is essential in all cancer registries: this is needed to prevent duplicate registrations of the same patient or tumour and to facilitate various functions of cancer registries, such as obtaining follow-up data and performing record linkage. *It is more important that for a given region sufficient identifying information be available than that the actual specific items be internationally standardized.*   The emphasis here is on adequate personal identification rather than on the specific items that contribute to personal identification, since these vary considerably from one country to another.

A number of other personal characteristics are described which are of interest both for personal identification and as independent, descriptive parameters in relation to cancer, e.g., date of birth and sex.   Precise date of birth is one of the most valuable items of personal identification and, if it is available, should always be recorded.   In describing cancer patterns, however, approximate age is sufficient.

Description of the neoplasm (items 17-21, 23 & 59)

A number of items deal with this central aspect of cancer registration and cover anatomical site (item 18), morphology (item 19), multiple primaries (item 20), pretreatment extent of disease (items 21, 23 and 59) and most valid basis of diagnosis of cancer (item 17).

Anatomical site is the most common axis for tabulations.   Its coding in a special adaptation of the *International Classification of Diseases for Oncology* (ICD-O) differs from the coding of topography in the current 8th and 9th editions of the *International Classification of Diseases* (ICD-8 and ICD-9).   In the ICD-O, the coding of topography and morphology must be considered together (Chap. 8).

Pretreatment extent of disease

Items 21 and 23 relate to two aspects of the extent of disease in the initial phases of diagnosis and therapy. The first, commonly referred to as 'clinical staging' (see item 21) pertains to the extent of disease, as assessed clinically, prior to the initiation of *any* treatment. The TNM classification (see below) is normally used at this time (item 59). The second (item 23) contains information on extent of disease that is available from initial surgical therapy, which will include histological information about lymph-node involvement, etc., or from autopsy, if the patient died before treatment could be given. This may be referred to as the surgical-cum-pathological extent of disease before treatment (sometimes referred to as surgical-pathological stage).

The clinical staging of neoplasms has a long history. That elaborated by the League of Nations (Heyman, 1937) for carcinoma of the cervix has stood the test of time, requiring only one addition, to take into account *in situ* carcinoma. Clinicians, however, have felt that this classification does not sufficiently describe other neoplasms; and additional classifications, such as that elaborated by Dukes & Bussey (1958) for the rectum, have gained widespread acceptance. The best-known system of clinical staging of malignant tumours is the TNM classification (item 59) promulgated by the International Union against Cancer (UICC, 1962). Davies (1977) has reviewed the spread and behaviour of cancer, and staging.

4.4 *Description and coding of items*

Items of patient information are described systematically in the following pages. These include a definition of each item and, for a considerable proportion of them, its relevance for a particular type of malignancy, for the registration process and for patient care and research. Each item may have several categories or classes. The recommended codes for each class are, in general, given not in the text but in Figures 4.1 and 4.2, which show the core and optional items on each side of the WHO Margin Punch Card[1]. Coding is an input operation and is described in Chapter 7, but it is more convenient to give the codes at the same time as the description of the items in this chapter. The coding of neoplasms is complex and is discussed separately in Chapter 8. Payne (1973) describes the practical problem, that 'Committees responsible for the design of national and international classifications and codes cause some inconvenience to cancer registries and similar organizations by too frequent changes. When such changes take place registries may either follow them but

---

[1] The WHO Margin Punch Card displays the items of information, core and optional, which may be collected by a hospital cancer registry.

only from the time changes become effective, or they may convert the coding of all existing records to conform to the changes. In the former case awkward discontinuities persist in the registry's data which complicate analyses extending over a long period; in the latter case, the conversion process may be time-consuming, expensive and possibly liable to introduce systematic errors'.

Information is held by cancer registries in two ways: as a record (in words) or as code (generally as numbers). Some of the items listed below, e.g., dates, are immediately entered as code, since they are not likely to undergo later change, and coding errors are likely to be minimal. Others are recorded in words, partly for reference and partly to ensure accuracy of coding.

Item 1: *Identification of the cancer registry*

The identity of the cancer registry should be recorded for each case notified. It may be considered superfluous for a hospital registry to have an identifying code number; however, many such registries contribute data to a larger system, which is often population-based, and this registry may in turn contribute to international compilations such as *Cancer Incidence in Five Continents*. Codes for countries and subdivisions within countries are available (see item 7).

Item 2: *Patient registration number*[1]

A registration number is assigned by the cancer registry to each patient. This number is given to all documents and items of information relating to the patient. If a patient has more than one primary tumour (item 20), each tumour is given the same registration number. These primary tumours can be distinguished by site (item 18), morphology (item 19) and incidence date (item 13). This question is discussed further under item 20. Use of a patient registration number rather than a tumour registration number is recommended, as this facilitates the analysis of multiple primaries and simplifies patient follow-up. One widely used numbering system includes the last two digits of the year in which the patient first registered together with a serial number for the year. For example,

| 7 | 8 | 0 | 0 | 0 | 0 | 1 |

is the registration number given to the first patient registered in 1978. The second patient registered in 1978 would be given the number 7800002. For computer-based registries it is useful to include an additional check digit to help ensure that updated information is assigned to the correct record.

---

[1] This item differs from the tumour registration numbers in the *WHO Handbook*. This item was modified after extensive consultation. In practice, it makes little difference to the internal operation of the registry, as each registered tumour has a separate tumour record.

FIG. 4.1 MODEL TUMOUR RECORD AND MARGIN-PUNCH CARD FOR HOSPITAL REGISTRIES - CORE ITEMS

This card is shown as an example only: the actual items collected will depend on local priorities (see section 4.2).

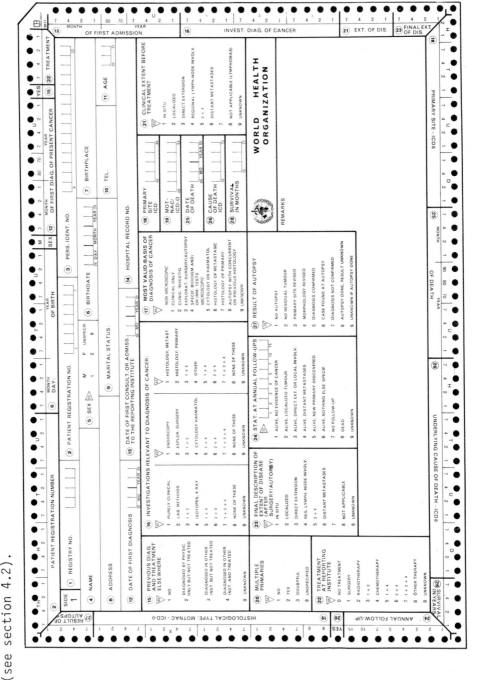

FIG. 4.2 MODEL TUMOUR RECORD FOR HOSPITAL REGISTRIES - OPTIONAL ITEMS

This card is shown as an example only. For a discussion of core and optional items, see section 4.2.

SIDE 2

51) DEPARTMENT OF HOSPITAL

52) NATIONALITY

53) RELIGION

54) ETHNIC OR RACE GROUP

55) OCCUPATION

56) INDUSTRY

57) REASON FOR PRESENTATION
1 ADVICE
2 SCREENING
3 DIAGNOSIS
4 INITIAL TREATMENT
5 COMPLEMENTARY TREATM.
6 SECONDARY TREATM.
7 OTHER
8 UNKNOWN

58) LYMPHOMA, INC. HODGKIN DISEASE AND LEUKEMIAS
LYMPHOMAS:
1 STAGE I
2 STAGE II
3 STAGE III
4 STAGE IV
LEUKEMIAS:
5 ACTIVE
6 IN REMISSION
7 NO DATA ON EXTENT
LYMPH. + LEUKEMIAS:
8 NOT APPLICABLE
9 UNKNOWN

59) TNM SYSTEM
T N M N+
N - = 1
N+ = 2

60) SITE(S) OF DISTANT METASTASIS
0 NONE
1 DISTANT LYMPH NODES
2 BONE
3 LIVER
4 LUNG/PLEURA
5 BRAIN
6 OVARY
7 SKIN
8 OTHER
9 UNKNOWN

61) CO-MORBIDITY
1 NO
2 YES
IF YES, ICD

62) CONDITIONS AFFECTING TREATMENT
0 NONE
1 PRECANCEROUS
2 OTHER DISEASE
3 1 + 2
4 COMPLICATIONS
5 1 + 4
6 2 + 4
7 1 + 2 + 4
8 OTHER
9 UNKNOWN

63) REASON FOR NON-CURATIVE TREATMENT
1 TREATM. ELSEWHERE
2 REFUSED TREATMENT
3 TOO ADVANCED
4 POOR CONDITION
5 AGE
6 DEATH
7 OTHER
8 NOT APPLICABLE
9 UNKNOWN

64) LATERALITY
1 RIGHT
2 LEFT
3 CENTRAL
4 BILATERAL
5 MULTIPLE
6
7
8 NOT APPLICABLE
9 UNKNOWN

65) SURGERY
1 SYMPTOMATIC
2 PALLIATIVE
3 CURATIVE INCOMPL.
4 CURATIVE COMPLETE
5
6
7
8 NO SURGERY
9 UNKNOWN

66) RADIOTHERAPY
1 SYMPTOMATIC
2 PALLIATIVE
3 CURATIVE INCOMPL.
4 CURATIVE COMPLETE
5
6
7
8 NO RADIOTHERAPY
9 UNKNOWN

67) CHEMOTHERAPY
1 SYMPTOMATIC
2 PALLIATIVE
3 CURATIVE INCOMPL.
4 CURATIVE COMPLETE
5
6
7
8 NO CHEMOTHERAPY
9 UNKNOWN

68) HORMONAL THERAPY
1 WITHDRAWAL BY SURGERY OR RADIOTHERAPY
2 ADDITIVE
3 ANTIHORMON THER
8 NO HORMONAL THER.
9 UNKNOWN

69) OTHER THERAPY
1 NO
2 YES, SPECIFY

70) SUMMARY OF TREATMENT
1 SYMPTOMATIC ONLY
2 PALLIATIVE
3 CURATIVE, INCOMPL.
4 CURATIVE, COMPLETE
5 UNCERTAIN
6
7 OTHER
8 NO TREATMENT
9 UNKNOWN

71) CHRONOLOGY OF TREATMENT
1 SURGERY
2 RADIOTHERAPY
3 CHEMOTHERAPY
4 HORMONAL THER
5
6
7
8 OTHER
9 UNKNOWN

72) DISEASE STATUS AT DISCHARGE
1 NO CANCER
2 IN REGRESSION
3 UNCHANGED
4 IN PROGRESSION
5
6
7
8 DIED IN HOSPITAL
9 UNKNOWN

73) DURATION OF HOSPITALISATION IN DAYS

74) PATIENT STATUS. Before, after first treatment + at annual follow-ups
1 WELL AND ACTIVE
2 WELL, NOT ACTIVE
3 SOME DISABILITY BUT ACTIVE
4 SOME DISABILITY, NOT ACTIVE
5 CONFINED TO BED
6 ALIVE, STATUS NOT DETERMINED
7 FOLLOW-UP NOT DONE
8 DEAD
9 UNKNOWN

75) ADDITIONAL CAUSES OF DEATH

76) CANCER ENTERED ON DEATH CERTIFICATE
1 NO
2 YES
9 UNKNOWN

REMARKS

The year of registration may be different from the year in which the patient was first admitted to hospital and diagnosed.   For instance, a patient admitted and diagnosed in October 1977 may not be registered until January 1978.   In this case the registration number will begin with 78, although the year for calculation of incidence will be 1977.

Item 3: *Personal identification number*

Many countries use a personal identification number that is unique to an individual; it may incorporate other personal information, such as date of birth and sex.   Some countries have no such personal identification number; others have more than one.   Examples include the national identity number in Scandinavian countries, the National Health Service number in the UK and the social security number in the USA.

The utilization of these identification numbers in medical records varies greatly.   They are more likely to be available when they serve an administrative purpose associated with medical treatment or hospital admission or with providing benefits to patients.   If a suitable number is available for only a very few patients, then it should not be relied on for patient identification; however, whenever such a number exists, the cancer registry should promote its inclusion in the hospital files (preferably at the time of admission).

The complete number should be obtained, including any check digits when these exist.   It must be noted that the number as written may be incorrect, since transposition of digits occurs commonly.

Item 4: *Names*

The full name is essential for identification in cancer registries. Although this item appears to be simple to obtain, there may be many problems with names, especially in developing countries.   It is recommended that names be copied from identity cards whenever possible.

Spelling of names.   There are often different spellings for names with the same pronunciation, e.g., Reid and Read, MacLennan and McLennan.   With regard to unwritten languages and dialects in developing countries, subtle distinctions in sound may not be expressed by the phonetic system used for medical records (English, French, Spanish), and the same name may be spelled differently on different occasions. Ambiguities due to spelling can be greatly reduced by use of a special code system, e.g., the 'Name Search Technique', using NYSIIS coding (Bureau of Systems Development, 1970).

Abbreviations.   Persons often, but not consistently, use abbreviations of names, e.g., the name James may be modified to Jim or Jimmy; Robert to Rob, Bob, Bobby, etc.

Titles.   Titles can be used to assist identification, although they may not be used consistently, e.g., Doctor; Father, Mother, Brother, Sister in certain religious orders; and Mrs, Miss or Ms in some English-speaking countries.

Changes of names.   The name on a birth certificate and on other official records may reflect the dominant culture of the country, whereas the name commonly used by the person may be a variant in his own language or dialect.   Thus, one name may be used in everyday life, whereas the death certificate may give the official name on the birth certificate.   For instance, in Scotland Malcolm (English) might be on the birth and death certificates, while Calum, the Gaelic equivalent, was used for all other occasions.   Names may also change: this occurs in many societies in which women change their family name following marriage; in many non-industrialized societies names are changed at other stages of life.   In many developing countries, additional information may be available, including affiliation, i.e., the father's name; in many Latin American countries the mother's family name is often given on documents.

Order of names.   Conventions vary as to the order in which names are written.   In western European cultures, the family name may be written either first or last, depending on the context, although in everyday speech the family name is given last.   In many parts of Asia, the family name is invariably given first.   The order in which names are written should be standardized for each registry and should reflect local practices.   Most registries will need to make provision for the recording of multiple names (to allow for changes, e.g., on marriage) and to cross index them.

Item 5: *Sex*

Sex is a further identifying item and is invariably found in hospital records; however, in many other sources of information, the sex may not be recorded.   Although sex may be inferred in some cultures from the given name or from the wording of the hospital summary, in others it is not easy to determine from the given or personal names, and there may be problems in determining sex in reports of cancer that are based on pathology reports only.   Persons who change their phenotypic sex by means of operations and drugs should be coded separately; although the cancer risk in such persons is of interest, it can only be assessed by pooling information from a number of cancer registries (Suggested codes for sex changes are: 7, male to female and 8, female to male.   These supplement those given in Fig. 4.1).

Item 6: *Date of birth*

Date of birth is of great importance in assisting identification, particularly when there is limited variation in names, or when other specific identifying information is lacking.   The related item, 11, age at date of tumour incidence, may be derived from the date of birth

(if known).   Alternatively, if the date of birth is not known, the
year of birth may be estimated in years from the approximate age.
This is useful in constructing birth cohorts.   The date of birth on
an identity card may be the result of a guess, but, provided it is
used consistently on all documents, it is useful for identification.

For purposes of international collaboration it is necessary to
convert any local dating system or convention to the standard system
used internationally, for instance, by United Nations organizations.
The date should be recorded, i.e., written, in clearly labelled boxes
as shown below:

25	May	1976

Day   Month   Year

The international convention is to write these in the order
illustrated   (The reverse order has certain advantages in data
processing, but this can readily be achieved during electronic data
processing.)   Day and year should be given in figures in full, and
month in words;   this will avoid ambiguities such as occur in data
received from the USA.

There is a distinction between the recording of a date and its
coding: thus, the date written above is coded as:

2 5	0 5	7 6

D   M   Y

Item 7:   *Place of birth*

Place of birth may assist in personal identification, and it may
provide clues to cancer etiology.   Studies of persons who move from
one environment to another may show differences in cancer incidence
in the two environments.   Such movement can be studied between
countries, e.g., Japan and the US, and also within countries, e.g.,
migration within Colombia from Nariño to Cali.   Whenever possible,
the precise birth-place in the country of origin and date of migration
(item 77) should be recorded;   this allows comparative studies to be
made in which the effects of possible genetic factors are largely
controlled.   Furthermore, national boundaries change, and an individual
born in 1910 in Breslau, then in Germany, would now live in Wroclaw,
Poland.   Sources of demographic data on migrant groups are discussed
by Staszewski et al. (1970).

This item is of lesser interest to a hospital registry but is of
great interest to the population-based registry, and codes used should
conform to those used in national vital statistics.   These may include
places within the geographical area covered by the cancer registry, in

addition to places in other parts of the country or in other
countries.   An example of the latter is the list of geocodes for
place of birth used by the US SEER programme.   WHO also has a list
of codes of countries for international use (Appendix).   The same
considerations apply to nationality (item 52), religion (item 53) and
ethnic group (item 54).

Item 8: *Address*

Although included here as part of the patient's identification,
address is also used in follow-up, in the planning of health services
and in examining possible variations in incidence by place of residence.

The address recorded should be the patient's usual residence, and
this must be distinguished from his address at the time of entering
hospital.   If there is an identity card, this will normally give the
patient's usual residential address, which may be copied by the
hospital.   This could help to distinguish residents from another area
who are staying temporarily with relatives.   Patients may intentionally
give an address in the area served by a specific hospital in order to
qualify for acceptance or free treatment by that hospital.   In some
areas identity cards may be borrowed for the same purpose.

It is generally regarded as desirable that every cancer patient be
examined physically at least once a year; the follow-up anniversary
date (item 13) is often a convenient time for this.   For follow-up
purposes, a number of other addresses may be required in order to be
able to contact a patient, e.g., address of a near relative, neighbour,
local doctor or person of influence or authority.   Such addresses may
be kept in the patient's hospital record or in a separate follow-up
file.

For population-based registries, the place of usual residence
should be coded, using the same classification and codes as used for
available population denominator data.   The most detailed codes
available should be used, in order to minimize the effects of changes
in administrative or political boundaries within a country or region.
Thus, detailed codes can be regrouped to conform to new boundaries or
definitions of denominator data (e.g., urban or rural).   Identification of 'non-resident' patients is important, and they must be excluded
from incidence (and survival) studies.   Unless this is done there may
be considerable distortion, particularly if the registration area
contains a treatment centre of renown.   Thus, the Tata Memorial
Hospital treats head and neck cancers from all over India; inclusion
of all patients would give a false picture of the importance of cancers
at these sites in the Bombay population.

Item 9: *Marital status*

Although suggested as an item of personal identification, it must
be remembered that marital status may change during the course of an
illness.   Such information is of interest since studies have shown

that women who have never married are frequently at lower risk for
cancer of the uterine cervix but at higher risk for breast cancer.
The social implications of civil status on medical care and follow-up,
especially when the patient is living alone, are of considerable
interest to the hospital registry, since they may influence patient
management.

If the registry is interested in this item, and fairly certain to
get accurate information in a sufficient number of cases, the codes
adopted should be those used in vital statistics.

Item 10: *Telephone number*

In some countries the patient's telephone number may assist in
identification as well as facilitating future contact for follow-up.
If the patient moves, it may be possible to trace his new address
through the telephone company (especially for follow-up purposes).
For follow-up, several telephone numbers may be used, if available:
home, place of work, physician, relatives, etc.

Item 11: *Age at incidence date*

This refers to the age in years at the incidence date (item 13).
In many populations, age may not be known accurately, or may delibe-
rately be stated inaccurately. If the birth-date is unknown, the
year of birth may be estimated from the stated age and recorded as a
fixed item (item 6).

Age is of great relevance in the description of cancer incidence,
but precise age is not needed. In developing countries, approximate
age may be estimated in a number of ways (Higginson & Oettlé, 1960);
for example, the person may have married at the time of some event
whose date is known. The Chinese and other groups in Asia follow a
system in which the names of animals are assigned to different calendar
years of birth in a 12-year recurring cycle. Thus, among Chinese, it
may be possible to validate reported age if the animal year of birth
is also recorded.

It is advantageous to have 'age' punched in the margin punch card
(Fig. 4.1) for easier sorting. In computerized registries this is
unnecessary, since age at incidence for each primary tumour can be
calculated from birth-date and date of incidence.

Item 12: *Date of first diagnosis by a physician*

There is considerable international variation in the definition
of the date of first diagnosis of a tumour, e.g., 'the date a physician
first made a diagnosis of cancer', 'the date a pathological diagnosis
of cancer was made' or 'the date of first admission to hospital where
a diagnosis of cancer was made' (Tuyns, 1970).

In hospital registries, it is recommended that the date of first diagnosis of cancer by a physician be recorded, even if histological confirmation is made only later or never. For example, a general practitioner feels a lump in the breast and makes a diagnosis of possible cancer. The patient is referred to a hospital where the diagnosis is confirmed. The date of diagnosis to be recorded is the date of the general practitioner's diagnosis. This date is used also if the physician writes 'tumour' and not 'cancer'. Combined with other information, this date of first diagnosis can be used to measure the delay between first diagnosis of cancer by a physician and its definitive treatment. The problem of 'delay' is of greatest interest to the hospital registry, since it may show the need for education of the public and/or of physicians and a need to search out and remove administrative difficulties in gaining admission to hospital.

A population-based registry is unlikely to be able to get reliable information on 'delay' for an adequate number of cases; it is therefore not advisable to strive to obtain this date, except where specified in item 13.

The complete day, month and year of first diagnosis are recorded by the hospital registry, but only the month and the last two digits of the year are coded.

Item 13: *Incidence date*

This is not necessarily the date of first diagnosis by a physician (item 12). For hospital registries, it is the date of first consultation at or admission to a hospital for the cancer· This item includes consultation at outpatient departments only; it is a definite point in time which can be verified from records and is the most consistent and reliable date available throughout the world. For these reasons, it is chosen as both the *anniversary date* for follow-up and survival computation purposes and as *the date of occurrence* for measuring incidence, henceforth referred to as the *incidence date*.

For population-based registries, if the above information is not available, other dates may have to be used. Thus, incidence date refers to, in order of priority:

(a) date of first consultation at, or admission to, a hospital, clinic or institution for the cancer in question;

(b) date of first diagnosis of the cancer by a physician or the date of the first pathology report;

(c) date of death (year only), when the cancer is first ascertained from the death certificate (item 76) and follow-back attempts have been unsuccessful; or

(d) date of death preceding an autopsy (item 27), when this is
the time at which cancer is first found and was unsuspected
clinically (without even a vague statement, such as 'tumour
suspected', 'malignancy suspected').

If there is a delay between first consultation and admission
for definitive treatment, the date of first consultation at the hospital
is selected (both consultation and treatment may be outpatient: for
example, in nasopharyngeal carcinoma).   If cancer is diagnosed during
treatment for another illness, e.g., a person being treated for a
chronic disease develops symptoms during inpatient or outpatient treatment and cancer is detected, the appropriate incidence date is the date
of diagnosis.

A special problem is posed by cases known to the registry only
from death certificates.   If the registry does not succeed in obtaining further information but nevertheless includes such cases (see item
80), the general rule is to take the year of death as the year of
incidence.   Thus, all such cases would, in the absence of special
analysis, have a 'survival' of less than one year.   However, occasion-
ally a death certificate may state, 'carcinomatosis, following mastectomy for cancer of breast'; in such cases, with no further information
forthcoming, the year of incidence might be left as 'unknown', or the
year of death may be used to simplify subsequent data processing.

Previous tumour at site of present malignancy (also discussed
under item 20).   There are three possibilities: (a) no histological
diagnosis is available for the previous lesion, which was stated to
be a neoplasm; (b) the previous lesion is of the same morphology but
benign (e.g., a 'benign' papilloma is removed, and the next papilloma
to appear is diagnosed as transitioned-cell carcinoma); (c) the
previous diagnosis of a benign neoplasm has, after review of the microscopic slides, now been changed to malignancy (e.g., 'metastic leiomyosarcoma in abdominal cavity' following simple hysterectomy for 'myoma'
is now corrected on review to 'leiomyoma with early malignant change').
The procedure and the codes adopted by a registry to assign an incidence
date in such cases must be unequivocal and consistent in such
situations.

A special, optional item may be required to specify 'previous
tumour at site of present malignancy' and coded according to the
three possibilities described above.

Previously diagnosed tumours in persons who move into an area
covered by population-based registration are not included in incidence
computations.

Item 14: *Hospital record number*

This item should always be recorded, in order to facilitate reference back to hospital files for additional information not included in the cancer registry. When separate records are kept, the hospital department may also have to be identified and coded.

This number is superfluous when personal identification numbers (item 3) are used routinely in hospital records; this practice is much to be recommended, when possible.

As the same patient may be reported by several hospitals, a population-based registry or a hospital registry serving several hospitals will have to code each hospital in addition to the record number.

Item 15: *Previous diagnosis and/or treatment elsewhere*

This item refers only to previous diagnosis and/or treatment for the particular tumour being registered in the hospital registry, as might occur when a patient moves from one hospital system to another of his own volition or on transfer for, say, super-voltage therapy. If information about previous diagnosis and treatment is lacking, such cases will be excluded from some analyses.

The population-based registry may be interested to know about previous diagnosis in order to check (and up-date, if necessary) the correctness of incidence date (item 13) and corresponding hospital and record number.

Item 16: *Investigations used for planning initial treatment*

This item is usually recorded by hospital registries only. It is used to assess the nature and quality of the investigation conducted to establish diagnosis *before* treatment was begun. Thus, it must not be up-dated (in contrast to item 17).

Item 17: *Most valid basis of diagnosis of cancer*

The information of greatest interest for the assessment of reliability of incidence rates is the most valid diagnosis made during the course of the illness. This should be clearly distin- guished from the investigations done prior to treatment (item 16). The most valid basis of diagnosis may be the initial histological examination of the primary site, or it may be the *post-mortem* examination (Sometimes corrected even at this point when histological results become available). This item must be revised if later infor- mation allows its up-grading.

When considering the most valid basis of diagnosis, the minimum requirement of a cancer registry is differentiation between neoplasms that are verified microscopically and those that are not. To exclude the latter group, as some pathologists and clinicians might be

inclined to do, means losing valuable information; the making of a
morphological (histological) diagnosis is dependent upon a variety of
factors, such as age, accessibility of the tumour, availability of
medical services, and, last but not least, upon the beliefs of the
patient and his attitude towards modern medicine. Cytological and
histological diagnoses should be distinguished.

A biopsy of the primary tumour should be distinguished from a
biopsy of a metastasis, e.g., at laparotomy, a biopsy of cancer of
the head of the pancreas *versus* a biopsy of a metastasis in the
mesentery. If it is not stated whether the biopsy is from a primary
or a secondary, code it as a primary (code 7). Such uncertainty is
reflected in the morphology code (item 24) with a 9 as the 5th digit.

Unrepresentative biopsies. Morphological confirmation of the
clinical diagnosis of malignancy depends on the successful removal of a
piece of tissue which is cancerous. Especially when using endoscopic
procedures (bronchoscopy, gastroscopy, laparoscopy, etc.), the clinician may just miss the tumour with his biopsy forceps, although he
sees it. These cases must be registered on the basis of endoscopic
and not morphological diagnosis. A special code may be used to
indicate 'unrepresentative' biopsies.

Care must be taken in the interpretation and subsequent coding
of autopsy findings, which may vary as follows: (a) the post-mortem
report includes the post-mortem histological diagnosis; (b) the autopsy
is macroscopic only, histological investigations having been carried
out only during life; or (c) the autopsy findings are not supported
by any histological diagnosis.

For coding, diagnoses have been divided into two broad categories,
'non-microscopic' and 'microscopic', each consisting of four categories.
These are given in approximate order of increasing validity in Figure
4.1.

Item 18: *Anatomical site: topography (ICD-0)*

The detailed topography of a tumour may be of importance in
relation to the feasibility of detection in screening and diagnosis, to
the choice of therapy and to prognosis and may provide clues to differences in etiology. It is thus the main axis of tabulation of registry
data.

The location of the tumour should be written in words, with as much
specific information as possible, i.e., with the full clinical diagnosis;
for instance, 'primary malignant neoplasm of left upper lobe of lung';
'malignant tumour of colon, hepatic flexure'; 'metastatic tumour in
lung, primary unknown'. The information for this item should be up-
dated whenever additional data become available; e.g., in the last
example, the primary site may be reported, leading to a change in the
coding of topography (but not in the incidence date, item 13).

When the special ICD for Oncology (ICD-0) (WHO, 1976b) is used (see Chap. 8), the topography code refers to the anatomical location only and does not distinguish, for example, between a primary malignant neoplasm of the lung (ICD-9 162.9) and a metastasis in the lung when the primary is unknown (ICD-9 197.0). In ICD-0 the distinction between these two is made with a behaviour code (5th digit of morphology code).

With ICD-0, topography is coded regardless of the behaviour of the tumour. Benign tumours and tumours of undefined behaviour are thus given the same topographical code as malignant neoplasms. Thus *the 5th digit of the morphology code must always be coded even if histology is not coded*. This topic is discussed further in Chapter 8.

Item 19: *Histological type: morphology (ICD-0)*

Although the anatomical site of a tumour is the main axis for the reporting of cancer registry data, the importance of detailed morphology is being recognized increasingly and not only as an index of confidence in the diagnosis. In the past, lymphomas, leukaemias, melanomas and choriocarcinomas were the only malignant, morphological diagnoses that could be identified in the ICD. However, morphology is often related to etiology and prognosis and, hence, must be considered in many epidemiological and clinical studies. An unusual histological type may be the first indication of a new environmental carcinogen, e.g., angiosarcoma of the liver following exposure to vinyl chloride. The choice of therapy and assessment of prognosis are increasingly influenced by the

The complete histological diagnosis must be recorded by cancer registries. The results of examinations must be recorded in words, as stated in the pathology report, including the date and type of specimen examined. It is also useful for the registry to record the identification numbers of the blocks used to make histological sections, since this may facilitate future access for review.

The wording of the histological diagnosis may pose problems in coding. Even for a common tumour, the diagnosis of which would give rise to no dispute, terminology may differ according to various schools. It would be of great help if pathologists could be persuaded to use the terms of the ICD-0 morphology chapter. These are given in Chapter 8 along with a discussion of the detailed coding of morphology.

The ICD-0 should be used universally for describing morphology, even by registries that continue to code anatomical site by the standard ICD. Indeed, the Index of the 9th Revision of the ICD contains the ICD-0 morphology codes (WHO, 1977).

Item 20: *Multiple primaries*

There are many problems concerned with the term 'multiple primaries'. More than one primary tumour may occur at different sites in the same organ or in different organs, with the same or different histology and at

the same or different times.   The registry's pathologist must decide if
multiple tumours are manifestations of a single neoplasm, i.e., one
primary with metastasis, or if they are different tumours.   The registry must have clear procedures for the classification and coding of multiple primary tumours.   Some multiple primary tumours, e.g., of the skin,
are coded as one tumour.   Possible combinations of multiple primary
tumours by site, histology and time sequence are illustrated in Figure
4.3.   Site is limited for practical reasons to 3-digit site codes, and
the figure is thus somewhat arbitrary.

FIG. 4.3   REGISTRATION OF MULTIPLE NEOPLASMS

No. of primary tumours	Site 3-digit	Histological type	Time	No. of tumours registered	Comments
2 or more	Same[a]	Same[b]	Same[c]	1	Multifocal
2 or more	Same	Same	Different	1	Multifocal
2 or more	Same	Different	Same	2 or more	
2 or more	Same	Different	Different	2 or more	
2 or more	Different	Same	Same	2 or more	Provided metastasis
2 or more	Different	Same	Different	2 or more	can be ruled out
2 or more	Different	Different	Same	2 or more	
2 or more	Different	Different	Different	2 or more	

[a] A registry may decide to separate multiple neoplasms at the 4-digit level e.g., to distinguish the caecum from the sigmoid colon, thus increasing the number of primaries registered. To maintain international comparability it is suggested that 4-digit multiples be not included in incidence rates.

[b] Within the same 3 digit ICD-O code e.g., 807 includes all variants of squamous carcinoma.

[c] Within 2 months

(a) *Same site and histological type*

More than one neoplasm with the same histology may be found at the
same site, either at the same time (synchronous) or at different times
(non-synchronous).   Tumours of the same histology occurring at the same
3-digit site are registered only once, regardless of their time of
occurrence; e.g., a second squamous-cell carcinoma of the skin or a
second adenocarcinoma of the colon[1].   For the pathologist it may be
difficult to say whether such second tumours are second primaries.

(b) *Same site but different histological type*

The main problem is to decide whether differences in histology represent variations in a single tumour or whether there is more than one
primary tumour.   For the latter, the differences in morphology must be
such that they cannot be explained on the basis of histological appearance: e.g., squamous-cell carcinoma and melanoma of the skin would be
coded as separate primaries, as would angiosarcoma of the liver and
liver-cell carcinoma or adenocarcinoma and leiomyosarcoma of the colon.

---

[1] See footnote to Table 4.3

In the case of the thyroid, papillary carcinoma and follicular carcinoma may exist at the same time (in which case a single papillary tumour would be diagnosed) or at different times. Since iodine deficiency is believed to be related to the follicular type, these two must be distinguished for etiological studies.

Pathologists may have different opinions as to whether there are one or two distinct tumours, depending on their interests and specialization, and at times an arbitrary decision will be required. In general, it is better to err on the side of conservatism, i.e., to record one rather than two.

(c) *Same histological type but different sites*

Neoplasms of the same morphology may appear in two different organs simultaneously or one after the other (e.g., adenocarcinoma of breast and adenocarcinoma of ovary). In such cases, registration of a second primary should be deferred until a pathologist has decided whether there are two primaries or whether one is a metastasis of the other. The pathologist will decide on the basis of his knowledge of the biology of the tumours. The occurrence of squamous-cell carcinoma simultaneously in the larynx and uterine cervix (e.g., in a prostitute who smokes heavily) would probably be regarded as two primaries.

(d) *Different sites and histological type*

Primary tumours of different histology may appear at different sites at the same time or at different times, e.g., malignant melanoma of the skin and hypernephroma of the kidney. These must be registered as two tumours. When it has been decided that two or more tumours exist, each will require its own tumour record (see Chap. 7) with individual date of incidence, survival and relation to cause of death. The patient registration number will however be the same.

(e) *Special problems of the skin and breast*

Skin cancers. In hospital registries skin cancers should be registered since they constitute a large demand on medical services in many countries. If the histology is the same (Fig. 4.3), only one registration is made, whether or not multiple primaries are found at the same time or at different times. Such multiple primaries could be regarded as multifocal tumours. In Queensland, Australia, up to 40 or 50 primaries may occur in one individual. If the histology is different (Fig. 4.3) a separate registration is made for each histological type. In this connection, histological type should not be interpreted to mean all the variants listed in the ICD-0 morphology but should be restricted to squamous-cell, basal-cell, adnexal or malignant melanoma.

In population-based registries skin cancers are usually not registered, except for malignant melanoma. Many are treated by general practitioners without biopsy, and the extent of under-reporting cannot be assessed. However, all reports of skin cancers made to the registry must be checked against the Patient Index File (Chap. 7), since they may contain follow-up information, e.g., a skin lesion may be biopsied if it is considered to be a possible metastasis of a previous tumour.

Skin cancers may constitute more than 25% of all registered cancers and thus comprise the commonest site.   But since basic information on age, sex, etc. is often missing, registration is very unsatisfactory. If it is decided to register all skin cancers, then special arrangements will have to be made with those who treat the disease, as has been done in El Paso, Texas (Waterhouse et al., 1976).

Breast cancers.   A common problem is the subsequent appearance of a second cancer in the contralateral breast.   Although some believe that this should not be considered as a new primary, others consider that under specified conditions - such as a lapse of several years, no evidence of metastasis from the first cancer and a clinical opinion that it should be treated as a primary by radical surgery - it might be better to register this second cancer separately in order not to lose the information.   Each registry must adopt a consistent procedure in dealing with this problem.   The recording of one rather than two neoplasms is recommended.

Item 21: *Clinical extent of disease before treatment*

The clinical extent before treatment reflects the clinical opinion of the doctor prior to treatment, except when there is a pathologists report indicating carcinoma *in situ*.   This item must *not* be changed by subsequent information; it is of interest to the hospital registry as an indication of the stage at which patients present themselves for treatment at the institution.

The 1-digit code proposed (Fig. 4.1) is identical with that for item 23.   The first code (*in situ*) is based on microscopy and thus has a different axis of classification from the other codes.   However, in practice they are grouped together.   Many hospital registries prefer the TNM system (item 59), which is explained for specific sites in UICC booklets, although not all sites have yet been defined in this system.

Proposed codes or internationally accepted staging systems are now in use for tumours of the female pelvis[1] and for malignant lymphoma (as an alternative to item 58) and may be developed for others.   The hospital registry is advised to conform to the stage classifications which best serve the interests of its cooperating physicians.

It must be stressed that whatever classification is used, item 21 (or item 59) can be accepted by a cancer registry only in so far as it is truthfully recorded in the medical file and has not been influenced by findings at surgery or autopsy, which are described in item 23.

---

[1] For instance, the staging system of the International Federation of Gynecologists and Obstetricians (FIGO) for primary cancer of the ovary, which was derived from American College of Obstetricians and Gynecologists (1973).

Item 22: *Initial treatment*

This item describes the definitive plan of treatment at the
reporting institution.   For some patients, part of the treatment
will subsequently be given elsewhere.   The classes of information
and codes are given in Figure 4.1.

Hospital registries may wish to go into much more detail, including
the recording and coding of treatment according to items 65–70 (Fig. 4.2).
This is an area of rapid development, in which new treatment schedules
and combinations of various techniques are being used.   Accurate recording is needed to assist evaluation.

The amount of information needed for clinical trials is beyond the
scope of this publication;   the hospital registry may serve as a focal
point for collecting such additional data, and the population-based
registry may assist follow-up.

For the *population-based registry*, this item should be 'planned
initial treatment', covering approximately the first four months or
longer with consecutive courses of treatment.   Since treatment practices vary from place to place, and even within one centre in the course
of time, it is advisable to collect data in very broad categories.
An alternative grouping to those given in Figure 4.1 could be

- radical[1] or non-radical surgery;

- radiation before and/or after surgery;

- chemotherapy;

- immunotherapy;

- hormonotherapy.

Special codes have been assigned (item 63) for patients who did not
receive initial tumour-directed treatment, since such persons are
important for survival studies and for studies of the natural history
of the disease.

Item 23: *Surgical-cum-pathological extent of disease before treatment*

This item serves to validate the staging assessed under item 21.
It does not deal with extent during follow-up (item 24).   Thus, item
23 describes the pretreatment extent of the disease in which clinical
observation (item 21) is augmented by the findings at surgery (including
microscopic examination), if this is part of the initial treatment, or
the findings at autopsy, if the patient died before treatment could be
given.   If there is no surgery or autopsy, this item is given the
code 8 (Fig. 4.1).

---

[1] Each institution should define what 'radical' means, preferably
annually, since techniques change.

Item 24: *Status at annual follow-up*

Hospital registries generally plan an annual follow-up by using the incidence date (item 13) as the anniversary date. The information to be collected and the codes used are straightforward (Fig. 4.1).

Population-based registries may only be able to obtain information as to whether the patient is alive or dead or of unknown status. To go further may be very costly. The date of last discharge from hospital (item 85) can indicate when a person was last known to be alive, thus enabling estimation of minimal survival.

Item 25: *Date of death*

The complete date of death, including day, month and year, should be recorded to facilitate tracing of death certificates and other information relating to the individual. This item enables computation of survival. The place of death (item 83) should also be recorded.

Item 26: *Cause of death (ICD)*

The cause of death recorded by registries should be the underlying cause as defined in the current manual of the *International Statistical Classification of Diseases, Injuries and Causes of Death* (ICD). The cause of death may include any disease; thus, the coding is different from ICD-0, which is restricted to neoplasms. An easier alternative for cancer registries may be item 84.

The coding of cause of death can be very complex since this embraces the full range of the ICD and involves the application of specific rules for the allocation of underlying cause. Special training is therefore needed. Hence, if registry staff are required to code cause of death, they should be trained in national vital statistics offices, and periodic checks must be made on the validity of their coding. The population-based registry will often know only that death has occurred and have no information on the cause, e.g., non-medical certification of death. If death certificates are received from national vital statistics offices, they may already be coded according to the ICD.

A special problem is posed by the diagnosis 'terminal acute leukaemia'. If the patient was known to be suffering from chronic leukaemia, that diagnosis will not be changed. If the former diagnosis was made for persons known to have 'malignant lymphoma' or 'polycythemia vera', doubts may arise as to whether to leave the original diagnosis as the only one or not. It is considered that 'terminal acute leukaemia' must be interpreted to be related to the diagnosis, just as generalized carcinoma is related to a known primary (see rule 3 of ICD-9, WHO, 1977, Vol. 1, p. 705). If desired, the registry could have an additional optional item, with a special code, to describe cause of death in these cases, e.g., 'morphology at death similar to that at initial diagnosis'; 'morphology at death different from that at initial diagnosis'.

There is no problem in attributing postoperative embolism to surgery, but it may be difficult to decide how to interpret death due to myocardial infarct during the recovery period after an operation or after a strenuous diagnostic procedure such as bronchoscopy. It can be argued that the myocardial infarct would probably not have occurred without the treatment for cancer; therefore, all such cases must be counted as cancer-related deaths, in order to avoid artificial 'improvement' of cancer survival data, provided death occurs within a period not exceeding one month after the operation (see rule 3 of ICD-9, WHO, 1977, Vol. 1, p. 705).

Item 27: *Result of autopsy*

This item refers to findings relative to cancer at autopsy. It should be remembered that autopsies vary considerably in their completeness: many are performed solely to establish a cause of death; on the other hand, in many centres necropsies are exhaustive, and early cancers, which may not have contributed to death, may be found.

The codes suggested for the results of autopsy are given in Figure 4.1. Code 2, 'no sign of residual tumour', indicates that the tumour had been completely removed or that the disease (e.g., leukaemia) was in remission; code 6 is for cancer found only at autopsy, when it was not suspected prior to death; code 7, 'cancer diagnosis not confirmed', refers to cases in which the autopsy examination suggests that the diagnosis of cancer prior to death was mistaken. It is desirable to keep such cases in a separate file in the registry (see section 7.9).

Item 28: *Survival in months*

Survival in months is calculated from the incidence date (item 13) to the month and year of death (item 25). Thus, with many data-processing systems it is not essential that this appear as a separate item.

Item 51: *Department of hospital*

This item is of interest mainly to hospital registries, especially those in which departments keep their own records (see item 14). Its coding is at the discretion of the registry: if it refers only to the department undertaking the main treatment, a 1- or 2-digit coding system will suffice; if it is to record each department concerned with the treatment of a patient, a more extensive coding system would clearly be required. Population-based registries should use item 79.

Item 52: *Nationality*

For most purposes, nationality is equivalent to citizenship, which is defined as the legal nationality of a person. There may be difficulties in obtaining accurate information about stateless persons, persons with dual nationality and other ambiguous groups. Nationality must be distinguished from residence (see item 8).

When calculating rates, the definitions of nationality used by the census bureaux for the population denominators must be used.

Item 53: *Religion*

The optional collection of information on religion as a separate item will depend on local conditions: the number of religions, feasibility of collection and possible relevance. Religion may determine the attitude towards, and the use of, modern medical services and thus influence knowledge about malignant disease; for instance, there are differences in utilization of medical services between Chinese and Malays in the Singapore population (Muir et al., 1971); women in some religious groups are reluctant to use medical services (especially examination by male physicians), and their reported malignancy rates may be incredibly low.

Religious beliefs may directly affect exposure to carcinogens or may be an indicator of cultural differences which affect exposure. The rarity of lung cancer in Seventh-day Adventists (Wynder et al., 1959), a religious group whose members do not smoke, has been important evidence in disproving a dominant role of genetic factors in the etiology of lung cancer.

Information on religion may be incorporated into the definition of ethnic group (item 54).

Item 54: *Ethnic group*

This is considered to be an essential item for many cancer registries.

Social and cultural differences between groups may be related to the utilization of medical facilities and to the acceptance of programmes for early detection. Ethnic group may be an indicator of differences in culture and habits which determine exposure to carcinogenic factors, since different ethnic groups may differ in occupational specialization, diet and other habits and customs. Information on subgroups within major ethnic groups may also be important, particularly for providing clues to etiology. Thus, in Singapore, information on the occurrence of cancer in various distinct groups speaking Chinese dialects has revealed important differences in cancer patterns (Shanmugaratnam & Wee, 1973). The castes in India are subgroups with important differences in genetic composition and culture; more information about possible differences in cancer patterns among castes is needed.

The ethnic characteristics about which information is needed in different countries depend on national circumstances. Some of the bases on which ethnic groups are identified are: country or area of origin, race, colour, linguistic affiliation, religion, customs of dress or eating, tribal membership or various combinations of these characteristics. In addition, some of the terms used, such as 'race' or 'origin', have a number of different connotations. The definitions and criteria applied by each registry for the ethnic characteristics of cancer cases must, therefore, be determined by the groups that it wishes to identify. By the nature of the subject, these groups will vary widely from country to country, so that no internationally accepted criteria can be recommended.

Because of the interpretative difficulties that may occur, it is important that when this item is recorded the basic criteria used be defined. The definitions of ethnic groups used by cancer registries should be compatible with official definitions used for census reports, but may need to be more detailed. Even if no population census figures are available, information on ethnic group is important for relative frequency analyses.

A problem may arise when an ethnic group is disguised for political or other reasons; this is the case with the Chinese in certain South-East Asian countries. They are not distinguishable on the basis of routine medical records, and documentation of their cancer patterns would need a special survey.

Item 55: *Occupation*

Item 56: *Industry*

Occupation refers to the kind of work done by an employed person (or performed previously, in the case of unemployed or retired persons), irrespective of the industry or of the status of the person (as employer, employee, etc.). An example might be: a lorry driver in transport or mining industries or in government.

Industry refers to the activity of the establishment in which an economically active person works (or worked) (United Nations, 1968). Some occupations are specific to an individual industry. The *International Standard Classification of Occupations* (ISCO) is published by the International Labour Office (ILO, 1968) and the *International Standard Industrial Classification of all Economic Activities* (ISIC) by the United Nations (United Nations, 1968). These classifications were created primarily for economic purposes and are thus often inadequate for studies of cancer. The *Classification of Occupations and Directory of Occupational Titles* (CODOT), published by the Department of Employment, UK (DOE, 1972) gives more specific details of occupation, which are more relevant to potential exposure.

Information on occupation is frequently poorly reported to registries. Often, the status at the time cancer occurred is reported, which is irrelevant to the occupational status some 20 to 30 years previously; the latter is more significant in relation to possible etiology. Nevertheless, although it must be treated with caution, even imperfect information of this kind may be of value.

The most satisfactory way in which population-based cancer registries can assist in the evaluation of risks of specific occupational exposures is by determining the incidence of cancer in cohorts of persons with a known exposure. For instance, the incidence of nasal cancer in nickel workers in Norway has been determined by linking a list of workers employed in the nickel industry with the cancer registry (Pedersen et al., 1973).

Item 57: *Reason for presentation of patient*

This item serves to evaluate the awareness of cancer in a population. It also gives information about screening activities and level of diagnosis. It distinguishes primary from secondary treatment (follow-up of treatment begun elsewhere). In the latter case, it may be difficult to document precisely the initial extent of the disease, due to differences in clinical description and staging, etc. It is also useful for hospital administrative statistics. Further details are given in Figure 4.2. The item is for hospital registries only.

Item 58: *Staging of lymphomas (including Hodgkin's disease)*
          and leukaemias

Registries will want to conform to the staging system preferred by physicians, e.g., the Ann Arbor staging scheme for Hodgkin's disease (Carbone et al., 1971).

The coding instructions for leukaemia in the *WHO Handbook* are meaningful only for coding follow-up information; for initial diagnosis, the morphology code of ICD-0 is sufficient.

Item 59: *TNM system*

The TNM classification of cancers at various sites is now well established on an international basis (Harmer, 1972). The International Union Against Cancer initially published brochures concerning cancers of the breast and larynx in 1958. Information on additional sites soon followed; and a total of 22 sites, classified by TNM, were amalgamated into a single booklet, the so-called *Livre de Poche*, which appeared in 1968. Over approximately the same period, the American Joint Committee on Cancer Staging and End Results Reporting brought out a total of ten fascicles dealing with about a dozen sites (Harmer, 1972).

The TNM system covers three aspects: the 'T' describes the site of the primary tumour; the 'N' whether or not regional lymph nodes are involved; and the 'M' refers to distant metastases. Additional

features of each field can be indicated by subscripts, e.g., microscopic findings.   For further discussion, the reader is referred to
Davies (1977).

This important item for the comparison of treatment and survival
is of highest priority for hospital registries.

Item 60:   *Site(s) of distant metastases*

This item is mainly of use to hospital registries.   Provision is
made for recording, after the conclusion of the first course of treatment, three separate sites of distant metastases (Fig. 4.2).

Metastases may also be observed during follow-up.   In this case,
they are recorded on the follow-up card together with the date (Chap.
7).

Item 61:   *Co-morbidity*

Hospital registries record conditions affecting treatment or survival (items 61, 62, 63), in order to document the reasons why conventional treatment has not been given.   This is part of the assessment
of the clinical evaluation that led to the choice of treatment.   Here,
the total patient, and not just the neoplasm, is considered.

Co-morbidity is suggested as an optional item for hospital registries only.   The ICD numbers of any coexisting diseases are recorded
here.   Certain precancerous conditions may also be coded, although
these are unlikely to be searched for systematically.   Suggested codes
are given in Figure 4.2 (see also item 82).

Item 62:   *Conditions affecting treatment*

Various categories of conditions are recorded and coded, either
singly or in combination (see Fig. 4.2).

Item 63:   *Reasons for non-curative treatment*

Important for both hospital and population-based registries, this
item lists broad categories of reasons why tumour-directed treatment
(item 22) is not given.   Categories and codes are given in Figure 4.2.

Item 64:   *Laterality*

In paired organs, such as breast, ovary and lung, the side involved
may be important in the choice of therapy, e.g., pneumonectomy is more
feasible for the right lung.   Data about which breast is involved may
be of epidemiological importance, e.g., in relation to the side usually
used for breast-feeding (Ing et al., 1977).

Some registries may wish to establish a further optional item in
order to register more detailed location within an organ.   This might
also be done by adding a 5th digit to the ICD-0 topography code (item
18).   Such coding is already in use for oral pathology (WHO, 1973).

Item 65: *Surgery*

Item 66: *Radiotherapy*

Item 67: *Chemotherapy*

Item 68: *Hormonal therapy*

Item 69: *Other therapy*

Item 70: *Summary of treatment delivered*

The categories described under items 65-68 and 70 (Fig. 4.2) give
the opinion of the treating physician at the time of completion of
definitive treatment, e.g., 'curative, completed' should be entered if
it is thought that the operation has completely removed all traces of
the tumour.   In some cases, time will show this opinion to be incorrect;
nevertheless, it is important that the opinion on completion of treatment be recorded, and this should not be changed because of subsequent events.

These items are important for hospital registries, but population-
based registries might collect item 70 as a summary of treatment.
'Curative, not completed' refers to treatment undertaken with curative
intent that was not completed because of operative complications or some
other problem.   'Palliative treatment' is that given without expectation of cure but with expectation of prolonging and improving life.
'Symptomatic treatment' implies no expectation of prolonging life.

Item 71: *Chronology of treatment*

This item gives the order in which the various component types of
treatment were given.   It allows for six successive items of treatment
(initial and subsequent treatments), and each is to be entered in its
appropriate position (starting from the left), identified by a number
according to the codes given in Figure 4.2.   For example, a patient
was treated first by surgery, then by radiotherapy and chemotherapy.
Subsequently he received a further course of radiotherapy, followed
by chemotherapy.   The coding would be:

1	2	3	2	3

Item 72: *Disease status at discharge from hospital*

This item should record the opinion of the doctor in charge of the
case at the time of discharge or at the end of hospitalization for the
first course of treatment.   It must not be changed by subsequent
events.   Codes are given in Figure 4.2.

Item 73: *Duration of hospitalization in days*

This item, recorded in days, refers to the initial course of treatment given.   In many hospitals, it may indicate the efficiency of organization or the extent of collaboration between different departments involved in treatment.   It may also be influenced by the home conditions of the patient.

Item 74: *Patient status (i) before and (ii) after first treatment and at anniversaries*

The importance of this item must be stressed, since it is the only one that expresses the 'quality of life of the cancer patient'.   As such, it can be recorded only by hospital registries or in information from general practitioners.

Codes for this item are given in Figure 4.2.   A scale of incapacity is given, ranging from 'well and active' to 'confined to bed'. This is a difficult item to code, as such grading is to some extent subjective.   Two digits serve to describe the patient's status before or after the first, or main and most important, treatment. The remaining eight digits refer to the patient's degree of disability after 1, 2, 3, 4, 5, 7, 10 and 15 years of follow-up.

Example: A woman presenting with a breast tumour was, at the time of diagnosis, disabled but active;   after treatment, she was well and active.   The first two digits would then be

3	1

For the first three years of follow-up her status remained unchanged ('well and active');   but in the fourth year she became disabled and inactive, and by the fifth year she was confined to bed.   The coding for this case would be :

Before treatment	After treatment	Years of follow-up 1	2	3	4	5	7	10	15
3	1	1	1	1	4	5			

Item 75: *Additional causes of death*

This optional item enables up to three additional causes of death to be coded (Fig. 4.2), each to 4 digits, using the ICD.   The underlying cause of death is coded as item 26;   item 75 enables coding of other causes that may be mentioned in a death certificate.

Item 76: *Cancer entered on death certificate*

This refers to any subsection of the international form of medical certificate of cause of death, including section II of the certificate.

For follow-up.   As with item 26 (cause of death), the use of
item 76 for the follow-up of known cancer cases is mainly of interest
to hospital registries.   It would be collected by population-based
registries only in special surveys, e.g., to determine how often
cancer is not mentioned on death certificates in known cancer cases:
nasopharyngeal carcinoma is said to be under-reported on death certificates of Hong Kong Chinese due to a belief that it is hereditary and
that 'public' mention of it could interfere with a daughter's prospects
for marriage (Ho[1]).

It is uncertain in what proportion of cases a hospital registry
will be able to obtain details of death certificates when death has
not occurred in the hospital itself.   The South Metropolitan Cancer
Registry informs treating physicians of cause of death to permit
completion of files.   Vital statistics offices generally code only
one of those causes stated on the death certificate, i.e., the underlying cause of death.   Any additional causes may be obtained only
from the actual wording on the death certificate, and special arrangements will have to be made to obtain this.   In many instances, the
word 'cancer' may not be mentioned, but there may be a statement such
as 'post-radical mastectomy' from which a diagnosis of previous cancer
can be inferred.

As a source of new cases.   This item is important for population-
based registries as a source of cancer cases not previously notified by
any other source.   It may thus be the first and perhaps the only
means of notification and in this sense is an essential item for population-based registries.   A death certificate notification may precede
other notifications which may await completion of an autopsy report
and histology before transmission to the cancer registry.

For quality control.   If cancer is reported FIRST *via* a death
certificate, this indicates the quality of the reporting system;
if reported ONLY *via* a death certificate, it indicates the quality of
the data.

Item 77: *Year of immigration*

This is of interest for registries dealing with migrant groups
including immigrant workers.   It is of importance to relate the date
of incidence to the date of immigration in order to assess the effect
of change of environment.   In a country with many migrants, e.g.,
Israel, a sudden rise in the incidence rates of cervical cancer soon
after an immigration period could be ascribed to an increase in
'diagnosis rate' rather than to a real increase in the incidence of
this disease in the population group.

---

[1] Personal communication

Item 78: *Country of birth of father*

The country of birth of the parents may be of interest in countries with immigrants. For example, first- and second-generation Japanese in the US show differences in the incidence of breast and stomach cancers.

Usually, country of birth of father is more often available in denominator data.

Item 79: *Name of first hospital or institution where definite diagnosis was made*

For a population-based registry, this item is comparable to item 51 (department of hospital). It is not restricted to hospitals, but may include other institutions such as tuberculosis clinics. This information may be valuable in planning case-control studies.

Item 80: *Documentation*

This optional item (for population-based registries only) grades the level and nature of the documentation of the case: the highest grade is given to a case summary with histological details, the lowest to a case where not more than a death certificate is available to the cancer registry.

A suggested set of codes in ascending order of priority is:

1. Case on printed list of deaths, but no death certificate received

2. Death certificate but no other document

3. General practitioner information

4. Hospital discharge diagnosis

5. Notification from specialist clinic

6. Case summary but no detailed report on histology

7. Case summary with detailed histology

Item 81: *Certainty of diagnosis*

It may be useful to include a code to express the certainty of the coded diagnosis. Even the pathologist, in making an autopsy report, may be unable to state the origin of the tumour but may give a choice of two or three possibilities. Coding rules exist for ICD-8 and ICD-9. This item could be used to indicate doubts as to the stated histological diagnosis or, on the other hand, to express confirmation after revision by a specialist. Thus, cancer registry data are qualified by most valid basis of diagnosis (item 17), by documentation (item 80) and by expression of certainty of diagnosis (item 81).

A suggested set of codes is:

1. Malignancy uncertain, site uncertain

2. Malignancy uncertain, site certain

3. Malignancy certain, site uncertain

4. Malignancy certain, site certain, histology uncertain

5. Histological diagnosis doubtful after revision

6. Histological diagnosis confirmed after revision

7. Malignancy certain, site certain, histology certain

Item 82: *Other pathology at site of cancer*

In addition to what was discussed under item 61, it is possible here to add chronic disease in the organ affected by cancer, e.g., lithiasis, schistosomiasis. These may appear in death certificates and would be mentioned in the clinical record.

Item 83: *Place of death*

This information is useful for both hospital and population-based registries. No codes are proposed, but should be developed by a registry to reflect local practice, e.g., death at home, in a death house (Singapore), in hospital, etc.

The population-based registry may use this information as an indication of certain aspects of medical care, e.g., a tendency to discharge terminal patients in order to diminish the number of deaths in hospital statistics. It may thus indicate the need for chronic hospitals.

For those deaths that occur in a hospital, it would be possible to obtain data on the frequency of autopsy in known cancer cases.

Item 84: *Relation of cause of death to cancer*

As an alternative or in addition to item 26, in which the cause of death is coded according to ICD rules, it may be much easier for both hospital and population-based registries to record the relation of the cause of death to the neoplasm.

Suggested groupings and codes are as follows:

1. Due to cancer (Information about multiple primaries will appear on the record of the primary that is believed to have caused death)

2. Due to treatment for cancer, e.g., as a result of surgery, chemotherapy or radiation

3. Due to another cause, unrelated to cancer, but with signs of cancer present (on the basis of clinical, surgical or autopsy findings)

4. Due to another cause unrelated to cancer, and with no clinical signs of cancer present

5. Due to another cause, with no surgical or autopsy evidence of cancer. This may be due to complete removal of the cancer or to a false diagnosis. In the latter event, the tumour record is placed in the file of rejected cases (section 9.10).

Item 85: *Date of last discharge from hospital*

This optional item is useful for population-based registries to assist in up-dating and follow-up.

Other optional items

The registry will frequently be asked routinely to collect additional items of information, such as specific hazards (e.g., radiation exposure), habits (tobacco, alcohol), blood groups, etc. Each request should be examined carefully in the light of cost, reliability of the item and the yield and utility of the information. It may be preferable to study the associations of such items with neoplastic diseases by means of special surveys or linkage studies (see section 2.6.1).

5. SOURCES OF PATIENT INFORMATION

5. SOURCES OF PATIENT INFORMATION

5.1 *Overview*

All the sources of information for a hospital registry are to be found in the hospital inpatient and outpatient departments and in its laboratories. The main source is often the hospital medical record department. The hospital registry should cooperate and be coordinated with any existing population-based cancer registry that covers the same population; some hospitals draw cases from a very extensive geographical area which may be covered by more than one population-based registry.

The task of a population-based registry is easier when there are collaborating hospital registries which contribute information on cancer cases, as in New York State (Burnett, 1976). The information required about all cancer patients in a geographical area can usually be found in those places in which the patients have been observed, examined or treated. In theory, every practitioner, every hospital and every laboratory may have such information; in practice, this information is sought in the files of hospitals, cancer centres, pathology institutes and haematology laboratories. Other sources, such as health insurance plans and death certificates, can be very useful in case finding (Chap. 6).

5.2 *Sources for the hospital registry*

5.2.1 *Medical record department*

A basic prerequisite for a hospital cancer registry is a functioning medical record department. There should be a medical record for each patient, containing all pertinent aspects of diagnosis and treatment. Such records are often kept in a single medical record department, although in some hospitals each specialized service may keep its own records, thus increasing the difficulties of registration (see section 5.2.5).

'The medical record department plays a major role in the efficient operation of a cancer registry by supplying identification of cancer patients having been discharged from the hospital and by making the records of these patients available promptly.' (American College of Surgeons, 1974a).

5.2.2 *Pathology and autopsy services*

Pathology services. These are considered by many to be the most important source of information, since it is the examination of tissue that permits prediction of whether a tumour is likely to behave in a malignant fashion or not. The files of pathology services usually contain the most complete information on the histopathological nature

-73-

of the neoplasm.   Some hospital pathology services may be located
elsewhere, e.g., in other hospitals or in private laboratories.

A frequent inconvenience in the exploitation of histological
material relates to the inaccuracy of other elements of information.
Very often the names of a patient are spelled incorrectly, or items
concerning sex and age are inaccurate or missing.   The reason for
this inadequacy is evident: the pathologist does not usually see
patients, and the clinician sends specimens without paying much attention to these items.   Therefore, it is sometimes difficult to connect
the very precise diagnosis made by a pathologist to the corresponding
patient record.

Autopsy services.   These are generally situated in the same place
as pathology services.   Autopsy files are a very valuable source of
information because of the generally exact description of the site of
the tumour, the extent of spread and histopathological appearance.
An autopsy may confirm or exclude doubtful diagnoses suggested by a
clinician or mentioned in a death certificate.

A histopathological examination may not have been carried out,
especially if a histological diagnosis was made previously.   In other
cases, a very active pathology department may defer the histopathology
for months, and a revised diagnosis may not reach the cancer registry.
Close cooperation with the pathology department is needed to uncover
such further information.   However, careful autopsies may give 'too
much' information.   Some tumours that are clinically unapparent may
only be detected on autopsy, death being due to another cause.   If
such a tumour is present and it has consequently to be registered, the
question may be raised of whether, for reasons of comparability, to
include these tumours in the computation of incidence.   A special code
for such cases enables a choice to be made of whether to include them
in incidence studies (item 27 - Code 6).

Incipient or *in situ* tumours may be discovered by post-mortem
examinations in, e.g., the uterine cervix, prostate and thyroid.

5.2.3 *Radiotherapy*

Large numbers of cancer cases are treated in these services, and
precise information is kept on types of treatment, mode of application
and dosage.   Such a service often forms the nucleus of a cancer centre
(see below);   it may treat considerable numbers of patients on an outpatient basis, e.g., those with skin, breast or nasopharyngeal cancers.

5.2.4 *Outpatient department*

In many hospitals, the medical record department codes diagnoses
only for inpatients and not for outpatients (Laszlo et al., 1976).
Due to the high cost of inpatient care, many cancer cases are seen
only as outpatients in various specialized services (see section 5.2.5).
Although many such 'outpatient only' cases will be ascertained by

means of a pathology report, those for whom pathology studies were
performed elsewhere will be missed by the hospital registry.   Thus,
'it is necessary that provision be made at the administrative level
to assure inclusion in registration of all cancer patients seen on an
outpatient basis.   Provision should also be made to inform the registry of subsequent follow-up visits' (American College of Surgeons,
1974a).

5.2.5 *Other specialized services*

Specialized departments of hospitals deal with patients with
cancer of specific anatomical regions or body systems.   Although
generally integrated administratively, such departments may be large
and administratively autonomous, with their own medical record libra-
ries;   they may have their own outpatient clinics and radiological
facilities.   In some countries, it is not uncommon for such departments, e.g., gastroenterology, to undertake their own diagnostic histopathology.   The importance of these sources is that some cancer
patients may be seen and treated only in these departments, and the
information will not be obtained elsewhere.

The tumours thus treated frequently belong to very specific groups.
Consequently, to disregard such sources risks under-registration
of certain sites.   Although the clinical and therapeutical information
is of great interest, giving, for instance, precise tumour localization,
the information is very often incomplete from the registry's view point:
complete identity or residence may be missing.   In the day-to-day
practice of cancer registration, the collection of data from the various
specialized services usually generates problems.

Pathology and radiotherapy services are discussed above.   The
list of other specialized services that follows does not exhaustively
cover every possible source.

(a) *Surgery* may accept the numerous types of cancer that are
considered to be operable, especially cancers of the digestive tract
and breast.   The existence of specialized surgical units may attract
patients whose tumours belong to this speciality;   for example, a unit
of thoracic surgery would deal with broncho-pulmonary and oesophageal
cancers.   Neurosurgery, orthopaedics and traumatology services are
discussed below.

(b) *Gynaecology* diagnoses and treats the majority of tumours of
the uterine cervix and corpus, ovary and lower genito-urinary tract
and the rarer tumours of the adnexae.

(c) *Obstetrics* normally diagnoses tumours of the placenta, hydati-
form moles and chorionepitheliomas, as well as the rare, congenital
tumours seen in the newborn.

(d) *Paediatrics* deals with the cases of cancer in children who,
for many reasons, are often not sent to cancer centres unless these
have their own paediatric services.

(e) *Orthopaedics and traumatology* receive the majority of tumours of bone and cartilage and, also, many bone metastases originating from primary tumours in other organs, since these are sometimes the first clinical manifestations of malignancy.

(f) *Odonto-stomatology* often diagnoses, in addition to the rare tumours of dental origin, cancers and precancerous lesions of the buccal cavity and of the salivary glands. Their role is of special importance in those countries in which tumours of the mouth are particularly frequent, as, for instance, in India.

(g) *Ophthalmology* may diagnose malignant neoplasms of the eye, orbit and adnexal structures such as the eyelids. The presence of an intra-cranial neoplasm may also be suspected in a patient presenting with a defect in vision.

(h) *Otorhinolaryngology* is equipped to diagnose tumours situated deeply within the inner ear and upper respiratory and digestive tracts, which are not easily accessible except to specialists in this field. This speciality also assists in the endoscopic diagnosis of bronchial, gastric or oesophageal tumours.

(i) *Dermatology* is very often equipped to give superficial radiation therapy, and it is here that the majority of cancers of the skin and related organs are seen. Depending on local custom, a vary-ing proportion of these neoplasms may not be biopsied.

(j) *Urology*, whether at the time of diagnostic exploration or of treatment, sees the majority of cancers of the urinary tract and of the male genital tract.

(k) *Neurology, neurosurgery and psychiatry* diagnose tumours of the nervous system and tumours of other origins that cause motor or sensory disturbance by extrinsic compression. In psychiatric patients, the occurrence of neoplasms in other sites should not be overlooked.

(l) *Endocrinology* may diagnose tumours in which the symptoms are due not to the physical effects but to an endocrine distrubance, e.g., tumours of the hypophysis, adrenals and parathyroid, and the rare tumours of the islets of Langerhans.

(m) *Haematology* often diagnoses leukaemias, certain malignant lymphomas and multiple myelomas.

(n) *Biochemistry and immunology* play a limited and somewhat accessory role within the chain of sources of information, the former by establishing the level of acid phosphatase in cancers of the pro-state, the latter in the search for alpha-fetoprotein in primary liver cancer, carcino-embryonic antigen in large-bowel cancers and chorionic gonadotrophins in chorionepitheliomas. Their role will probably become more important in the future.

The practical use of information from biochemistry and immunology services to a population-based cancer registry is doubtful.

Firstly, these exist not only as hospital services but also as
private laboratories or in conjunction with health insurance schemes.
They may cover a wide range of examinations, and the results that
interest the cancer registry will be interspersed among a vast amount
of other non-relevant data.   Moreover, identifying information is
usually insufficient for later location of a patient.

5.3   *Sources for the population-based registry*

5.3.1 *Hospital registry or its sources*

The sources for the population-based registry include those
described above for the hospital registry and may include hospital
registries.   In addition, there are other sources which may not
contribute to hospital registries but which are very important for
comprehensive registration.

5.3.2 *General hospitals*

Patients are generally referred here for diagnosis, either
directly from the general practitioner or after initial screening in
an outpatient department or clinic.   There is a world-wide trend
towards team care of cancer cases.   This must be carried out in a
hospital, and, hence, in the future, the sources of information for
cases will become concentrated in hospitals and will depend less on
private practitioners.   Malignancy can be diagnosed in practically
every department of a general hospital (internal medicine, surgery,
gynaecology, paediatrics, and the special services - urology, otorhinolaryngology, traumatology, etc.), and the most detailed medical
histories can be found in their files.   The routine medical documentation of the hospital does not, however, generally meet the
demands of a cancer registry.   This is understandable, since cancer
patients constitute only a minor fraction of all admissions.   There
may be little knowledge of and little attention paid to the particulars
of special interest to the cancer registry.   The patient may have
been transferred for further investigation and/or therapy to another
ward in the same hospital or to another hospital where more specialized
facilities are available (e.g., neurosurgery).

It must be emphasized that for a sizeable proportion of cancer
patients there may be only a single hospitalization: (a) the patients
may be followed up in the respective outpatient department, which may
be a quite independent service, or referred to an oncological hospital
(e.g., cancer centre, see below); or (b) death may occur during the
first hospitalization (e.g., after a very late diagnosis or in the
event of a post-surgical death).

To make full use of general hospitals, a cancer registry must
become acquainted with administrative practices and procedures, from
admission to discharge, and with the existing filing systems.   The
admission clerk is responsible for recording identifying items and
for their correctness and completeness.   The person responsible for

patient files may be the nurse in the ward, the nurse in the corresponding outpatient department, or a trained medical record librarian
in a record room connected with all departments.   The filing system
must be understood, e.g., whether files of patients relating to
successive hospitalizations are combined, and how it can be used to
check the completeness of reporting on all cancer cases seen in the
hospital.   In the case of an emergency admission, only minimal data
may be on hand: it is not always realized that cancer patients may be
admitted as emergencies, with obstructed bowel, perforated malignant
gastric ulcer, etc.

5.3.3 *Cancer centres*

The term 'cancer centre' is applied to medical facilities, varying
in scope, activities and equipment, that care for cancer patients from
diagnosis through all stages of their disease.   Common to all is a
striving for the best possible treatment, awareness of new methods,
continuous care, follow-up and evaluation of the treatment given.
Many of the best hospital registries are found in cancer centres.
In most countries, basic and clinical research is an integral part of
the work.

In principle, this is an excellent source of information, because
patients have been seen there many times or may have stayed in the
centre.   They have been examined and diagnosed, and all pertinent
information can be found in the medical files; the available documentation in these files generally exceeds that required by the population-
based registry.

Cancer centres are a source of information in which the physicians
are particularly motivated from the point of view of cancer registration; it is thus generally easy to get their cooperation or the
cooperation of the staff.   Many cancer centres have their own
registries, which may be regarded as sources for the population-based
registry (see section 5.3.1).   As noted in Section 2.3, cancer centres
often selectively attract patients from a wide geographical area.

Because of the scope of the information available in these cancer
centres, the population-based cancer registry may use this documentation for complementary research, especially for studies on the diagnosis and treatment of patients or for certain etiological studies.

5.3.4 *Specialized hospitals and services*

The pathology, radiation therapy and other specialized services
of hospitals described above (sections 5.2.2 to 5.2.5) may have
analogues in separate hospitals or institutes, which must be covered
by the population-based registry.   Perhaps the most common of such
specialized hospitals are those for obstetrics, paediatrics, psychiatry and ophthalmology.   Cancer cases may also be found in hospitals
for the treatment of tuberculosis; in many parts of the world cancer
patients may be found in long-stay institutions such as leprosaria.

Such sources are important since they may have records of cancer patients who do not appear at cancer centres or in death certificates.

Forensic services are a potential source of cancer cases, although their purpose is to establish the cause of death and not necessarily to report incidental cancer. A proportion of accidental deaths, and some suicidal ones, occur in persons with cancer, and contact should be maintained with the medico-legal services.

5.3.5 *General practitioners and other sources of primary medical care information*

Physicians are often the first to see cancer patients and to suspect the malignant nature of the illness. In most developed countries as soon as there is a suspicion of cancer, general practitioners will send the patient to a hospital or cancer centre. The information available to the general practitioner is usually limited, except for that concerning the first symptoms of the illness and, possibly, antecedent data concerning the patient and his family.

Cancer patients may appear at the physician's office with a very advanced stage of cancer, when all therapy would be futile, and the physician may decide against examinations, sometimes painful, which may be of minor diagnostic value. This applies especially to older people in developed countries and to people of all ages in developing countries. For such patients, general practitioners are the only source of information and would normally be the certifying physician on the death certificate, which in these cases is the source of information for the population-based registry. It, in turn, follows the case back by asking the general practitioner to complete the notification form or to describe the case (see item 76).

5.3.6 *Health insurance (workmen's compensation funds, etc.)*

In many countries, systems of health insurance have developed either as complete national services, as obligatory insurance for an important fraction of the population or as voluntary insurance.

In such insurance systems emphasis is placed on administrative documentation in relation to the refunding of benefits to the insured. Information of a medical character may be sparse and not very accurate; on the other hand, information concerning the identity items, the correct spelling of the name, date of birth, residence and successive occupations may be exact. In this respect, even if the medical information leaves much to be desired, insurance organizations are, in some countries, an important source for verifying data on the patient. Under certain circumstances, the health insurance organizations serve as middle-men between the various sources of information at the cancer registry, since they assume the task of assembling all documentation relating to the insured. In this case, these organizations are a very valuable source of information, on condition that the obstacle of confidentiality can be overcome.

These schemes often have one major drawback from the point of
view of registration, namely, that the identifying data pertain to
the insured, while the illness may be in one of his dependants, e.g.,
his wife.

5.3.7 *Screening programmes*

Such programmes have been set up in the course of the last 20
years to detect cancer as early as possible.   These campaigns are
designed mainly for detection at 'accessible sites', such as the
uterine cervix and breast.   Programmes have also been organized to
detect and examine cancers in other organs, such as the bladder in
workers in the aniline dye industry.   Information from such programmes
is held by those organizing them, especially with reference to cases
of cancer diagnosed within the operation.   It is generally easy to
obtain information from these programmes, but differentiating, invasive
cancers from cancers *in situ* and other precancerous lesions usually
require further investigation elsewhere.

Detection schemes for other diseases may become an important
source of information;   thus, the search for tuberculosis by X-ray
examination results in detection of some cancers of the lung and media-
stinum.

With the acquisition of knowledge in certain new areas of oncology,
as, for instance, in immunology, other, systematic ways of detecting
certain types of tumour may be developed in the future.   At present,
the occurrence of alpha-fetoprotein in the serum is used in the diagnosis of primary cancer of the liver.   The evidence for the presence
of other embryonic proteins in cancers of the digestive organ has not
yet reached the same degree of specificity, and the same is true for
tests for antibodies against the Epstein-Barr virus in Burkitt's
lymphoma and cancers of the nasopharynx.   Nevertheless, the progress
made within the last few years in these areas allows speculation that
in the future serological services may become a potential source of
information for the cancer registry (see section 5.2).

Although valuable as sources of cases, the effects of such programmes on the comparability of incidence rates of cancers detected
in this way should be borne in mind.

5.3.8 *Death certificates*

Most countries have a system of death registration.   The cause
of death is generally noted on a certificate, which is used as the
basis for issuing a burial licence.   As mentioned in the discussion
on confidentiality (section 3.4), however, the diagnosis may be
entered on a detachable slip, which, if separated, makes this source
useless for cancer registration.

A model death certificate was initially devised by WHO in 1948;
many countries have adopted this model, adapting it to their own needs
but conserving the principle of differentiating between the immediate

cause of death, the underlying cause of death and other pathological conditions present at the time of death but which did not directly cause it.

The cause of death is coded according to WHO codes, using classification rules agreed upon internationally since 1948. The publication of results is likewise subject to precise rules, and the tabulations refer to the underlying cause of death.

From the point of view of using these items as a source of information about cancer, the principal goal of the system, which is to give the cause of death, may present difficulties: thus, for those patients who die of cancer there are no problems; however, for cancer patients who die from other conditions or due to an accident, cancer may or may not be mentioned on the certificate, and even if it is noted it will only rarely be coded. These details are important in obtaining the information sought by the cancer register.

The diagnosis of the cause of death is often given in vague terms, and with regard to malignancies, the localization is very often mentioned but is not always correct. As this document is often made out by administrative authorities themselves, items of identity, such as dates of birth and of death and residence, are generally accurate. These elements are of particular importance if survival analysis of cancer patients is made one of the objectives of the registry, as is usual for hospital registries. The wording of the death certificate does not, however, always infer whether the death was due to cancer or to another cause. Scrutinizing original (or copies of original) death certificates is much better than relying on the diagnostic lists of the vital statistics bureau, because the latter are often coded only according to the underlying cause of death and may not include those deaths for which cancer was not the underlying cause.

Information on death is always of major interest for population-based cancer registries. Very often it is found that deaths from cancer, with cancer, or occurring after an operation for cancer relate to persons who have not previously been registered, and a 'follow-back' must be started:

(a) For each death certificate relating to a death in hospital or to an autopsy, the pertinent clinical abstract will be requested from the hospital or pathologist.

(b) A physician certifying death from or with, e.g., a 'post-malignancy state' will be asked to fill in a form indicating the basis of the diagnosis and if and when the patient had been seen previously at a hospital. Great care must be taken in formulating the letter to the physician; he may learn to avoid being approached, by the simple expedient of not writing a diagnosis of cancer. Some physicians respond much better to a telephone call than to a registry form. Since he may have been called in only at the terminal stage, his information that the patient 'has never been hospitalized' may prove later

to have been incorrect.   For a population-based registry, it is
recommended that all cases be registered, even if no other document
is forthcoming, and that 'registration from death certificate only'
be noted (item 80, Code 2).

Such cases may prove to be worth separate analysis.   Since they
may concern special groups of people, such as the elderly and ethnic
or religious groups, avoidance of the use of medical services may be
suspected.   The validity of observed 'incidence' rates (which, in fact,
are always 'diagnosis' rates) for such groups might then be questioned
in the light of the proportion of home cancer deaths not reported from
any other source.

Cases in which cancer is recorded on the death certificate and in
which the diagnosis is later proven wrong (e.g., by autopsy) should
be kept on a special file (see section 7.10).   A person with confirmed
cancer may have been treated successfully but the death certificate may
nevertheless give the cause of death as cancer.   If necropsy is performed and no trace of cancer is found, the cause of death should be
updated on the tumour record (item 27).

6. CASE-FINDING AND COLLECTION OF DOCUMENTS

6. CASE-FINDING AND COLLECTION OF DOCUMENTS

6.1 *Overview*

The identification of all cancer cases is essential to ensure completeness of coverage. The sources of such cases were described in Chapter 5. Case-finding is relatively simple for the *hospital registry*, involving regular checking by the registry staff of various sources of cases. Case-finding by a *population-based registry* is often done chiefly by means of voluntary notification to the registry: a notification form is completed by physicians (in hospitals and general practice), hospital administrators, etc. Some registries use field clerks to collect essentially the same information. Such case-finding is supplemented by the systematic investigation, by registry staff, of the other sources of cases described in Chapter 5.

Cancer registries may arrange to have various types of documents forwarded regularly, e.g., lists of deaths, including those in which cancer is mentioned on the death certificate. Such documents may serve not only for case-finding, but may contain information about the patient or his tumour. 'Hospital Activity Analysis' systems can assist case-finding but cannot replace cancer registries, because they have limited coverage and have problems in linking successive admissions of the same patient.

Although there are typical patterns of patient referral and treatment which facilitate case-finding, for some patients there may be a very different pattern, related to local medical conditions and to their own temperament. It is evident that a valid measure of cancer incidence in a population can be made only with all the relevant information. Its quality will vary with the source. Complete case-finding inevitably results in the collection of multiple reports about the same patient (see Chap. 7). There is a lack of comparability between some items of information received from different sources. Uniformity of techniques, diagnosis and nomenclature can only partially compensate for this variation in quality.

6.2 *Hospital registries*

6.2.1 *Development of a reportable list*

'A reportable list is an integral part of a cancer registry. It is a statement of those diagnoses which are included in the registry. It should also state those diagnoses which are excluded. This list should be compiled by the registrar in consultation with the hospital cancer registry committee' (American College of Surgeons, 1974a). The *International Classification of Diseases for Oncology (ICD-0)*,

1976 (WHO, 1976b) may be used as a basis for the reportable list.
All diagnoses that have a behaviour code of 2 or higher (5th digit of
the morphology code) are reportable.   Those with a behaviour code
of 1 (uncertain whether benign or malignant;   borderline malignancy)
should be reviewed by the cancer registry committee to determine
whether they should be reportable.   Those not reportable should be so
marked in the alphabetical index of ICD-O.   Some registries may wish
to register benign tumours (behaviour code 0), although these are
usually excluded.   The ICD-O, 1976, gives a list of tumour-like
lesions and conditions which would not normally be included in the
reportable list.

6.2.2 Case-finding[1]

Case-finding is a systematic method of identifying all reportable
cases.   It is effected by regular checks by the registry staff of
all departments in hospitals, including outpatients, which have
information on cancer patients.   The details of such checking vary
with the registry.

(a) Medical records department

This department, when it exists, is probably the most complete
source in the hospital for case identification.   Arrangements may be
made whereby medical records personnel help identify cases and make
their records accessible to registry staff.   If this can be arranged,
the personnel involved must be few in number and must be thoroughly
familiar with which diagnoses are reportable to the registry by using
a copy of the registry's reportable list.

(b) Pathology department

Since most cancer patients have undergone a biopsy or surgical
resection, case-finding procedures must involve the pathology
department.   Several methods of identifying reportable cases are
outlined below.   When this department is used for case-finding, it
is important that all pathology reports, including autopsy, bone
marrow and cytology reports, are screened.   In a large hospital
there may also be separate speciality departments (e.g., oral pathology,
eye pathology).

  1. The most effective case-finding method is screening by the
registrar of all pathology reports.   This is best done by use of the
pathology departments chronological file, to ensure that every report
is reviewed.   Since not all biopsies result in detection of malignancy, even when it is present, screening of these reports will allow
identification of those cases which have a clinical diagnosis of

---

[1] This section is based very closely on the publication of the
American College of Surgeons (1974a).

malignancy.   The corresponding patient record can later be screened
to determine whether a definite clinical diagnosis of malignancy was
established.

2. In some hospitals, the pathology department sends copies
of pathology reports to the registry.   Some send copies of all
reports, others send only reports of malignant diagnoses as selected
either by the pathologist or by a clerk, who should, of course, be
using the reportable list.   For doubtful cases the pathologist or
the registrar should decide whether the case is reportable.

3. A third method involves a listing or a card made for the
registry for each reportable case.

(c) *Radiotherapy department*

This department treats cancer patients almost exclusively.   Since
many patients receive radiotherapy on an outpatient basis and are never
admitted to the hospital, a case-finding system is essential for this
department.   Two methods of identifying cases are used by registries:

1. The most effective method is for the registry to receive a
copy of the radiotherapy summary for all patients.   This summary not
only identifies the case to the registry but also serves for abstracting information in those hospitals where this information is not incorporated into the main patient record.   The summary may be a letter
to the referring physician or it may be a special form.

2. Some registries receive only a list of cases;   or they may
review the radiotherapy department's log book and make a list of
cases for themselves.   This is an acceptable method but is usually
more time-consuming than that described above.

(d) *Outpatients department*

Outpatients departments may be located physically in the inpatient
service to which they pertain, and under such circumstances records
are usually maintained in those outpatients departments.   Under other
circumstances, outpatients clinics may be held in a separate outpatients block or floor, and records may either be centralized or
brought to a clinic session by the staff of the particular service
holding the clinic.   The registry will have to determine how outpatients records are kept - and this may vary within hospitals and
between hospitals - and design an appropriate method of case-finding.

6.2.3 *Preparation of a cancer registry abstract*

A cancer registry abstract is a summary of information about a
cancer patient, including his tumour.   It is completed by the registry,
generally following case-finding and registration of the tumour (Chap.
7).   It is analogous to the notification form for population-based
registries (section 6.3.2).

An example of a cancer registry abstract is given in Figures 4.1 and 4.2, which comprise the WHO Hospital Cancer Registry margin-punch card. This abstract is completed by the staff of the registry following case identification. The WHO abstract card contains all the items of information in the *WHO Handbook*. However, the amount of information included on an abstract form is a matter for local decision. The format of the card can also be modified , but the numbering of the items should not be changed.

When developing a form to meet the requirements of an individual hospital, the American College of Surgeons (1974a) recommends the following guidelines:

1. It should satisfy the needs and desires of the medical staff, giving thoughtful consideration to the availability and subsequent use of all information collected.

2. Data should be easily retrieved, whether manually or by machine.

3. Data should be basically simple and used to stimulate new areas for research:

   (a) High-priority items (Tables 4.1, 4.2, 4.3), plus any additional information desired by the hospital staff should be collected.

   (b) Information, such as dosage in chemotherapy, special epidemiological data (e.g., smoking history), is usually collected only for special studies, and then under the close supervision of the interested physician.

4. Each item on the form should be clearly defined, either on the form itself or in the procedure manual (section 7.10.1), thus ensuring consistency in the collection of data.

5. Every abstract form should be developed with reference to a procedure manual.

6. In areas where a central registry exists (section 2.2) it may be practical to use the abstract form of the central registry in each collaborating hospital.

6.2.4 *Use of field clerks*

If a hospital registry serves several hospitals, it may use field clerks, who are useful for case-finding and abstracting and are most important in follow-up. The number of field clerks on the staff of a cancer registry depends upon the size of the geographical area covered by the registry, the number of cancer cases in the various hospitals and on the cooperation of the hospitals. It might sometimes be advantageous to use someone living near an important source of information (e.g., a cancer centre) if there are sufficient cases.

6.3 *Population-based registries*

6.3.1 *Case-finding*

While a reportable list must be developed both for population-based and for hospital registries (section 6.2.1), use of such a detailed list is impracticable for those who send spontaneous notifications to the registry. The Singapore cancer registry (Fig. 6.2) asks for notification of 'all cases of cancers (i.e., carcinomas, sarcomas, leukaemias and all other malignant tumours)'.

Case-finding in the population-based Singapore cancer registry is as follows:

(a) *Spontaneous notification*

This is the major source of cases registered. A modified notification form (Fig. 6.1) is described below (section 6.3.2).

(b) *Biopsies*

All pathology laboratories in Singapore are visited regularly by a clerk from the registry. The major source is the Institute of Pathology, comprising both government and university laboratories. The institute keeps a log book, which is scanned daily, and a list is made of all biopsies reported to be cancerous. Private laboratories are visited regularly but less frequently.

(c) *Autopsies*

Copies of all autopsy summary sheets are collected once a week.

(d) *Haematology*

The accession book of the haematology laboratory is scanned twice a year.

(e) *Lists of deaths*

A listing of all deaths in Singapore, including those in which cancer is mentioned on the death certificate, is sent to the registry every three months.

(f) *Hospital discharge summaries*

All government hospital discharge summaries in which cancer is mentioned are sent to the registry three times per year.

For other populations, it may be necessary to cover further sources of cases, described in Chapter 5. Other modes of collection may need special administrative arrangements; an administrative order issued by the director-general of the ministry of health to medical records officers is the basis for their submitting carbon copies of pertinent case summaries to the cancer registry.

6.3.2 *Notification*

A notification form is a summary of information on a cancer case.
It is usually sent spontaneously and is not filled in routinely by
registry staff.

A model notification form, modified from that used in Singapore,
is given in Figure 6.1.

The items have been changed slightly to conform to the terms used
in Chapter 4.   The number of items requested is limited, and some of
the specific items relate to local conditions in Singapore, which is
a multiracial society, although predominantly Chinese, including many
immigrants, especially in the older age groups.   The Chinese consist
of a number of distinct dialect groups which have been shown to have
different patterns of cancer incidence, hence, the inclusion of
'dialect group' (Shanmugaratnam & Wee, 1973).   Explanatory notes
are given on the reverse side of the form (Fig. 6.2).   When the
registry began, the chairman of the cancer registry committee wrote
to all doctors in Singapore, giving information about the registry
and enclosing copies of the notification form and postage-free envelopes.   The letter is reproduced in Figure 6.3.   Notifications to
the Singapore cancer registry are made by doctors in government and in
private hospitals or clinics in Singapore.   When information is
missing or needs clarification (section 7.2), a request is made by
post, using a standard form (Fig. 6.4).

Notifications may not only be spontaneous but may also be requested
by the cancer registry when cases have been found from other sources,
such as biopsy reports, lists of deaths or hospital discharge diagnoses
(see section 6.3.1).   All available information is completed by
the registry, and the notification form (Fig. 6.1) is sent to the
doctor concerned with the case, together with a standard letter
(Fig. 6.5).   If there is no response to the request for notification,
the notification form is completed by registry staff.

The above scheme is used in Singapore, but each registry would
need to design a procedure appropriate to local circumstances.

The sending of notification forms by post is often the best means
of collecting information;   some registries are allowed free mailing
by the postal services, while others arrange for postage-paid envelopes.

6.3.3 *Collection of information at source*

A population-based registry may assume the responsibility of
obtaining the information at the place where the patient has been seen.
This is much more costly, forbiddingly so, for large-scale registries,
and specially trained personnel are needed.   Of course, the consent
of the treating institution must always be obtained for an 'outsider'
to find cases and to abstract information.   The advantages are that
the forms are filled in by a person who knows exactly what information
is needed and in what form.   Further, this person may supplement or

FIG. 6.1 CANCER NOTIFICATION FORM

CANCER NOTIFICATION FORM
(Explanatory notes overleaf)

CONFIDENTIAL

FOR REGISTRY USE

(2) ☐☐ ☐☐☐☐

1 ☐ Spontaneous

2 ☐ On Request

3 ☐ Registry Staff

☐ Abstract Card
☐ Register   ☐ Previous

(1) ....Cancer Registry
(Address) ....
....
Tel. ....

A.

(4) PATIENT

Name ....
      Please underline family name

Maiden name ....

(3) Identity
    Card No. ....

(6) Date of
    birth .... Age ......

(5) SEX   (54) ETHNIC GROUP

1 ☐ Male   Race   Dialect group
2 ☐ Female   1 ☐ Chinese   1 ☐ Hokkien
                  2 ☐ Malay   2 ☐ Teochew
                  3 ☐ Indian   3 ☐ Cantonese
                  9 ☐ Other*   4 ☐ Hainanese
                                    5 ☐ Hakka
                                      ☐ Other*
                  ....
                  * please specify * please specify

(6) PLACE OF BIRTH

                  1 ☐ Singapore
                  2 ☐ Malaysia
                  3 ☐ China
                  4 ☐ Indonesia
                  5 ☐ India/Pakistan
                  9 ☐ Other*
                  ....
                  * please specify

(8) PERMANENT
    RESIDENTIAL
    ADDRESS ....

LOCAL
ADDRESS
(if different) ....

B.

(79) HOSPITAL/CLINIC ....

(51) UNIT ....   Unit No. ....

(14)   ☐ In-patient-Hosp. No. ....
       ☐ Out-patient-Ref. No. ....

HOSPITAL, UNIT OR CLINIC RESPONSIBLE FOR SUBSEQUENT TREATMENT
OR FOLLOW-UP

       ☐ Same as above

       ☐ Other

D.

(15) HISTORY OF PREVIOUS DIAGNOSIS

Was cancer previously diagnosed in this
case? ....

       ☐ Yes

       ☐ No

If Yes,
Date cancer first diagnosed ....

C.

(18) DIAGNOSIS (specify primary organ or site of cancer and exact
               location if possible)

....
(13) DATE OF DIAGNOSIS ....
(17) MOST VALID BASIS OF DIAGNOSIS

Non microscopic   *Microscopic*

1 ☐ Clinical only   5 ☐ Cytology or hematology

2 ☐ Clinical investigation   6 ☐ Histol. of metastasis**
                                 (No. .....)

3 ☐ Exploratory surgery or   7 ☐ Histol. of primary**
    autopsy   (No. .....)

                               8 ☐ Autopsy with concurrent
                                 or previous histology
4 ☐ Specific biochemical   (No. .....)
    and/or immunological
    tests   9 ☐ *Not known*

(19) **HISTOLOGICAL DIAGNOSIS

By whom diagnosed ....

E.

(24) PRESENT STATUS

       1 ☐ Alive   2 ☐ Dead

If Dead
(25) Date of Death ....

(83) Place of Death ....

(26) Cause of Death ....
....
....

REMARKS (if any) ....

Date of Notification ....

Notified by ....

FIG. 6.2 EXPLANATORY NOTES FOR MODEL NOTIFICATION FORM

EXPLANATORY NOTES

CASES TO BE NOTIFIED

   Please notify all cases of cancer (i.e., carcinomas, sarcomas, leukaemias and all
other malignant tumours) diagnosed in your hospital, clinic or practice.

   Please notify confirmed cases of cancer as well as cases of 'probable cancer' in
which the diagnosis is based only on clinical findings (i.e., without histological,
radiological or other methods of confirmation.)

   Please notify all cases diagnosed in Singapore regardless of citizenship or place
of permanent residence of the patient.

   Please notify a case even if you think it may have been notified by some other
doctor previously.

PROCEDURE

   Please notify cases as soon as they are diagnosed, even if the diagnosis is
based only on clinical findings.

   If you are unable to provide all the items of information requested please
submit as much information as is available at the time of notification.
Please notify the Registry if there is a change in diagnosis.

   Where boxes are provided please mark ☒ as appropriate.

   When information is not available, please mark "?" against the item.

ITEMS OF INFORMATION

   Please obtain the items of information requested in Section A from the Identity
Card whenever possible.   The members in parentheses before each item are
international codes assigned by the World Health Organization.

   "Diagnosis" - This refers to the diagnosis at the time of notification.   The
diagnosis may be stated as "carcinoma of the stomach", "sarcoma of the left femur",
"cancer of left lung", "cancer of liver", etc.

PLEASE WRITE OR PHONE THE REGISTRY IF YOU REQUIRE ANY ADDITIONAL INFORMATION

Address: . . . .   Telephone: . . . .
         . . . .

FIG. 6.3 LETTER TO DOCTORS IN SINGAPORE

SINGAPORE CANCER REGISTRY

Committee

Prof. K. Shanmugaratnam
        (Chairman)
Dr. Chia Kim Boon
Dr. Goon Sek Mun
Mr. I. Nadarajah
Dr. S.R. Sayampanathan
Dr. Tan Kheng Khoo
Mr. Tye Cho Yook

University Dept. of Pathology
General Hospital
Singapore 3.
Tel: 7214 ext 378

25th January 1968

Dear Doctor

    A Cancer Registry has been organized in Singapore with support from the International Agency for Research on Cancer which has established a Regional Centre in the University of Singapore with the approval of the Ministry of Health.

    The Registry will seek to obtain information on the epidemiology, diagnosis and survival of cancer cases in Singapore that will assist in the evaluation of local cancer problems.   Cancer Registries exist in most progressive countries for this purpose.   Singapore is particularly suitable for the organization of such a Registry because it has well developed medical services and reliable vital statistics.

    The Registry will aim to obtain information on every case of 'cancer' or 'probable cancer' diagnosed in Singapore from 1st January 1968, regardless of the citizenship or place of domicile of the patient. We would be most grateful if you would notify the Registry of all new cases in your hospital, clinic or practice as soon as they are diagnosed, even if the diagnosis is based only on clinical findings (i.e., without histological, radiological or other methods of confirmation).   Please notify a case even if you think that it may have been notified by some other doctor previously.   It is not necessary to notify cases that were diagnosed before 1st January 1968.

    Copies of the notification form and postage-free envelopes are enclosed and more will be sent periodically.   If you are unable to provide all the items of information requested, please submit as much information as you can. Some explanatory notes are given on the reverse of the notification form. Please write or phone the Registry if you require any further information or a fresh supply of forms and envelopes.

    The success of the Cancer Registry depends on the cooperation of the whole medical profession in Singapore and we rely on your support.   We would like to stress that the information is required only for academic and professional purposes and will be treated in the same confidential manner as other hospital records.

                         Yours sincerely,

                         K. Shanmugaratnam

FIG. 6.4 STANDARD FORM
FOR OBTAINING CLARIFICATION OR MISSING INFORMATION

SINGAPORE CANCER REGISTRY

Department of Pathology, University of Singapore

Outram Road · Singapore 3 · Tel: 919050, 72141 Ext. 378

Dear

Name of Patient . . . .

Hosp/Unit/Adm. No.   . . . .

Diagnosis . . . .

Date of Notification . . . .

Thank you for your notification on the above patient, a copy of which is enclosed.

The following item(s) of essential information has been omitted/ needs clarification.   I would be most grateful if you could please return this letter to us with the information requested.

Items	Please fill in your information in this section

Thank you for your cooperation in this matter.

Yours faithfully,

K. Shanmugaratnam
Head, Singapore Cancer Registry

FIG. 6.5 ACCOMPANYING LETTER TO NOTIFICATION FORM (FIG. 6.1)
FOR CASES OBTAINED ELSEWHERE

SINGAPORE CANCER REGISTRY
Department of Pathology, University of Singapore
Outram Road · Singapore 3 · Tel: 919050, 72141 Ext. 378

Dear

     The enclosed forms refer to cases from your
_____ that have not been notified to the
Cancer Registry.   These cases were picked up from the

_____

     We have filled in some of the available information
and would be most grateful if you would complete the forms
and return them to us as early as possible to enable us to
register the cases.

     If any of these cases has been notified previously,
or is not a case of cancer, please state this under
"Remarks" and return the form to us.

Yours sincerely,

K. Shanmugaratnam
Chairman

Encl:

correct information about previously reported cases.   Such 'field clerks' are of great importance to a registry: their efficiency depends upon their competence, upon the reputation of the cancer registry and, last but not least, upon their personal ability to get themselves accepted by the various hospitals, cancer centres, laboratories and physicians from whom they request information.   Such persons are used to abstract data for the New Mexico and Recife Cancer Registries in several hospitals.

6.3.4 *Advantages of multiple sources for case-finding*

The multiple source approach secures a more complete coverage of diagnosed cases.   Cross-checking is essential, since none of the individual sources can be relied upon to notify all of its cases. It is well known from the reporting of infectious diseases that notification required by law also needs supervision and checking.

There is another advantage in taking in information from various sources.   A cancer registry requires detailed demographic, identifying and medical information, which is rarely to be found in a single source, e.g., a pathology report.   On the other hand, because of the absence of a standard manner of recording identifying items, there is a danger of duplication.   The dangers of both over- and under-registration must constantly be guarded against.

6.3.5 *Voluntary and legally required notification*

Persuasion is better than compulsion, even when notification is required legally, although the latter facilitates reporting by helping to overcome the barriers of medical secrecy.   *It is strongly advised that payment should not be made for notifications from individual physicians*, although this has been the practice in some registries. Registries may pay hospitals to provide data on cancer patients; payment may be withheld if the quality of the reports is not adequate (this is done at the Connecticut Tumor Registry).

There seems to be little relation between the existence of legislation and the efficient operation of a cancer registry.   There are numerous examples of first-class registries that function on a purely voluntary basis;   there are even more examples of registries in which, in spite of adequate laws and rules, good and complete reporting is not ensured and registration does not function properly.   This clearly indicates that the interest of the medical profession is of greater importance than legislation.   In some countries however, a legal basis for reporting may help or even be indispensable.

6.4 *Improving completeness of coverage*

One of the main problems of cancer registries is making sure that the cases notified represent all diagnosed cases.

The hospital registry should check all potential sources of cases within the hospital(s) (see sections 4.4 and 4.5). The population-based registry should check all potential sources in the population covered. Even so, no cancer registry can ever be sure of having 100 per cent coverage, certainly not of those groups of patients who are likely never to have been hospitalized and whose malignancy is not stated officially on the death certificate (old people, deaths at home). Furthermore, cancer cases that are not diagnosed can never be registered.

Completeness of coverage can be improved in various ways:

(a) A field clerk can check the list of cases admitted to a cancer centre or hospital with a diagnosis of cancer during a specified time, separating re-admissions from first admissions. This is facilitated if there is a diagnostic index. In pathology institutes, the names and numbers of biopsies and surgical specimens pertaining to cancer patients are checked; however, patients coming for first biopsy may already be registered, with an unverified diagnosis.

(b) Death notifications are also checked. The hospital registry may detect deaths during follow-up, but the population-based registry will have to scan lists of all deaths, preferably in alphabetical order by names. In some Scandinavian countries, the 'death tape' is matched against the registry tape by the unique identity number, thus avoiding much manual work.

The percentage of malignancies that is registered but for which there is no subsequent information may be an indication of the performance and reliability of a population-based cancer registry (Waterhouse et al., 1976).

(c) The population-based cancer registry may check whether interesting cases reported in the medical literature have been registered. The physician who wrote the paper may have withheld the patient's file from the records room, and the cancer registry may, therefore, have missed the case. A request for information may be made to the author.

7. INPUT OPERATIONS

7. INPUT OPERATIONS

The input activities in a cancer registry, outlined in Figure 7.1, are universal and are primarily concerned with getting data ready for tabulation and analysis.

FIG. 7.1 SCHEMA OF INPUT OPERATIONS IN THE CANCER REGISTRY

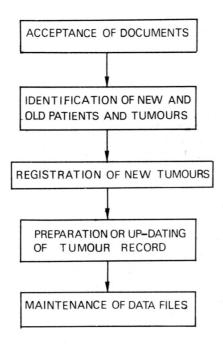

Documents coming to the registry are inspected for completeness and consistency. If accepted, the next step is to decide if they relate to a person or tumour previously registered or 'old'. If not, the tumour is registered. The next step is the preparation, or up-dating, of the tumour record. This activity constitutes part of the routine maintenance of files.

The above activities should be clearly distinguished from the means whereby they are accomplished, which vary from country to country.   These two distinct concepts are discussed at the end of this chapter (see section 7.9).

One of the problems in running a large registry is to decide whether its various activities should be specialized and carried out by narrowly-trained staff or whether there should be a greater elasticity in their training and in the assignment of work.   The latter may be preferable in view of the frequent necessity for replacement (sickness or holidays), which must not be allowed to interrupt the flow of work in the registry.   This must be considered in planning for staff (see section 3.9).

This chapter is concerned more with concepts and principles that apply to all cancer registries than with a detailed description of procedures in one or more prototype registries.   For specific registries readers are advised to obtain additional expert advice, preferably from a number of sources.

The diagrams which accompany the text are not intended to cover comprehensively every aspect of registration, but rather to illustrate the various procedures.   In general, standard flow chart symbols are used, a diamond representing the need for decision and a small circle referring to the continuation of a diagram elsewhere.   Optional procedures are indicated by interrupted lines.

7.2 *Acceptance of documents (Fig. 7.2)*

7.2.1 *Recording the intake*

Regardless of the source (Chap. 5) or method of collection (Chap. 6), it is advisable to stamp the date of arrival at the cancer registry on all documents   (As an optional procedure, a log book may be used to record intake by source and type of document).   This will help to detect irregularities or deficiencies of specific sources, to initiate appropriate requests and to assess, for administrative reasons, the volume of intake.

7.2.2 *Check for completeness and consistency*

All documents that arrive at the registry must be scrutinized for missing or wrong information.   Incomplete documents may be sent back (or, better, kept and a copy sent back) for completion.   Alternatively, they may be put aside for completion by a field clerk, or they may be processed and the missing items added later.

Documents are also checked for consistency of information.   Thus, for instance, it is impossible for a male to have a cancer of the uterine cervix and rare, although possible, for a male to have breast cancer.   A remark on incomplete or inconsistent items is added to the document.   This may simply be a ' ! ' which is circled when corrected.

FIG. 7.2 ACCEPTANCE OF DOCUMENTS

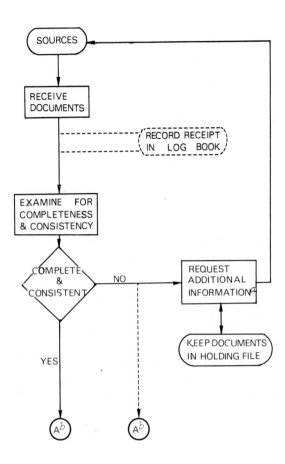

a A source other than the original one may need to be
contacted.

b The next steps are shown in Figure 7.3.

7.2.3 *Decision to accept a document*

Following the examination for completeness and consistency (Fig.
7.2), a decision is made to accept the document as received or to
request additional information from the source.   This may also be
recorded in the log book.

7.2.4 *Holding files*

The flow of registration may be interrupted at various points due to lack of information or to enable more efficient batch processing. Thus, incomplete or inconsistent documents may be held in alphabetical order in a holding file (Fig. 7.2), pending receipt of further information. Alternatively, complete and consistent documents could be held in a different holding file for batch processing. Many of the case-finding procedures described in Chapter 6 initially yield only incomplete information, e.g., in a hospital registry, the patient record may not be available until the discharge of the patient, and the incomplete information may be held in a holding file.

7.3 *Identification of new* versus *old patients and tumours* (Fig. 7.3)

7.3.1 *Avoiding multiple registration*

Due to the multiplicity of sources of information, multiple documents may be received for the same tumour. Hence, each individual declaration of a new case must be suspected as referring to a patient or tumour already registered. All notifications must be compared systematically, 'matched' with existing information in the files of the registry and registered as a new tumour only after all likelihood of previous registration has been excluded. In spite of all precautions, multiple registrations may still be detected later during file maintenance or data processing. Registries must thus be continually on the alert for duplication in order to reduce it to a minimum.

In a population-based registry, the documents pertaining to an apparently new tumour case are scrutinized carefully to determine if the diagnosis is on the reportable list (see section 6.3.1), and if it is really a new case. If the information in the documents suggests that the patient may already have been registered, further efforts are made (see below) to avoid multiple registration. Documents are kept in holding files to await further information, i.e., whether they refer to a new patient or a new tumour. Most population-based registries prefer to collect and assemble documents for periodic work-up. Such batch processing may reduce costs, but it causes delays in supplying information from the registry.

7.3.2 *The patient index file*

The patient index file (PIF) is the master reference file and is composed of one patient index card for each registered patient. These cards are filed alphabetically by name, living and dead cases together, and when in the file[1] are never removed.

---

[1] When a file has been in existence for a long time, it will include a disproportionately large number of dead cases. It is advantageous to cull such cards from the file and to transfer them to another file - the dead file - where they will be used less. It is preferable to

FIG. 7.3 MATCHING OF NEW MATERIAL
TO IDENTIFY NEW OR OLD PATIENTS AND TUMOURS

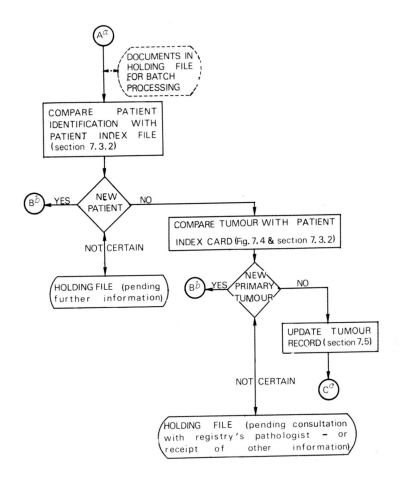

^{a} Continuation of Fig. 7.2

^{b} Continues in Fig. 7.5

^{c} Continues in Fig. 7.7

remove cards referring to dead cases only after a lapse of at least
two years from the date of death, since during that period the cards
may be needed due to the late arrival of some documents concerning
the case.

The patient index card (Fig. 7.4) contains a record of information relevant to identification: name, sex, birth-date, residence, personal identification number, etc. It also has the registration number and primary sites of all previously registered tumours for this patient. In some registries the PIF is generated by computer.

FIG. 7.4 PATIENT INDEX CARD

NAME SEX	MEDICAL RECORD NUMBER	PATIENT REGISTRATION NUMBER
ADDRESS	DATE OF BIRTH	IDENTITY NO.
CITY PHONE	INCIDENCE DATE(S) 1.	PRIMARY SITE(S) WITH MORPHOLOGY 1.
DATE OF DEATH PLACE OF DEATH	2.	2.
	3.	3.
CAUSE OF DEATH		
PATIENT INDEX CARD[a]		

[a] Adapted from American College of Surgeons (1974)

File order

(a) *By name*.   The PIF is ordered firstly by family name and secondly by personal name.   Many of the problems encountered with names are discussed under item 4 in Chapter 4.   When women adopt the husband's family name on marriage, the PIF may have two cards - the first with the husband's name and the second with the woman's maiden name, with a cross-reference to the first.   When the spelling of names is variable, a system of phonetic spelling of names is used; this has been used successfully in cancer registries (see Chap. 4, item 4).

(b) *By birth-date*. In countries in which births have been registered officially for at least 80 years, the date of birth (item 6) can be used as the first axis in ordering the PIF, with family name as the second

axis.   An official date of birth (whether exact or not) is a means of
identification that is more stable than the spelling of family names.
The use of a personal identification number (item 3) as the first axis
in ordering the file is not recommended for most countries as it may
not always be available, but its inclusion on the patient index card
may be very useful in detecting multiple registrations due to changes
of name.

Comparison of documents with patient index file

All documents coming into the registry are organized for matching
with the PIF.   They are arranged in the same order (usually alphabetical), and the identification of the patient is compared with
the file to determine whether or not he is a new patient (Fig. 7.3).
If he is, the case is registered (see section 7.4).   If he is not,
the documents are placed in a special holding file.

An alternative to patient index cards stored in a file is a strip
index which has one line for each patient.   Strips are inserted in
special vertical holders and can be scanned easily.   Individual strips
can be colour-coded, e.g., blue strips for cases which occurred prior
to the establishment of the registry.   A disadvantage is the extra
time taken to rearrange strips when holders are full.

If the documents pertain to a patient registered previously, a
further comparison is made with the patient index cards, in order to
ascertain whether a new primary tumour is involved (see discussion of
item 20).   If it is a new primary tumour, it is registered with the
existing patient registration number (Fig. 7.5).   If it is a previously
registered tumour, the tumour record is updated (Fig. 7.3).

7.4 Registration of new tumours (Fig. 7.5)

7.4.1 Tumour accession register

New primary tumours are entered in the tumour accession register,
(Fig. 7.6), which is a permanent list of registered tumours arranged in
order of registration.   The accession register is used to assign a new
patient registration number to all new patients, the number being the
next in a series (see p. 41).   The patient registration number that is
assigned to the new tumour is written on all documents referring to the
case, and the relevant information is abstracted to prepare the tumour
record (see below).   *New primary tumours in a previously registered
patient are given the same patient registration number.*   The latter is
to be found on the patient index card.

If the case is a new patient (as distinct from another primary tumour
in an old patient), a patient index card is prepared and filed in the
patient index file (see section 7.3).   As noted above, a new primary
tumour in an old patient is recorded on the existing patient index card.
A follow-up card is also prepared for new patients (see section 7.6).
The site and incidence date of a new tumour in an old patient is noted
on the existing follow-up card to avoid multiple follow-up letters and
multiple dates for follow-up examinations of patients with more than
one tumour.

FIG. 7.5   REGISTRATION OF NEW TUMOURS

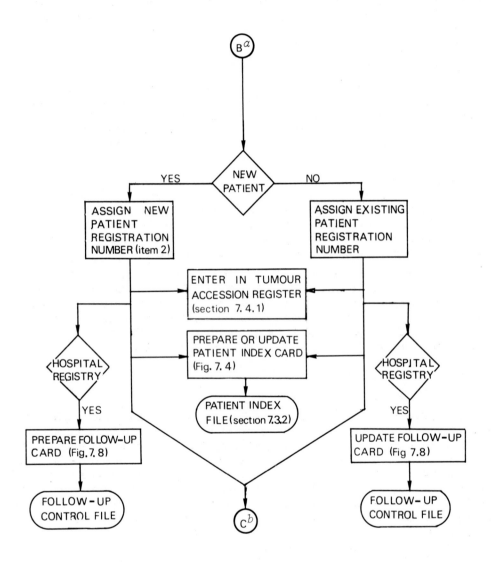

^a Continuation of Fig. 7.3
^b Continued in Fig. 7.7

FIG. 7.6   TUMOUR ACCESSION REGISTER

YEAR	PATIENT REGISTRATION NUMBER (Item 2)	HOSPITAL RECORD NUMBER[a] (Item 24)	PATIENT'S NAME (Item 4)	PRIMARY SITE (Item 18)	REMARKS

[a] Optional for population-based registries

7.4.2 *Special registration problems*

Hospital registries are advised to decide whether they will
include basal-cell and squamous-cell carcinomas of skin in their
registration and, if so, whether they will treat the appearance of
a new lesion as a new primary with a separate registration number or,
as most prefer, will register them only once (see item 20).

All cases that come to the attention of the population-based cancer
registry must be registered, regardless of the incidence date (item 13),
even if this is before the start of cancer registration: such cases
will not appear in incidence reports but are likely to appear in lists
of deaths, and they must be registered with the incidence date in
the tumour file.   They will be analysed separately from newer cases.
Cases notified from death certificates only, for which the registry
has not succeeded in obtaining clarifying information, must also be
registered, e.g., generalized metastases, 'post-radical mastectomy for
cancer'.   Likewise, non-residents diagnosed and treated in the region
covered by the registry and immigrants diagnosed as cancer patients
before immigration must be registered.   They can be excluded, when
appropriate, from certain analyses (see item 8).

The accession register is also used to record under 'remarks'
the removal of names, due to multiple registration or cancellation of
the diagnosis of malignancy.   Re-use of these numbers is most strongly
contraindicated.

7.5 *Preparing and up-dating the tumour record* (Fig. 7.7)

7.5.1 *Content of tumour record*

A separate tumour record is created for each registered primary tumour; thus, a patient with multiple primary tumours will have multiple tumour records. A special code, e.g., item 20, can be used to indicate the presence of multiple primaries, but this is not essential as the existence of multiple primary tumours can be detected from the patient registration number, incidence date, site and morphology.

FIG. 7.7 PREPARING AND UP-DATING THE TUMOUR RECORD

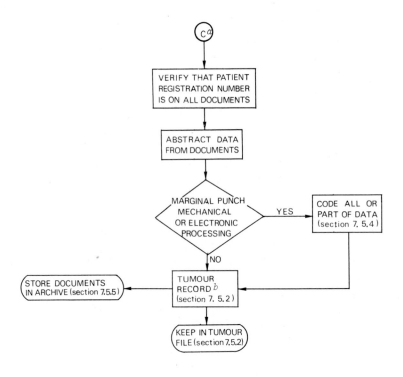

[a] Continued from Figs 7.3 and 7.5

[b] The tumour record may consist of an abstract card, coded cards, 80-column punch cards, computer tape, etc.

The list of items contained in the tumour record depends on the type of registry (see Chap. 4). Details used by hospital registries in making follow-up contacts are recorded on the follow-up card and not on the tumour record. Many registries find it useful to record an abbreviated version of the patient's name as a check on identification, and some also record in a coded fashion the institution or physician who made the original notification of the case, as well as the one responsible for follow-up.

7.5.2 *Types and order of tumour records and files*

A tumour record may take various forms: a registry abstract form, a margin-punched card (Figs 4.1 and 11.1), an 80-column punch card, a computer tape, etc., as discussed in Chapter 10. In hospital registries, tumour records are kept in a tumour file, which is ordered firstly by topography (see footnote to Table 7.1) and secondly by patient registration number; this order facilitates responses to the common request to the registry for a listing of all persons with a particular cancer, e.g., all colon cancer seen in the past three years. Population-based registries may further order the tumour file by hospital at which the tumour was diagnosed. With modern electronic data processing, copies of the file may be kept in different orders.

Especially when manual processing is used, tumour files are conveniently separated into living and dead sections; this reduces work in file management (see also footnote to section 7.3.2).

A new tumour record is created for a new tumour, whereas the existing tumour record is up-dated for an old tumour. The principles of the input operations are the same, whatever mode of data processing is used. The simplest tumour record consists of an abstract in words without coding, on some type of form or card. This would be used only by very small registries, and coding is nearly universal.

7.5.3 *Coding*

The coding is divided, so that non-medical terms are coded by a clerk and medical terms are coded by the medical director or the registrar. After the abstracting and coding, an independent check is made to ensure that all the necessary terms and correct codes have been entered into the appropriate places. After input of new information, the tumour record is inserted into the tumour file, and the documents are stored in an archive (see section 7.5.5).

7.5.4 *When and how to code*

Coding should begin when there are no apparent errors or inconsistencies in the data. It must be realized that it may be necessary to recode during up-dating. Later reports may not always contain a more valid basis for diagnosis. The most valid basis of diagnosis (item 17) may be the first report that describes surgery; in other cases, the correct diagnosis may only be made at the time of histological work-up at autopsy. Similarly, every item recorded initially may be subject to change at up-dating, e.g., name, age and even sex.

Recommended codes for almost all items of patient information are given in Chapters 4 and 8. Where these codes do not apply locally, different codes will have to be used. These may already exist, but otherwise will have to be developed.   The codes for any item must be comprehensive as a whole, and each code must be mutually exclusive. In general it is better to code as finely as possible, since codes can be combined during data processing.   This however may be more expensive.

7.5.5 *Storage of documents*

The space used to store documents is termed an archive.   It must be secure and inaccessible to unauthorized persons.   Documents should be kept indefinitely (possibly on microfilm) for the following reasons:

(a) Diagnosis and date of diagnosis may differ in later documents from those stated originally.   Medical judgement is often needed, when comparing new with old material, to decide what to accept as the correct diagnosis, and a pathologist or clinician may have to be consulted.

(b) Researchers in certain fields very much appreciate finding documents from various agencies concentrated in one place, especially when the original information may not be traceable at the source.

Documents should be stored in order of patient registration number, as in the record-keeping system of hospitals.   It is preferable that documents for each patient be kept in individual folders, but this requires rapidly increasing storage space and entails considerable work when new material is to be added.

Copies on microfilm can only be made after all documents pertaining to a deceased person are available.   The equipment necessary for photography and reading is rather expensive, and considerable time is required.   It may also be difficult to relocate an abstract on the film without rather expensive equipment.

7.6 *Active and indirect follow-up*

Follow-up of cancer patients is an integral part of patient care, since early detection of the spread of disease enables more effective measures to be taken.   Active follow-up is generally limited to hospital registries, whereas population-based registries usually undertake indirect follow-up by determining survival from date of death or by referring to active follow-up by hospitals.   A few population-based cancer registries remind treating physicians of anniversary dates, e.g., Birmingham (UK) and South Metropolitan (UK).

For active follow-up, a follow-up card (Fig. 7.8) is prepared for all new living patients.   This contains information necessary for contacting the patient and the 'anniversary date' on which the patient is asked to come for examination.   The so-called 'anniversary date' is accepted as a reference date, e.g., the month the patient was first seen at the treatment hospital.   In most cases, this is equivalent to the month of diagnosis.   Follow-up cards are stored in a follow-up control file in chronological order of follow-up.

FIG. 7.8 FOLLOW-UP CARD

NAME SEX	MEDICAL RECORD NUMBER	PATIENT REGISTRATION NUMBER
ADDRESS	DATE OF BIRTH d ⎸ m ⎸ y	IDENTITY NO.
CITY PHONE	INCIDENCE DATE(S) 1. 2. 3.	PRIMARY SITE(S) 1. 2. 3.
NAME OF RELATIVE OR FRIEND	DATE THIS FOLLOW-UP REMARKS	
ADDRESS		
CITY PHONE		
OTHER SOURCES		
NAME OF PHYSICIAN(S)		
FOLLOW-UP CARD[a]		

[a] Adapted from American College of Surgeons (1974a)

It is up to the clinical oncologist to decide whether, and how often, for the benefit of the patient, he must insist on examining him, or whether he can be satisfied with obtaining adequate information from the patient's physician. Every effort must be made to avoid unnecessary investment by the patient in time and/or travel expenses to come to the hospital and to avoid making him feel, subsequently, that he has been invited for statistical purposes only. In Madras, India, for example, travel expenses by rail are met by the government.

7.7 *Maintenance of files*

Maintenance of files is essential in all cancer registries; the activities involved are summarized in Table 7.1. The three major files (patient index file, tumour file and follow-up control file) are discussed above.

Although similar in principle, maintenance activities vary in feasibility, in the speed with which they are carried out, and with the type of data-processing equipment available (see Chap. 10).

Table 7.1 Maintenance of files

File	Sorting	Merging	Editing	Up-dating
Patient index file	Alphabetical	Add new patients (sorted in same order)	Identify duplication of patients	Correct data; add new primary tumours
Tumour file	(1) Primary site[b] (2) Patient registration number (within site)	Add new tumours (sorted in same order)	Identify duplication of patients and/or tumours and errors	Add new data; correct old data; construct active file periodically
Follow-up control file[a]	(1) Month of follow-up (2) Alphabetical (within month)	-	-	Add remarks on follow-up

[a] Usually only in hospital registries

[b] For manual systems using the ICD-O, tumours are sorted first by behaviour and then by 3-digit topography, to avoid confusion between, e.g., primary tumours and metastases.

7.7.1 *Sorting and merging*

It has already been noted that data files are arranged in a particular order to meet specified needs. This implies that they have previously been arranged or sorted into the specified order and that new records are entered into the file accordingly. Therefore, it is important first to sort the incoming file into the same order as the existing one, using the sorting tools available, and then to merge the two files.

A complete re-sorting of certain files may be required periodically in order to perform some of the other operations discussed below. For example, if a check is to be made that all live patients in the tumour file also appear in the patient index file, and that the primary sites listed on the patient index card for a patient correspond to those found in the tumour file, there must be a re-sorting of at least one of the two prior to matching. The specialized sorting techniques used in the three types of data processing (Chap. 10) are used.

7.7.2 *Editing*

Editing consists of checking each of the records in a file for completeness, legality of codes and internal consistency[1]. As discussed in section 7.2, incoming documents are checked for consistency on reaching the registry and prior to coding. However, there will inevitably be omissions or inconsistencies, which may be detected when further information is available; additional errors will occur in coding and punching operations and in transcribing data. Thus, the tumour record must be edited systematically prior to, or at the time of, its entry into the tumour file. Special editing checks may also be made periodically on the entire file, for example, on the alive section.

Legality of codes. The simplest type of editing check on a coded and punched record card is verification that each item has a permissible code. Thus, a female coded 3 would be incorrect (Fig. 4.1). For

[1] Editing procedures from the United States SEER programme are given in Appendix 2.

manual and punch-card operations, this is accomplished by sorting or tabulating each item in succession.   Records that contain inadmissable codes or lack data are returned to be punched or coded again by the appropriate person.   With a computer-based system, it is possible to edit the record by matching each item against an internally stored directory of codes, so that records that have inadmissable codes are rejected prior to entry and printed on an 'error' list.

Logical verification.   Internal consistency checks compare different items on the same record or items on different records for the same patient in one or more files.   The possible number of such checks is large, and the scope of checking will be limited by time and cost. The internal consistency checks commonly made are of:

(a) identity items such as name, sex and birth-date on all
     records for a given patient;

(b) demographic items such as marital status and age;

(c) certain diagnoses and stated sex (see section 7.2 above);

(d) certain sites with age at onset;   e.g., sites other than
     central nervous system, bone marrow, lymph nodes, bone,
     kidney, retro-peritoneum, connective tissue and eye could
     be flagged for children under 15 years;

(e) date of birth, date of onset, age at onset, date of last
     follow-up, date of death;

(f) site and stated morphology, e.g., squamous-cell carcinoma
     of the mandible;   and

(g) ICD-O behaviour code with site, morphology or extent of
     disease.

Not all inconsistencies are errors, e.g., lung cancer may occur at 10 years of age, but the records of such a case should certainly be double-checked for accuracy.

When editing an entire computer-based file, it is generally preferable to make a list of all errors and to correct them subsequently. In the interim, the source documents for the case may be consulted to determine exactly which corrections are necessary.

7.7.3 *How to deal with duplication*

Multiple registration may be discovered at any stage in registry operations, from the identification of new patients and tumours (section 7.3) to notification of death.

When duplication is discovered, all existing documents for the case must be drawn together in order to up-date one tumour record and cancel the other.   A new abstract may be made using one of the registration numbers.   The fact and reason for cancellation of a registration number are best recorded in the tumour accession register (section 7.4.1). In a manual operation, the cancelled tumour cards will have to be removed from the tumour file, but the patient index cards might serve as a cross-reference, e.g., if two names refer to the same person, such as before or after marriage, divorce or remarriage, this should be noted on two patient index cards.

A rarer and sometimes very annoying event is the erroneous combination of information from two cases (mostly with the same name and a similar diagnosis at approximately the same time) into one tumour record.   The separation requires very careful attention to particulars in the documents, in order to decide which details apply to which patient, and then to create two tumour records.

7.7.4 Up-dating

This activity involves the addition of new or missing information to an existing record and the correction of old data after careful review.   The tumour file may be up-dated periodically by moving dead patients from the living section to the dead section.   This would normally be done at least two years after death.

7.8 Special files

For doubtful cases and for epidemiological studies a number of independent files may be created and matched periodically with the patient index file or followed up more actively.   These are not necessarily part of the routine operations of a cancer registry. Thus:

7.8.1 Rejected cases

The cancer registry may receive a pathology report (biopsy or surgery) that gives a clinical diagnosis of a malignancy, e.g., stomach cancer, but the histological examination after gastrectomy clearly and unequivocally denies this diagnosis.   At a later time, a case summary, perhaps from the internal medicine department, may come in, referring to the period before the histological examination was carried out.   In order to avoid confusion and an unnecessary request for the pathology report, the case is designated a rejected case and filed.   It is not given a patient registration number and is therefore not entered in the tumour accession register.   In other words, this group includes all excision biopsies which are negative. However, a negative liver biopsy from a clinically diagnosed case of primary liver cancer, e.g., with positive alpha-fetoprotein, is registered and is not rejected.

It must be kept in mind, however, that the same patient may later develop a malignancy, so that each later report must be checked carefully to ascertain whether it refers to the site and period covered by the 'rejected case'.

A registered case diagnosed clinically as having cancer, e.g., cancer of the oesophagus, may, on autopsy, be found not to have cancer, but to have, perhaps, an aneurysm of the aorta.   A death certificate

written prior to autopsy may give the clinical diagnosis.   Such cases
will stay permanently in the patient index file, with a note on the
change in diagnosis.   They are removed from the tumour file to the
file of rejected cases.

7.8.2 *Precancerous lesions*

These may be diagnosed during screening programmes and optionally
notified to the registry.

7.8.3 *Persons suspected of having a tumour*

Cases may be reported in which there is only a suspicion of a neoplasm and which are 'under observation'.   A request may be made for
additional information, and the cases may be kept in alphabetical
order in a special file.   In hospital registries, they may also be
included in the follow-up file; thus, they are not registered, and
are therefore not included in the patient index file, but are matched
with it periodically.

7.8.4 *Survey persons*

Cancer registries may be associated with surveys of persons
without cancer, such as control subjects in case-control studies or
larger population groups surveyed for some type of exposure.   Such
survey persons may be kept in a special file and matched periodically
with the patient index file.   Although an important activity, this
is not part of cancer registration.

7.9 *Activities and corresponding structures in the registry*

The main activities concerned with input into a cancer registry are
listed in Table 7.2, together with their corresponding structures.
Only those not discussed already will be discussed here.

7.9.1 *Procedure manual*

From the first, it is useful to have a manual for registry staff
and for outside users that gives an exact and detailed description
of the registry's operations and of the codes used.   It should be
based on the information and techniques outlined in this monograph.
This manual will for a long time be 'preliminary', since only experience
will show what to change and what to add.   Nevertheless, having everything down in writing avoids later confusion arising from oral instructions which only some of the registry staff remember and others forget
or have never heard.   The manual can be based on flow charts such as
those given here.   Whenever a decision about operations or coding is
made, this must be added to the manual.

The manual will serve as a reference for handling doubtful situations that are likely to recur frequently and involve major decisions
and will also help in training new staff.

Table 7.2 Activities and corresponding structures within the
cancer registry

Activity	Structure
Document in detail all procedures of the registry	Procedure manual (manual of operations)
Record receipt of documents	Log book
Match documents with existing files	Patient index file; tumour file
Register new tumours	Tumour accession register
Prepare and file patient index card	Patient index file
Prepare and file follow-up card	Follow-up control file
Code data	Code lists
Maintain files	All data files
Create and up-date tumour record	Tumour file
Store documents	Archive
List data sources	Directories

7.9.2 *Conventions manual*

In the course of coding and other registry operations many
difficulties arise which require the making of judgments.   When a
decision has been made (often after consultation with a specialist
adviser), it should be recorded, together with the relevant circumstances, so that the same decision will be made in the same circumstances in the future.   The correctness of the decision taken is often
of less importance than the consistency of the coding or other action
taken in specific circumstances.   Such decisions may be incorporated
in future editions of the registry's procedure manual.

7.9.3 *Directories*

Many registries maintain directories of the names and addresses of
the institutions or individuals on whom they rely for notification of
pathology and with whom they maintain contact for follow-up.   Names

of responsible physicians at each institution are also listed. These
directories are consulted prior to generation of requests for follow-
up or other data to be used to correct, or bring up to date, a
patient's record. In a computer-based operation, they may be stored
on tape or disc and linked with other files, so that names and
addresses can be provided automatically for letters requesting additional data.

8. CLASSIFICATION AND CODING OF NEOPLASMS

8. CLASSIFICATION AND CODING OF NEOPLASMS

8.1 *Classifications of neoplasms in the past*

8.1.1 *Introduction*

Registry personnel must understand the evolution of the present classification system in order to adapt former systems and to apply the new International Classification of Diseases for Oncology (ICD-0), which was referred to briefly in Chapter 4, items 18 and 19.

The International Classification of Diseases (ICD) is universal and helps to improve international comparability. It is revised every ten years to incorporate and express progress in medical thinking. The ICD is multipurpose and its rubrics may cover broad categories. To satisfy the needs of oncologists, the ICD-0 has been developed by the WHO (1976b), with the assistance of international and national agencies. It provides considerable detail about a cancer but is nevertheless convertible to the parent ICD.

8.1.2 *Anatomical location and behaviour of neoplasms*

The anatomical location of a neoplasm determines in no small measure the biological effects on the bearer, since each site may differ in ease and route of spread and in interference with vital functions. The 8th Revision of the ICD (in effect since 1968) allots rubrics 140 to 239 to neoplasms. Rubrics 140 to 199 are reserved for malignant neoplasms, rubrics 200 to 209 for neoplasms of lymphatic and haematopoietic tissues, rubrics 210 to 228 for benign neoplasms, and neoplasms of uncertain nature are allocated rubrics 230 to 239.

The 8th Revision of the ICD has now been replaced by the 9th Revision which comes into operation on the 1st of January 1979 (see section 8.2.3).

Certain problems are posed for cancer registries that want to use the ICD as it stands. The first axis of classification in the ICD is behaviour, and more rubrics are allotted to malignant neoplasms (140 to 209) than to benign neoplasms and those of an undefined nature; thus, it is more difficult to code precisely the anatomical location of the latter two (the greater topographical precision of ICD-0 is illustrated with lymphosarcoma in Table 8.2). Furthermore, the second axis of classification of the ICD is a mixture of the two axes: the majority of rubrics refer to anatomical location, but others refer to histological type of neoplasm (melanomas of skin, lymphomas and leukaemias). A cancer registry should distinguish between topography and morphology, and solutions to this problem are discussed below.

Problems are also caused by the periodic revisions of the ICD.
A cancer registry must be prepared to compare data over long periods,
and it is very difficult and time-consuming to re-code neoplasms coded
according to an earlier revision of the ICD and to re-train registry
staff to use the new classification.   If the cancer registry's code
is sufficiently detailed, it is possible to translate it to more than
one revision of the ICD without loss of information, but this may be
tedious.

8.1.3 *Histological classifications of neoplasms*

The histological classification of neoplasms has been bedevilled
by lack of an internationally accepted system.   The elaboration of
such a system is by no means easy, in that differing national or
medical school ideas about the histogenesis of tumours or, indeed,
about the existence of groups of tumours render the creation of such a
classification difficult.   There have been four serious contenders
in this field:

1. *UICC illustrated nomenclature.*   The UICC illustrated nomenclature of neoplasms (Hamperl, 1969) constitutes a major step forward
in this field in that it provides illustrations for a fairly large
spectrum of common neoplasms, each labelled with the appropriate
diagnostic label in English, French, German, Spanish, Russian and
Latin.   The publication, however, is not comprehensive and does not
incorporate a coding scheme.

2. *WHO histopathological classification.*   The *International
Histopathological Classification of Tumors* covers comprehensively the
histological nomenclature of neoplasms, taking into account international opinions.   These publications, the so-called 'Blue Books'
(WHO, 1967-1978) are profusely illustrated in colour, and colour
slides may be purchased.   A major drawback to these publications is
the lack of a coding scheme, and, although the nomenclature is classified, the classificatory indexing is such that there is no comparability between sites.   WHO therefore prepared a summary of all the
histological entities which will appear in the 1967-78 series of the
International Histopathological Classification of Tumours, supplying
each term with the corresponding ICD-0 code.

3. *Systematized nomenclature of pathology (SNOP).*   The systematized
nomenclature of pathology (College of American Pathologists, 1965),
often referred to as 'SNOP', provides a comprehensive coding scheme
for all pathology.   There are four fields: topography, morphology,
etiology and function, and each field comprises four digits.   While
anatomy can be described in very great detail, only 200 rubrics are
available in the morphology section to describe neoplasms, although
both the 8 000 and 9 000 series are set aside for this disease category.
The 8 and 9 do no more than indicate that a neoplasm is being coded, and
the terminal (4th) digit describes the presumed behaviour of the neoplasm.

This 4th digit of SNOP corresponds to the 5th digit of ICD-0, as
indicated in Table 8.5; this restriction to 200 rubrics is a major
disadvantage.   Nevertheless, the system has been so well designed
that it has attracted widespread support from pathologists in many
countries, and the neoplasms section, at least, has been translated
into French, German, Japanese, Spanish, Italian and Portuguese.   Not
all of the possible code numbers are used by SNOP, and the remaining
ones have often been used to incorporate national concepts (e.g., by
INSERM (1971) in France).   SNOP has recently been replaced by SNOMED
which now includes a 'procedural field' in addition to the topography,
morphology, etiology and function fields in SNOP.   The neoplasms
codes are identical with those used in ICD-0.

   4. *Manual of Tumor Nomenclature and Coding (MOTNAC)*.   The *Manual
of Tumor Nomenclature and Coding* (MOTNAC) of the American Cancer
Society (Percy et al., 1968) constitutes an amalgam of the morphology
rubrics of SNOP (slightly modified), as they pertain to cancer, with
the ICD rubrics (again slightly modified to give greater anatomical
detail) of the 8th revision of the ICD.   The ICD rubrics 200 to 239
are suppressed, since the information contained in them is expressed
in the morphology code.   Special 'topographical' rubrics were created
to describe neoplasms of the haematopoietic system.   MOTNAC is now
superseded by ICD-0 (see section 8.2 and Appendix 3).

8.2 *International Classification of Diseases for Oncology (ICD-0)*

8.2.1 *Development of ICD-0*

   The International Classification of Diseases for Oncology (ICD-0)
is an extension of the neoplasms chapter of the new (9th) revision
of the ICD (ICD-9).   It permits the coding of all neoplasms by topography, histology (morphology) and behaviour, i.e., malignant, benign,
in situ, of uncertain behaviour or metastatic, but is convertible to
ICD-9 (with loss of information).   It also permits grading of
differentiation.

   In 1968, the International Agency for Research on Cancer (IARC)
was asked by the WHO to make recommendations concerning the content
and structure of the neoplasms chapter of ICD-9, in consultation with
the Cancer and ICD Units of the WHO and various national bodies.   In
collaboration with a large number of consultants and committees from
various countries, the world-wide need for a detailed histopathology
code for neoplasms was recognized.   A code based on the morphology
section of MOTNAC was proposed, and a particular effort was made to
incorporate all the terms used in the WHO histological classifications
(see above).   ICD-0 is an official WHO publication supplementing the ICD.

   It is hoped that the ICD-0 will serve to promote international
cooperation in the field of cancer in accordance with the resolution
of the 28th World Health Assembly that requested the Director-General
'to consider ... steps to fulfill the need to accelerate ...

international coordination of cancer research and the elaboration of
information systems ... to support the comprehensive cancer research
programme, taking into account the proposals of national and international organizations interested in participation in this programme'
(WHO, 1975).

8.2.2 *Structure of ICD-0*

The topography section of ICD-0 was adapted from the malignant
neoplasms section of ICD-9, and the morphology section is a revised
and expanded version from MOTNAC.   The publication has numerical
indices that show the structure of the coded nomenclature and are
the primary reference for retrieval or decoding.   The general alphabetical index, combining both topography (anatomical sites) and morphology (histological terms) in a single list, would primarily be used by
coders.

The following abbreviations are used throughout ICD-0:

T - topography
M - morphology
NOS - not otherwise specified

Two symbols other than numerical digits are used in the codes:

Decimal point (.) in topography
Oblique (/) in morphology

In topography, the decimal point indicates subdivisions of basic
3-digit rubrics;   these are illustrated in Table 8.1.   In morphology,
the first 4 digits indicate the specific histological term, and the 5th
digit, after the oblique (/), is a behaviour code (see section 8.2.5).

The topography terms, prefixed by a T, have 4-digit code numbers
which run from 140.0 to 199.9;   the morphology terms, which may be
prefixed by an M, have 5-digit code numbers which run from 8000/0 to
9990/6.   Therefore, 10 digits are necessary for the complete identification of the topographical site, morphological type, behaviour of
a tumour and grading of differentiation.

Each topographical and morphological term appears only once in the
numerical indices.   The first term listed under a particular code
number (rubric) is either the preferred term or an inclusive term
appropriate for retrieval.   Example:

     194.0 Suprarenal gland
            Adrenal gland
            Adrenal, NOS
        Adrenal cortex
        Adrenal medulla

In this example, 'suprarenal gland' would describe all cases coded to
T-194.0.   The synonyms, 'adrenal gland' and 'adrenal, NOS' are
indented under 'suprarenal gland'.   The non-indented terms, 'adrenal
cortex' and 'adrenal medulla' are not synonyms but are linked under the

Table 8.1   Topography codes in ICD-O: basic 3-digit rubrics

Code no.	Topographical site
T 140-149	Lip, oral cavity and pharynx
T 150-159	Digestive organs and peritoneum
T 160-165	Respiratory system and intrathoracic organs
T 169	Haematopoietic and reticulo-endothelial systems
T 170-171	Bones, joints and connective tissue
T 173	Skin
T 174-5	Breast
T 179-189	Genito-urinary organs
T 190	Eye and lacrimal gland
T 191-192	Nervous system
T 193-194	Endocrine glands
T 196	Lymph nodes
T 199	Unknown primary site

same code number because they are topographical subdivisions of the
first term, 'suprarenal gland'.   Similarly, the presentation of:

    9540/3 Neurofibrosarcoma
           Neurogenic sarcoma
           Neurosarcoma

indicates that the preferred term is 'neurofibrosarcoma'.

The morphology code is extended by a sixth digit to express
'histological grade' or 'differentiation'.   This code is useful,
since a clinician's decision about management of a patient may hinge
on information about whether a tumour is stated to be well-differentiated or anaplastic.   Thus, for instance, gynaecologists may decide on
different treatments for well-differentiated endometrial carcinoma
(panhysterectomy with or without post-surgical irradiation) and for
anaplastic endometrial carcinoma (pre-surgical irradiation).   However
'the use of grading varies greatly among pathologists throughout the
world, and in many instances malignant tumours are not routinely
graded' (WHO, 1976b).

8.2.3 *Coding of topography in ICD-0, ICD-9 and MOTNAC*

In ICD-0, the topography code numbers or rubrics 140.0 to 199.9
are based on the malignant neoplasms section of ICD-9 and are used to
code the site of origin of all neoplasms. The rubrics 200.0 to 239.9
of the neoplasms section of ICD-9 are not used in ICD-0 because the
neoplasms coded to these rubrics are identified by morphology code
numbers. These sections in ICD-9 are:

200-208 Malignant neoplasms of lymphatic and haematopoietic tissue
210-229 Benign neoplasms
230-234 Carcinoma *in situ*
235-238 Neoplasms of uncertain behaviour
239   Neoplasms of unspecified nature

The ICD-9 rubrics 140-199 include a few categories based on morphology or behaviour; these also are omitted from ICD-0 because they are
identified by morphology codes. The ICD-9 categories that are not
used in ICD-0 are:

155.2   Malignant neoplasm of liver, not specified as primary or
        secondary
172   Malignant melanoma of skin
197   Secondary malignant neoplasm of respiratory and digestive
        systems
198   Secondary malignant neoplasm of other specified sites.

In ICD-9, the rubric 196 is used only for secondary and unspecified
malignant neoplasms of lymph nodes (primary malignant neoplasms of
lymph nodes are classified as 200-208), but the corresponding ICD-0
rubric, T-196, is used for both primary and metastatic neoplasms of
lymph nodes. ICD-9 rubric 159.1, 'malignant neoplasm of spleen, not
elsewhere classified', does not appear in ICD-0, which uses a different
code number for the spleen (T-169.2). The rubric, 169, is not used
in ICD-9, but in ICD-0 it is used to designate several topographical
sites within the haematopoietic system, as follows:

169   Haematopoietic and reticuloendothelial systems

169.0   Blood
169.1   Bone marrow
169.2   Spleen
169.3   Reticuloendothelial system, NOS
169.9   Haematopoietic system, NOS

These ICD-0 rubrics can be used as the topography code for many
of the neoplasms (mainly leukaemia) coded to rubrics 200-208 in ICD-9.

The final difference between ICD-0 and ICD-9 is that 'Hydatidiform
mole, NOS' (T-181.9, M-9100/0 in ICD-0) is not classified with other
neoplasms in ICD-9 but with 'complications of pregnancy, childbirth
and the puerperium' (rubric 630).

As mentioned above, the topography section of MOTNAC was based on the malignant neoplasms section of ICD-8 and was expanded by the inclusion of additional 4-digit subdivisions. In general, the expansions developed for MOTNAC have been incorporated into ICD-9 and then into ICD-0. Thus, there is a high order of comparability between the topographical classification in ICD-9 and ICD-0 and that in ICD-8 and MOTNAC. Since many cancer registries may change from ICD-8 or ICD-9 to ICD-0, examples of differences between ICD-0, ICD-8 and ICD-9 are given (Table 8.2).

Table 8.2   Some differences between ICD-0, ICD-8 and ICD-9 codes

Neoplasm	ICD-0		ICD-8	ICD-9
	Topography	Morphology		
Lymphosarcoma of axillary gland	T-196.3	M-9610/3	200.1	200.1
Lymphosarcoma, diffuse, of small intestine	T-152.9	M-9610/3	200.1	200.1
Endotheliomatous meningioma of brain, frontal lobe	T-191.1	M-9531/0	225.2	225.2
Malignant melanoma of skin of trunk	T-173.5	M-8720/3	172.6	172.5
Metastatic melanoma in lung (primary unknown)	T-162.9	M-8720/6	197.0	197.0
Amelanotic malignant melanoma of anal canal (rectum)	T-154.2	M-8730/3	154.2	154.2
Acute myeloid leukaemia	T-169.1	M-9861/3	205.0	205.0

8.2.4 *Coding of morphology in ICD-0 and MOTNAC*

As noted in section 8.1.4, the morphology section of MOTNAC was revised and expanded by the addition of many terms, for more detailed coding of histological types and subtypes of neoplasms, to create the morphology section of ICD-0. This expansion necessitated the use of an additional digit in the morphology code numbers used in ICD-0. To illustrate this expansion, the MOTNAC and ICD-0 entries for various types of 'squamous-cell carcinoma' are compared in Table 8.3.

It will be noted that the '807' series in MOTNAC has been expanded to 8070, 8071, 8072, 8073, 8074 and 8075, which describe several variants of squamous-cell carcinoma and hence, if desired, could be again collapsed into the MOTNAC equivalent. Three of the MOTNAC synonyms, 'cancroid', 'acanthoma, malignant' and 'prickle-cell carcinoma', were considered to be obsolete or not desirable and were therefore not included in ICD-0. Elimination of obsolete or undesirable terms does not in any way produce incompatibility between MOTNAC and ICD-0 code numbers.

Table 8.3   The ICD-O expansion of a MOTNAC rubric

Code	MOTNAC Neoplasm	Code	ICD-O Neoplasm
8073	Squamous-cell carcinoma, NOS Epidermoid carcinoma, NOS Cancroid Acanthoma, malignant Prickle-cell carcinoma Spinous-cell carcinoma Squamous carcinoma	8070/3	Squamous-cell carcinoma, NOS Epidermoid carcinoma, NOS Spinous-cell carcinoma Squamous carcinoma Squamous-cell epithelioma
		8071/3	Squamous-cell carcinoma, keratinizing type, NOS Squamous-cell carcinoma, large-cell, keratinizing type Epidermoid carcinoma, keratinizing type
		8072/3	Squamous-cell carcinoma, large-cell, non-keratinizing type Squamous-cell carcinoma, non-keratinizing type, NOS Epidermoid carcinoma, large-cell, non-keratinizing type
		8073/3	Squamous-cell carcinoma, small-cell, non-keratinizing type Epidermoid carcinoma, small-cell, non-keratinizing type
		8074/3	Squamous-cell carcinoma, spindle-cell type Epidermoid carcinoma, spindle-cell type
		8075/3	Adenoid squamous-cell carcinoma Pseudoglandular squamous-cell carcinoma

A few histological terms in ICD-O have been assigned code numbers different from those in MOTNAC, so that some incompatibility between the two has resulted. Equivalence tables[1] for converting data from ICD-O rubrics to MOTNAC code numbers and ICD-9 rubrics are of great use to cancer registries.

---

[1] Copies can be obtained from Mrs Constance Percy, Landow Building, Room B506, National Cancer Institute, 7910 Woodmont Ave, Bethesda, MD 20014, USA

8.2.5 *Behaviour code in ICD-0 morphology*

The 5th digit of a morphology code number, which appears after the oblique, is the behaviour code. The 5th digit behaviour code numbers used in ICD-0 are listed below; these distinguish between, e.g., benign and malignant neoplasms at the same site (which have the same topographical code in ICD-0).

/0 Benign
/1 Uncertain whether benign or malignant
   Borderline malignancy
/2 Carcinoma *in situ*

     Intraepithelial
     Non-infiltrating
     Non-invasive

/3 Malignant, primary site
/6 Malignant, metastatic site
   Secondary site
/9 Malignant, uncertain whether primary or metastatic site

8.2.6 *Coding of 'no microscopic confirmation'*

A set of code numbers, M-9990, has been provided in ICD-0 morphology to record cases that have a clinical diagnosis of neoplasia or cancer but have no microscopic confirmation. ICD-0 states that these code numbers can be used when it is known that no histological or cytological specimen has been examined microscopically and that the neoplasm has thus not been classified histologically. The 5th digit in this set of code numbers should be selected in accordance with the clinical evaluation of the malignancy of the tumour. The listing of these code numbers appears in ICD-0 as follows:

    999   No microscopic confirmation of tumour

    9990/0   No microscopic confirmation;
                clinically benign tumour

    9990/1   No microscopic confirmation;
                clinically tumour, NOS

    9990/3   No microscopic confirmation
                clinically malignant tumour
                (cancer)

    9990/6   No microscopic confirmation;
                clinically metastatic tumour
                (cancer)

8.3 *Use of ICD-0 by cancer registries*

8.3.1 *New registries*

There can be no doubt that ICD-0 represents a definite improvement over existing coding schemes, and new cancer registries should certainly use it.   While utilization of the topographical code poses few problems (other than conversion to the ICD-9 equivalents), the usefulness of the morphological information depends on the willingness of pathologists to use either the nomenclature or, preferably, the ICD-0 number in their reports.   This implies a major educational and organizational effort among the pathologists of a country.   Despite the international effort made in creating the morphology code, there may be pathologists who would not agree with the terms used.   This is of little importance if their own term can be given an appropriate morphology code number.

8.3.2 *Established registries*

For established cancer registries that are using previous revisions of the ICD (ICD 7 or ICD 8) or MOTNAC, conversion to a new modification poses problems of staff re-training, space on abstract forms and punch cards, and time.

Cancer registries that have been in existence for a long time may decide to retain their old topography code, with slight adaptations corresponding to the topography code of ICD-0.   They would be well advised to code morphology, as well;   however, coding according to the ICD-0 morphology code could be relatively time-consuming, and this may be reflected in demands for additional staff which not every registry will be able to meet.   Once experience is gained and code numbers for the common terms are learned, this may not be such a serious problem.

An abbreviated version of the ICD-0 morphology code listing frequently encountered terms would certainly facilitate routine work in cancer registries.   Examples are given in Table 8.5;   these are intended as a guide only and may, of course, be modified by individual cancer registries.   They complement but in no way replace the ICD-0 manual.

8.3.3 *Other general aspects*

The analysis of cancer registry data often covers longer periods than the relatively frequent changes of ICD, necessitating the choice between conversion or staying with an outdated classification.   If a very detailed system has been adopted from the start, conversion is a minor problem.

The very detailed information in the ICD-0 morphology section, necessary for detecting and tracing very specific neoplasms (which may be indicative of an occupational hazard), is of minor importance for incidence tabulations (see section 9.3.8).   For statistical information, the topography code plus grouped, inclusive categories of the morphology code would probably be used to allow comparison with previous publications and to result in meaningful numbers.   Thus, the *Third US National Cancer Survey* (NCI, 1975b) lists the number of cases by primary site (ICD-8) and detailed histology.   Although there were nearly 150,000 cases with histological confirmation, using the MOTNAC 4-digit code, for many of the histological diagnoses there were often only one or two cases.

Dentists and ophthalmologists are not satisfied with having 4 digits to code topography and have introduced further subdivisions with a 5th digit.   We suspect that other specialities may follow suit and would therefore advise new cancer registries to plan for a 5-digit topography field expanding on the topographical rubrics of ICD-0 (or 4 digits, if the first digit is suppressed as in SEER[1] codes). The last digit would thus be left blank for possible future use.

Instructions must be given to cancer registries so that comparable tabulations can be made;   these will obviously not correspond to those given for conversion to ICD-9.

8.4 *Practical problems in the coding of tumours*

The application of any ICD classification poses problems, some of which are dealt with below.   The 9th revision of the ICD and the ICD-0 have attempted to resolve some of these as indicated.   It is axiomatic that no classification can overcome the problems raised by imprecise diagnostic statements.

8.4.1 *Lip*

LIP ICD-8 140	LIP ICD-9 140
Although this rubric specifically excludes malignant neoplasms of the skin of lip, which should be assigned to ICD-8 173.0, in practice there are four difficulties:	Certain of the problems posed opposite cannot be solved if imprecise diagnostic statements are made; however, ICD-9 permits more precise coding.
(a) failure to specify skin of lip when this is the site of origin;	Problem not resolved, but basal cell carcinoma can only occur on skin of lip.
(b) the difficulty in the determination of the border between the lip and the oral mucosa;	While there is now provision for coding vermilion border, or external lip (ICD-9 140.0 and 140.1), and the inner oral aspect of the lip (ICD-9 140.3, 140.4, 140.5) separately, the determination of the border between the inner aspect of the lip and the oral mucosa (ICD-9 145.0 and 145.1) remains open to subjective interpretation.
(c) the determination of the point of origin for sizeable neoplasms; and	Problem not resolved at the topographical level, but basal-cell carcinoma can only occur on skin of lip
(d) ambiguity between commissure of lips, assigned to 140.9, and both lips, 140.2, since a commissural neoplasm must involve both upper and lower lip.	Commissure is coded 140.6, and there is no entry for both lips.

---

[1] US programme of Surveillance, Epidemiology and End Results

8.4.2 *Colon and rectum*

It is comparatively easy to decide whether a neoplasm is situated in the lower rectum or in the descending colon. The ICD requires neoplasms of the 'recto-sigmoid (junction)' to be assigned to the rectum (ICD 154), yet it may be very difficult to decide whether a neoplasm is in the sigmoid colon proper (ICD 153.3) or in the recto-sigmoid area (ICD 154.0). Even the name 'recto-sigmoid junction' makes little sense, since a junction is by definition a plane and, thus, cannot be occupied by a three-dimensional neoplasm. This is no academic point, since up to half of large-bowel neoplasms may be found around this region, and the incidence of colon cancer in comparison with rectal cancer can be significantly altered by local custom. The problem is further complicated by the fact that 'pathologists, surgeons and radiologists often use the terms "sigmoid colon" and "recto-sigmoid junction" interchangeably' (Puffer & Griffith, 1967). However, a study by De Jong et al. (1972), using material contributed by 13 cancer registries, has shown that the problem may not be as important as has hitherto been considered.

A major fault in the classifications is the impossibility of distinguishing between neoplasms in the upper rectum and those found in the lower rectum, a point of considerable importance for surgical treatment of the patient and for the evaluation of therapy. It is possible that there are geographical and, hence, etiological differences in the relative proportions of upper and lower rectum neoplasms. ICD-9 has not resolved this problem.

8.4.3 *Larynx and hypopharynx*

Neoplasms straddling the aryepiglottic fold present fairly insoluble problems of classification in that by the time diagnosis is made it is impossible to say whether these arose within the supraglottic portion of the larynx or in the hypopharynx. The continued use by many otorhino-laryngologists of the terms 'laryngopharynx' and 'intrinsic, extrinsic and external larynx' may well result in the misassignment of some hypo-pharyngeal tumours.

These neoplasms are handled somewhat differently in ICD-8 and ICD-9, as shown in Table 8.4. The problem of the aryepiglottic fold neoplasm has been tackled, since, if NOS, these are attributed to the hypopharynx. Neoplasms of laryngeal cartilages, admittedly very rare, are separated from the others.

8.4.4 *Malignant neoplasms of liver and intrahepatic bile ducts*

In ICD-8 only those neoplasms specified as primary were assignable to rubric 155, secondary neoplasms of liver being coded to ICD-8 197.7 and malignant neoplasms unspecified as to whether primary or secondary were coded 197.8. In ICD-9 primary liver cancers are coded to 155.0 and those not specified as primary or secondary to 155.2, secondary neoplasms being again assigned to 197.7. This change in coding may affect the apparent incidence of primary liver neoplasms.

Table 8.4 Coding of laryngeal and hypopharyngeal neoplasms in ICD-8 and ICD-9

Code	ICD-8 Neoplasm	Code	ICD-9 Neoplasm
148.0	Postcricoid region	148.0	Postcricoid region
148.1	Pyriform fossa	148.1	Pyriform sinus
		148.2	Aryepiglottic fold, hypopharyngeal aspect (excludes aryepiglottic fold or interarytenoid fold, laryngeal aspect T-161.1)
		148.3	Posterior hypopharyngeal wall
148.8	Other specified parts	148.8	-
148.9	Part unspecified	148.9	Hypopharynx, unspecified
161.0	Glottis, true vocal cord	161.0	Glottis
		161.1	Supraglottis Aryepiglottic fold or interarytenoid fold, laryngeal aspect
		161.2	Subglottis
		161.3	Laryngeal cartilages
161.8	Other specified parts	161.8	
161.9	Part unspecified	161.9	Larynx, unspecified

8.4.5 *Connective tissue and other soft tissue*

The coding of the admittedly rare malignant neoplasms of cartilage is somewhat confusing and has changed between ICD-8 and ICD-9. Articular and costal cartilages are coded to bone (ICD-9 170), neoplasms of tracheal cartilage to trachea (ICD-9 162.0), those of the laryngeal region to larynx (ICD-9 161.3) (see also section 8.4.3) and those of the nose to nose (ICD-9 160.0), whereas neoplasms of the cartilage of the external ear and eyelid are assigned to ICD 170.0, i.e., connective tissue.

Major problems arise in the coding of these neoplasms in regions such as the leg or trunk. Although the index to ICD-8 gives specific instructions concerning their handling, these are difficult to follow. The instructions in ICD-9 are somewhat clearer, and the whole subject is dealt with carefully in ICD-O.

8.5 ICD-0 codes for commonly used morphological terms[a,b]

ICD-0 M-code	Morphological term
	Adenomas and adenocarcinomas
8140/3	Adenocarcinoma, NOS
8141/3	Scirrhous adenocarcinoma
8143/3	Superficial spreading adenocarcinoma
8160/3	Cholangiocarcinoma (T-155)
8170/3	Hepatocellular carcinoma, NOS (T-155.0)
8180/3	Combined hepatocellular carcinoma and cholangiocarcinoma (T-155.0)
8200/3	Adenoid cystic carcinoma
8230/3	Solid carcinoma, NOS
8240/1	Carcinoid tumour, NOS
8250/3	Bronchiolo-alveolar adenocarcinoma (T-162)
8260/3	Papillary adenocarcinoma, NOS
8312/3	Renal-cell carcinoma (T-189.0)
8330/3	Follicular adenocarcinoma, NOS (T-193.9)
8340/3	Papillary and follicular adenocarcinoma (T-193.9)
8380/3	Endometrioid carcinoma
	Basal cell neoplasms
8090/3	Basal cell carcinoma, NOS (T-173)
	Blood vessel tumours
9120/3	Hemangiosarcoma
9140/3	Kaposi's sarcoma

---

[a] Site-specific morphology terms are given.

[b] This table gives only the preferred term. ICD-0 lists several synonyms, thus, for 8000/3: Tumour, malignant, NOS; malignancy; cancer; unclassified tumour, malignant. The terms are in alphabetical order at the group level only.

ICD-O M-code	Morphological term
	Bone tumours, miscellaneous
9260/3	Ewing's sarcoma (T-170)
	Burkitt's tumour
9750/3	Burkitt's tumour
	Chondromatous neoplasms
9220/3	Chondrosarcoma, NOS (T-170)
	Cystic, mucinous and serous neoplasms
8440/3	Cystadenocarcinoma, NOS
8441/3	Serous cystadenocarcinoma, NOS (T-183.0)
8450/3	Papillary cystadenocarcinoma, NOS (T-183.0)
8470/3	Mucinous cystadenocarcinoma, NOS (T-183.0)
8480/3	Mucinous adenocarcinoma
8490/3	Signet-ring-cell carcinoma
	Ductal, lobular and medullary neoplasms
8500/3	Infiltrating duct carcinoma (T-174)
8510/3	Medullary carcinoma, NOS
8511/3	Medullary carcinoma with amyloid stroma (T-193.9)
8520/3	Lobular carcinoma, NOS (T-174)
8530/3	Inflammatory carcinoma (T-174)
	Epithelial neoplasms, complex
8570/3	Adenocarcinoma with squamous metaplasia
	Epithelial neoplasms, NOS
8010/3	Carcinoma, NOS
8041/3	Small cell carcinoma, NOS
8042/3	Oat cell carcinoma (T-162)
	Germ cell neoplasms
9080/1	Teratoma, NOS

ICD-O M-code	Morphological term
	Gliomas
9380/3	Glioma, malignant (T-191)
9400/3	Astrocytoma, NOS (T-191)
9440/3	Glioblastoma, NOS (T-191)
9450/3	Oligodendroglioma, NOS (T-191)
	Gonadal neoplasms, specialized
8600/3	Theca-cell carcinoma (T-183.0)
8620/1	Granulosa-cell tumour, NOS (T-183.0)
8621/1	Granulosa-cell-theca-cell tumour (T-183.0)
	Haematopoietic tissue disorders, miscellaneous
9950/1	Polycythemia vera (T-169)
9960/1	Chronic myeloproliferative disease (T-169)
9970/1	Chronic lymphoproliferative disease (T-169)
	Hodgkin's disease
9650/3	Hodgkin's disease, NOS
9651/3	Hodgkin's disease, lymphocytic prodominance
9652/3	Hodgkin's disease, mixed cellularity
9653/3	Hodgkin's disease, lymphocytic depletion, NOS
9656/3	Hodgkin's disease, nodular sclerosis, NOS
	Leukaemia, NOS
9800/3	Leukaemia, NOS (T-169)
9801/3	Acute leukaemia, NOS (T-169)
9802/3	Subacute leukaemia, NOS (T-169)
9803/3	Chronic leukaemia, NOS (T-169)
9804/3	Aleukaemic leukaemia, NOS (T-169)
	Lobular - See *Ductal*
	Lymphoid leukaemias
9820/3	Lymphoid leukaemia, NOS (T-169)
9821/3	Acute lymphoid leukaemia (T-169)

ICD-0 M-code	Morphological term
9822/3	Subacute lymphoid leukaemia (T-169)
9823/3	Chronic lymphoid leukaemia (T-169)
9824/3	Aleukaemic lymphoid leukaemia (T-169)

Lymphomas, nodular or follicular

9690/3	Malignant lymphoma, nodular, NOS

Lymphomas, NOS or diffuse

9590/3	Malignant lymphoma, NOS
9610/3	Lymphosarcoma, NOS
9620/3	Malignant lymphoma, lymphocytic, well differentiated, NOS
9630/3	Malignant lymphoma, lymphocytic, poorly differentiated, NOS

Medullary - See *Ductal*

Melanomas

8720/3	Malignant melanoma, NOS
8730/3	Amelanotic melanoma

Meningiomas

9530/0	Meningioma, NOS (T-192)

Mesothelial neoplasms

9050/3	Mesothelioma, malignant

Microscopic confirmation, no

9990/3	Clinically malignant tumour (*cancer*)

Mixed and stromal neoplasms, complex

8940/3	Mixed tumour, malignant, NOS
8960/3	Nephroblastoma, NOS (T-189.0)
8970/3	Hepatoblastoma (T-155.0)
8980/3	Carcinosarcoma, NOS

Monocytic leukaemias

9890/3	Monocytic leukaemia, NOS (T-169)
9891/3	Acute monocytic leukaemia (T-169)

ICD-O M-code	Morphological term
9892/3	Subacute monocytic leukaemia (T-169)
9893/3	Chronic monocytic leukaemia (T-169)
9894/3	Aleukaemic monocytic leukaemia (T-169)
	Mucinous - See *Cystic*
	Mucoepidermoid neoplasms
8430/3	Mucoepidermoid carcinoma
	Myeloid leukaemias
9860/3	Myeloid leukaemia, NOS (T-169)
9861/3	Acute myeloid leukaemia (T-169)
9862/3	Subacute myeloid leukaemia (T-169)
9863/3	Chronic myeloid leukaemia (T-169)
9864/3	Aleukaemic myeloid leukaemia (T-169)
	Myomatous neoplasms
8890/3	Leiomyosarcoma, NOS
8900/3	Rhabdomyosarcoma, NOS
8910/3	Embryonal rhabdomyosarcoma
	Neoplasms, NOS
8000/3	Neoplasm, malignant; Cancer
8001/3	Tumour cells, malignant
	Nerve sheath tumours
9540/3	Neurofibrosarcoma
	Neuroepitheliomatous neoplasms
9500/3	Neuroblastoma, NOS
9510/3	Retinoblastoma, NOS (T-190.5)
	Osteosarcomas
9180/3	Osteosarcoma, NOS (T-170)

ICD-O M-code	Morphological term
	Papillary and squamous cell neoplasms
8050/3	Papillary carcinoma, NOS
8070/3	Squamous-cell carcinoma, NOS
8071/3	Squamous-cell carcinoma, keratinizing type, NOS
	Plasma cell tumours
9730/3	Plasma cell myeloma
	Reticulosarcomas
9640/3	Reticulosarcoma, NOS
	Sarcomas - See *Soft tissue*
	Serous - See *Cystic*
	Soft tissue tumours and sarcomas, NOS
8800/3	Sarcoma, NOS
8850/3	Liposarcoma, NOS
	Squamous cell - See *Papillary*
	Stromal - See *Mixed*
	Transitional-cell papillomas and carcinomas
8120/3	Transitional-cell carcinoma, NOS
8130/3	Papillary transitional-cell carcinoma

9. OUTPUT OPERATIONS AND REPORTS

9. OUTPUT OPERATIONS AND REPORTS

9.1 *Overview*

The output operations of the registry are those which provide information or service to users of the registry. Output is divided into routine and *ad hoc*, as shown in Figure 9.1.

FIG. 9.1 OUTPUT OPERATIONS OF CANCER REGISTRIES

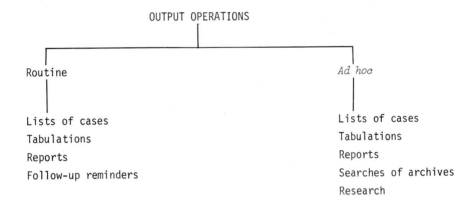

OUTPUT OPERATIONS

Routine

Lists of cases
Tabulations
Reports
Follow-up reminders

Ad hoc

Lists of cases
Tabulations
Reports
Searches of archives
Research

9.2 *Reporting hospital registry data*[1]

Reporting of the data collected is one of the most important functions of a properly operated registry. In smaller hospitals this function is often considered to be fairly useless, since 'we have such a small data base'. While it is true that the figures reported from a very small group of cases would rightly be considered to be statistically invalid by experts, evaluation of the figures in small hospitals can certainly be of value.

This section is for persons with little or no formal instruction in statistical methodology. It is not meant to replace such training, as much is omitted that would be included in a course on statistical methods.

---

[1] Adapted from American College of Surgeons (1974a)

The emphasis is on *reporting* cancer registry data, and only statistical terms necessary for that purpose are included.. Those in day-to-day charge of hospital registries are, of course, encouraged to make use of courses offered in local colleges, not only in statistics but in any relevant subject.

Reports from the registry should always be prepared with the guidance of physicians in order to assure proper content and balance. A cancer committee is usually asked to make reports to its administration. All information included in such a report need not be repeated in the annual report, but items of interest to the entire staff should be excerpted and included.

It is important that registry reports be distributed to all members of the medical staff. Even though some specialized physicians see few cancer cases, all physicians must be informed of cancer experience in the hospital. The reports should also be made available to administrators and to allied health professionals in the hospital who might benefit from the information; these groups would include nurses, cytotechnologists, radiation therapy technicians and medical social workers.

Physicians on the hospital staff and allied health professionals may wish to use registry material for professional papers, clinical investigations and other studies. These studies are often based on the registry's regular reports. Research publications based on registry material should be mentioned prominently in the registry report.

9.2.1 *Definition of terms*

The terms *mean* and *median* are frequently used in statistical reports. The *mean* is the average of a group of observations, whereas the *median* is the middle number of a group of observations. In order to determine the middle number, it is necessary to arrange the observations in ascending order. The median age of five patients of ages 25, 30, 37, 40 and 43 is 37. The median is just as simple to determine if there is an even number of observations, since it is then the number halfway between the middle two observations. Thus, in four patients of ages 28, 32, 36 and 40, the median age is 34.

The mean and median are *measures of central tendency* or methods of showing the 'average' observation in a sample, or group of patients. In a given case, one may be considered to be a better method than the other. For example, in a group of numbers such as 5, 7, 8, 9 and 45 the mean will be 14.8, whereas the median is 8; the one exceptionally large observation distorts the sample, making the median more descriptive of the group as a whole. In general, however, the mean is the more useful index.

At this point we would refer the reader to the simple statistical methods in TNM General Rules (UICC, 1974b) describing the evaluation of results and the presentation of end-results. It also gives definitions of the crude survival rate and the corrected or adjusted survival rate.   It discusses direct and actuarial methods of calculation, accuracy of results, etc.

9.2.2 *Tabulating the data*

The first step in preparing a report is to define the group of patients to be included and the variables to be studied.   It is important to report on each site of cancer rather than on all sites combined.   The years to be covered should be determined: it may be considered desirable to include only one year's cases, or several years' cases or two different groups of years for comparison.   In defining a year's cases, it is important to include only those with an incidence date between January 1 and December 31 inclusive.

The next step is to set up a master table, which should include all the variables to be included in the report.   Assuming that a report will include information on treatment by stage and sex, the tables for each site might be as illustrated in Figure 9.2.

FIG. 9.2 SAMPLE MASTER TABLE
ON TYPE OF TREATMENT BY EXTENT OF DISEASE BEFORE TREATMENT

The codes are those given in Chapter 4.

Type of treatment (item 22)	Extent of disease before treatment for cancer of _____ (item 21)												
	1. *In situ*		2. 3. Localized		4. 5. Regional		6. Distant		9. Unknown		Totals	
	M	F	M	F	M	F	M	F	M	F	M	F
0 None												
1 Surgery only												
2 Radiation only												
3 Surgery plus radiation												
4 Chemotherapy only												
5 Surgery plus chemotherapy												
6 Radiation plus chemotherapy												
7 Surgery plus radiation plus chemotherapy												
8 Other therapy												
9 Unknown												
Totals												

On the basis of the tumour records, the cases would then be entered in the appropriate boxes. After all the cases have been tabulated, they should be counted, and the boxes added horizontally and vertically, to verify accuracy.

Many registries have found it helpful to prepare a small card for each case to be included in the report, listing only those variables that will be analysed, each with a fixed position on the card (Fig. 9.3). A key card, listing the position of each item as well as the abbreviations used, is essential, e.g., squamous-cell carcinoma can be abbreviated to SCC; radiotherapy to RT; dead or alive to D or A.

FIG. 9.3   SAMPLE TABULATING CARD

	Age	*Sex*	
	61	Male (M)	
Name	JONES, Donald P.	Oesophagus	*Primary site*
Histology	Squamous-cell carcinoma, Gr. II (SCC)	Radiotherapy (RT)	*Initial treatment*
Incidence date	4 July 70	Dead (D)	*Vital status*
		With	*Cancer status*
Date of latest information	5 Jan 72 Caucasian	24	*Completed months of survival*

Ethnic group

These cards may be helpful if the report requires many tabulations, since their use will save wear and tear on the tumour records.

Some registries have available a diagnostic index, which is a listing of cases by primary anatomical site, by year of diagnosis and, possibly, by histological diagnosis. This index may be prepared either manually or by computer and includes other information pertinent to the diagnosis, including stage, treatment and survival time. It may also be more convenient to use in tabulating data (see also section 11.5 and Fig. 11.2).

The automated registry, which has information available on punch cards, can use a card sorter to tabulate the information. Computerized registries can prepare programmes that will tabulate the data automatically. In some circumstances (particularly for a small series of cases), a card sorter may be more convenient and much faster than a computer.

9.2.3 *Preparing survival reports*

The process of calculating survival rates is really a simple mathematical process. The direct method for computing observed survival is described here; in other words, those patients who have survived the specified time period (e.g., three, five, ten years, etc.) are included, and no adjustments are made for deaths due to causes other than cancer. More sophisticated calculations may be made using the actuarial method, which allows inclusion of cases not exposed to the risk of dying for the entire time period and takes into account deaths from other causes. Since this method is well described in *Reporting of Cancer Survival and End Results* (American Joint Committee for Cancer Staging and End Results Reporting, 1963), it is not repeated here. For those hospital and central registries with access to computers and appropriate programmes, relative survival rates (adjusting for so-called normal mortality) are possible.

Survival rates for cancer patients are almost always computed from the incidence date (item 13).

The first step is to tabulate the necessary information; a master table, similar to the one shown in Figure 9.4, should be made.

FIG. 9.4 SAMPLE SIMPLE STAGE/SURVIVAL TABLE

The codes of item 21 are those given in Figure 4.1.

Clinical stage (item 21)	Number of months surviving (item 28)					
	< 12	12-	24-	36-	48-	60 or more
1. *In situ*						
2. 3. Localized						
4. 5. Regional						
6. Distant						
9. Unknown						
Total (all stages)						

Each patient is entered once only in the appropriate box, which indicates the number of months of completed survival. Thus, a patient who survived 42 months would be entered under the column labelled '36-'. A patient who survived only eight months would be entered in the '< 12' (less than twelve) box (Survival may be expressed in single months if this is more appropriate to the site being studied, e.g., acute leukaemia).

Once all the cases have been tabulated and the totals verified, survival rates can be computed. The completed table for localized cases can be assumed to be as in Figure 9.5:

FIG. 9.5 SAMPLE STAGE/SURVIVAL TABLE, LOCALIZED CASES

Clinical stage (item 21)	Number of months surviving (item 28)					
	< 12	12-	24-	36-	48-	60 or more
Localized	20	20	20	10	5	25

It must be remembered that each patient appears in the table only once. Patients who survive 60 months or more, however, also survived 48 months, 36 months, 24 months, etc.; therefore, in calculating survival rates all patients surviving 60 months should be added to each preceding interval, and all those surviving 48 months should be added to each preceding interval, etc. This can be accomplished in the following manner (Fig. 9.6):

FIG. 9.6 SAMPLE SURVIVAL TABULATION

	Number of months surviving					
	< 12	12-	24-	36-	48-	60-
Number surviving	20	20	20	10	5	25
	25	25	25	25	25	
	5	5	5	5		
	10	10	10			
	20	20				
	20					
	100	80	60	40	30	25

It will be noted that the total of the '< 12 months' column
should agree with the total number of patients in the study, since all
patients survived 'less than one year', even if they died the day
after diagnosis.   Thus, the survival rate for the '< 12 months'
column will always be 100%.   Using this figure as the denominator,
one calculates the survival percentages for each interval.   The survival percentage for the data presented in Figure 9.6 would be:

    80 patients survived 1 full year   80/100 = .80 = 80%
    60 patients survived 2 full years   60/100 = .60 = 60%
    40 patients survived 3 full years   40/100 = .40 = 40%
    30 patients survived 4 full years   30/100 = .30 = 30%
    25 patients survived 5 full years   25/100 = .25 = 25%

When the percentages have been calculated, they can be plotted
on a graph to make a survival curve (Fig. 9.7).   The graph should
then be labelled appropriately.

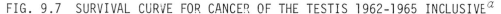

FIG. 9.7   SURVIVAL CURVE FOR CANCER OF THE TESTIS 1962-1965 INCLUSIVE[a]

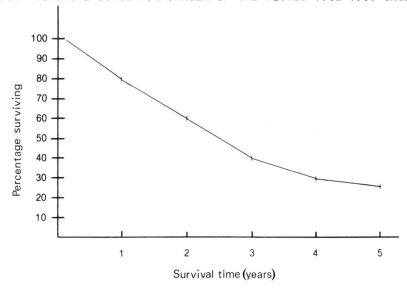

Survival time (years)

[a] This is not a typical curve, which would, in general, fall more
steeply in the first year.

9.2.4   *Graphical presentation*

When possible, information from the registry should be presented
clearly as a graph or pictogram;   suggestions for the construction of
various types of graphs and pictograms are given below.   All graphs

should be labelled clearly and titled and, in most cases, augmented
with a narrative description in the text.

The bar graph (histogram).   Whenever possible, this type of graph
should be arranged to read from left to right.   As with all other
graphs, it should be labelled concisely and clearly.

A simple bar graph has two axes, one representing the variable
presented, the other representing the number of observations for the
variable or the percentage of observations.

FIG. 9.8 AGE DISTRIBUTION OF 90 MALE PATIENTS WITH CARCINOMA OF

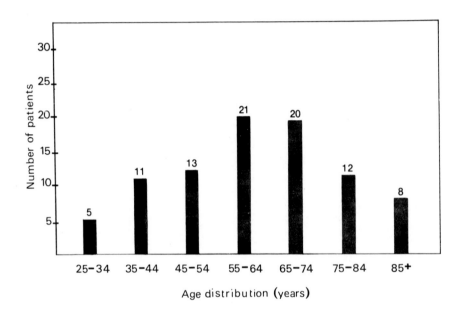

Each bar should be equal in width, unless the size of the age
group changes; in that case, the width of the bars may be changed.
For clarity, the number of observations should be printed at the top
of the bar, as in Figure 9.8.

A bar graph can be used to portray more than one variable, such as
in a stage/treatment distribution, using different colours or cross-
hatchings for different variables.   An example is shown in Figure
9.13.

Circle or pie charts.   A pie chart is simply a circle which has
been divided into wedges, each representing the percentage of one
variable compared to the entire sample.   It is best used when there

is only a small number of variables, such as in stage distributions, histological distributions and treatment distributions.

To prepare a pie chart, the variables should be converted to percentages; then, the percentage of each variable is multiplied by 360 (the number of degrees in a circle) and rounded off to full degrees.

Example: 20% = 360° × .20 = 72.00 = 72°

20% 33% = 360° × .33 = 119.00 = 119°

To draw the pie chart, make a circle, draw a radius from the centre of the circle to the right-hand outer rim and measure 72° from the radius with a protractor (Fig. 9.9).

FIG. 9.9   SAMPLE PIE CHART

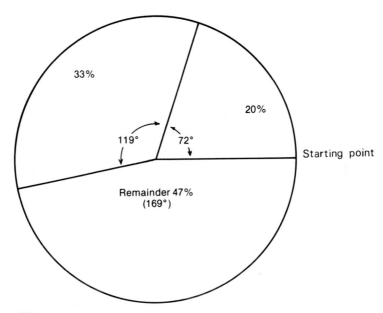

33% = 119°
20% = 72°
47% = 169°

100% = 360°

Line graphs.   One type of line graph, a survival curve, is illustrated in Figure 9.7.   Line graphs can also show other types of time trends, such as the number or percentage of cases of a particular site of cancer in different years (Figs 9.10 & 9.11).

FIG. 9.10   CASES OF CANCER OF THE BREAST
AS A PERCENTAGE OF ALL FEMALE CANCER DIAGNOSED,
1970-1974 INCLUSIVE

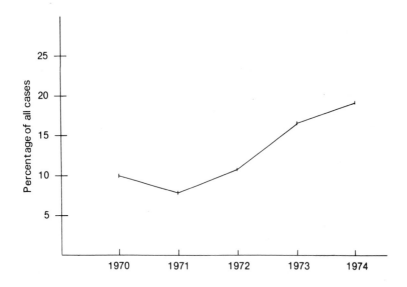

FIG. 9.11   CASES OF CANCER OF LUNG AND STOMACH
AS A PERCENTAGE OF ALL CANCERS DIAGNOSED: MALES
1955-1975 INCLUSIVE

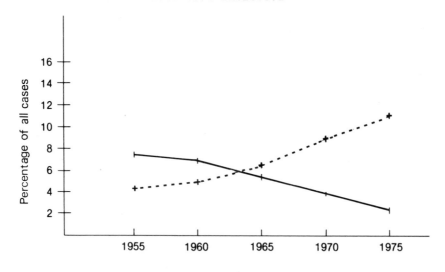

Lung cancer - - - - - ;   Stomach cancer _____ .

On the graph shown in Figure 9.11, two different sites are presented;   these show an increase in the percentage of lung cancer cases
and a decrease in the percentage of stomach cancer cases over the
period of years considered.

9.2.5 *Compiling the report*

When reporting information from the cancer registry, it is not
enough to count up some numbers, draw a graph and send it around.
The information should first be presented in rough draft form to the
cancer committee (or to a physician or group of physicians designated
by the committee) for review.   At this point, the committee may ask
for clarification or that additional information be included.   It is
also customary to accompany the report with a brief narrative description of the group of cases in the report, along with any unusual observations on the data presented.   It is recommended that this description be written by a member of the cancer committee or by the medical
director.

The American College of Surgeons' Commission on Cancer requires
reporting on at least an annual basis.   For this reason, many registries make annual reports, which may be of many types.   Since no particular format is required, registries are encouraged to be imagina-
tive and innovative in reporting.   Although reporting is required
'on at least an annual basis', a registry should prepare as many
reports in a year as required by the hospital cancer committee.
Registries should report the following at least annually:

(a) total number of new cancer cases seen in the year, including
    a distribution of the ten most frequent sites;

(b) total number of old cases: alive only and plus dead
    (need not be reported by site distribution);

(c) a follow-up report, including percentage of cases lost to
    follow-up;

(d) a complete study of at least one site each year, including
    survival;

(e) an administrative report covering requests for information,
    papers and publications and utilization of registry data; and

(f) some sort of comparative study to be used by the cancer
    committee as a yardstick for measuring the impact of the
    cancer programme on the cancer experience in the hospital.

A sample annual report is shown in Figure 9.12;   a sample statistical report is given in Figure 9.13.

FIG. 9.12   SAMPLE ANNUAL REPORT

XYZ GENERAL HOSPITAL CANCER REGISTRY

1978 Annual Report

SUMMARY OF REGISTRY ACTIVITIES

The cancer registry of XYZ General Hospital has now been in operation for 15 full years. Since 1963, over 5000 cases have been included in the registry, and over 2000 cases are under active follow-up. Only 2% of the 5000 cases have been lost to follow-up at this time.

In addition to this annual report, quarterly statistical reports for specific sites of cancer are prepared by the registry staff and the cancer committee. These reports were distributed to the entire staff and were the subjects of tumour conferences in February, June and November. Subjects covered in the past year were pancreatic and lung cancer and Hodgkin's disease. Additional copies of these reports are available.

The registry also assisted Doctors Smith and Jones in a special study on thyroid cancer, which is being prepared for publication. Any physicians wishing to use registry data for special studies should contact the chairman of the cancer committee.

The medical staff bulletin now includes information from the cancer registry as a regular feature.

REVIEW OF 1977 REGISTRATIONS

421 new cases were added in 1977; the distribution of the 10 most frequently diagnosed sites is presented here. 29 old cases and 14 reportable benign cases were registered, but these are not included in this analysis. Carcinomas of the skin other than melanoma are included.

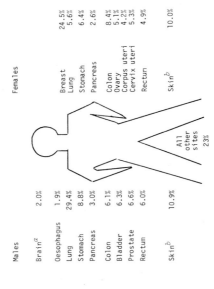

Males		Females	
Brain[a]	2.0%	Breast	24.5%
		Lung	5.6%
Oesophagus	1.9%	Stomach	6.4%
Lung	29.4%	Pancreas	2.6%
Stomach	8.8%		
Pancreas	3.0%	Colon	8.4%
		Ovary	5.1%
Colon	6.1%	Corpus uteri	4.2%
Bladder	6.3%	Cervix uteri	5.3%
Prostate	6.6%		
Rectum	6.0%	Rectum	4.9%
Skin[b]	10.9%	Skin[b]	10.0%

All other sites 23%

[a] Includes benign and unspecified neoplasms
[b] Other than melanomas

There was no appreciable increase in numbers of cases from previous years. The ratio of males to females was nearly 1:1.

FIG. 9.13 SAMPLE STATISTICAL REPORT

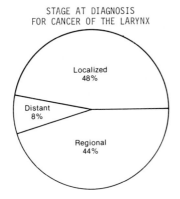

STAGE AT DIAGNOSIS
FOR CANCER OF THE LARYNX

CARCINOMA OF THE LARYNX
100 new cases
1968-1972

The statistics presented in this report were
compiled from data collected on the 100 cases
of carcinoma of the larynx that were initially
diagnosed and/or treated at this hospital
between 1 January 1968 and 31 December 1972.
The ratio of males to females was 19:1.
The median age of the male patients was 60 years.
The five females are excluded from the analyses
given here.
The histological diagnosis of all 95 males cases
is squamous-cell carcinoma. A distribution of
the histological grade at original diagnosis is
available from the cancer registry, as is other
more detailed information, such as survival by
treatment and more detailed information on
stage.

INITIAL COURSE OF TREATMENT
FOR CANCER OF LARYNX

OBSERVED 5-YEAR SURVIVAL BY CLINICAL
STAGE PRIOR TO TREATMENT

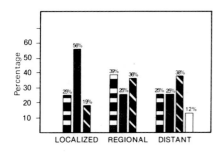

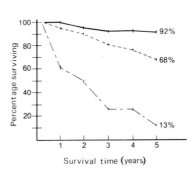

Surgery only ▪▪▪▪; radiation only ▬▬ ;
Surgery + radiation ▰▰▰; no treatment ▭.

Localized ——— ; regional ----- ;
distant — —— .

9.2.6 *Cancer committee report to staff*

Reports to the medical staff should include a résumé of the cancer
activities during the years; in addition to preparing the report of
registry data, the registrar should assist the cancer committee in preparing their report.   The report should include at least the following:

(a) average or actual number of cancer cases presented at tumour
    conferences;

(b) average or actual number of physicians attending
    conferences;

(c) reports on special projects (e.g., routine Papanicolau
    smears or routine rectal examinations on patients of a
    certain age, rehabilitation programme, etc.);

(d) proposed goals for the future, enlisting the aid and
    cooperation of the staff, administration and local
    cancer society or other health organizations in the
    community.

9.3 Reporting population-based registry data

9.3.1 Description of the registry

This should indicate the name and address of the registry and
indicate to whom correspondence should be addressed.   An outline
of the organization of the registry such as appears for registries in
Cancer Incidence in Five Continents (Waterhouse et al., 1976) should
be given at least every few years, with cross-reference to it in other
years.   The professional staff of the registry should be listed,
with their specific fields of interest or responsibility, e.g., oncologist, epidemiologist, statistician, etc.

9.3.2 Population covered by registration

Each issue of the periodic report should contain a description of
the geographical area covered by the registry and contain a table
giving population denominator data used for the computation of rates.
A detailed description of the characteristics of the population should
be given, e.g., geographical or ethnic origin, access to health services,
etc.   Population data obtained from a census report should give a
detailed reference, including volume number, page numbers, table numbers
and the location in the report of narrative or comment concerning
completeness of the census.   If the figure for the population denominator is an estimate based on a census, the method of derivation should
be given, together with an unequivocal statement as to how migration in
and out of the registration area has been estimated.   If migration
figures are based on an 'informed guess', this should be noted.

When rates are given for subdivisions of the population, e.g.,
geographical regions within a country or ethnic groups, the source of
the population-at-risk should again be fully documented.   When urban/
rural rates are given, the definitions used for 'urban' and 'rural' must
be specified and attention drawn to local administrative practices that
permit the incorporation of small districts within a conurbation, thus
creating units which meet the definition of 'rural' although located in
built-up areas.

9.3.3 *Statistical terms*

These need not be defined unless local customs or practices make
statements ambiguous; e.g., by the Chinese calendar, a new-born child
is one-year old at birth, and if the new year begins shortly after his
birth he is considered to be two-years old, although by occidental
convention he may be only two-weeks old (see item 6, Chap. 4).
In other circumstances, age might have been determined by indirect
methods, such as a calendar of important local events, which must
be described.   The same applies to other items, such as residence.

9.3.4 *Definition of cancer*

'Cancer' should be limited to those neoplasms defined by ICD-0
under topography codes 140-199, corresponding to rubrics 140-209 and
230-239 of ICD 8 and ICD 9 (see Chap. 8).   The inclusion of some
groups of neoplasms may be controversial, e.g., so-called 'benign'
papillomas of the urinary tract.   For such lesions, the total number
of neoplasms of the urinary tract should be given, together with the
number reported as 'benign' papillomas (ICD-0 M-8210/1 or, as pathologists may now prefer, 'transitional-cell carcinoma grade 0').   The
general rule should be to allow removal of controversial diagnoses from
a tabulation if desired.   The same considerations apply to carcinoma
in situ.

It is advisable to have a clear statement about ways of handling
certain problems for which there is no general ruling, for instance,
whether cancers detected as incidental findings (e.g., at autopsy) are
included in incidence tabulations, whether cytological diagnosis is
included under microscopic confirmation, whether benign and undefined
tumours of the central nervous system are reported together with those
diagnosed as malignant, whether bladder tumours include papillomas,
etc.   Cancer registry procedures and coding instructions should allow
for flexibility in presentation of results on these debatable points.

Many registries also keep records of a variety of lesions which are
recorded as premalignant or of doubtful malignancy.   Under no circumstances should these be added to the 'cancer' tabulations, although they
may be tabulated separately.

The histologically benign tumours of the central nervous system
(ICD-0 morphology '/0') are often added to those that are unequivocally
malignant, on the grounds that these neoplasms are a danger to life and
that histological differentiation between 'benign' forms and those of
low-grade malignancy is difficult.   If it is possible to distinguish
them, these should be tabulated separately and not included in the
total malignancies for ICD-0 T-192.   Similar arguments apply to neoplasms of the central nervous system of unspecified malignancy (with
behaviour code '/1').

9.3.5 *Neoplasms of uncertain malignancy (coded morphology '/1' in ICD-0)*

The biological behaviour of a substantial number of neoplasms is difficult to predict on morphological grounds alone.   Neoplasms such as granulosa-cell tumours of the ovary are usually coded '/1' in ICD-0 (rubrics 230-239 in ICD-8 and 9).   Because of interest in these neoplasms and the fact that a variable proportion of them spread locally or metastasize, there has been a tendency to class them all as malignant and code them 140-209.   In our opinion, this is incorrect, and these neoplasms, if they show no signs of malignancy, should be tabulated separately.

9.3.6 *Ten most common sites*

This information should be presented in two tables, one giving the frequency of the 10 most common sites by sex, the other the age-adjusted rates (see section 9.3.8) by rank order.   Such tables summarize the cancer problems in the population in question and are most useful to the informed lay public and to those who make decisions about priorities (e.g., prostatic cancer in Sweden).

9.3.7 *Tabulations of numbers of new cases diagnosed within a specified period, by sex and site*

This information should be given by five-year age groups from 5-9 to 85+.   For the first five years of life, it may be useful to use 0 and 1-4.   When numbers are small, 10-year age groups may be used;   these must follow the WHO recommended age-intervals, i.e., 0-4, 5-14, 15-24, 25-34, etc.   Anatomical site should be given at the 3-digit level.   Tabulations at the 4-digit level should be done where possible.   If there is any departure from the ICD classification, this should be footnoted prominently.   Figures for males and females must be given separately, preferably in separate tables. Figure 9.14, from the report of the Finnish Cancer Registry (1976), illustrates the tabulation of the number of new cases.

9.3.8 *Tabulations of age-specific incidence rates*

These are most important and should normally be presented for the age groups given in section 9.3.7 as rates per 100,000 by primary site, sex and age group.   The formula for calculation is as follows:

$$\text{Age-specific incidence rate per 100 000} = \frac{\text{number of new cases (in age group)}}{\text{population (in age group)}} \times 100\ 000$$

The rate is valid for a specified time period.   It is rounded off to one decimal place.   Some registries prefer to publish rates per million, in order to avoid the decimal.

The reporting of incidence rates for 4th digits of an ICD rubric depends on the number of cases;   it is not worth tabulating rates based on a total of less than 10 cases of all ages.

FIG. 9.14 TABULATION OF NEW MALE CANCER CASES IN FINLAND, 1973

ICD 1977 code	0-4	5-9	10-14	15-19	20-24	25-29	30-34	35-39	40-44	45-49	50-54	55-59	60-64	65-69	70-74	75-79	80-84	85-	All ages
All sites	29	19	22	30	48	68	54	87	149	274	415	666	992	1188	961	615	298	133	6048
140-148	-	-	2	-	-	3	-	5	10	21	25	11	39	48	24	13	5	3	209
140	-	-	-	-	-	1	-	2	7	11	14	9	23	31	19	7	4	2	130
141	-	-	-	-	-	-	-	-	1	2	5	-	2	4	2	1	-	-	17
142	-	-	-	-	-	1	-	1	-	2	1	1	1	-	-	-	-	-	7
143-144	-	-	-	-	-	-	-	-	2	2	-	1	4	1	3	-	1	-	14
145-148	-	-	2	-	-	1	-	2	-	4	5	-	9	12	-	5	-	1	41
150-159	-	-	1	3	4	8	11	20	43	68	112	167	239	321	295	216	111	37	1656
150	-	-	-	-	-	-	-	1	2	-	7	12	17	24	16	13	6	2	100
151	-	-	-	-	1	2	6	7	20	32	47	67	91	139	141	119	51	20	743
152	-	-	-	-	-	-	-	-	1	4	4	4	3	3	-	3	-	-	22
153$^\alpha$	-	-	-	2	3	2	3	6	6	9	11	22	26	35	29	21	12	3	190
154$^\alpha$	-	-	-	-	-	3	1	2	5	9	15	17	26	41	44	19	20	2	204
155.0	-	-	1	1	-	1	-	2	1	2	5	8	21	15	11	4	5	1	78
155.1	-	-	-	-	-	-	1	1	2	2	2	4	4	10	9	10	3	-	48
157	-	-	-	-	-	-	-	1	6	10	19	30	43	47	34	24	11	5	230
156, 158-159	-	-	-	-	-	-	-	-	-	-	2	3	8	7	11	3	3	4	41
160-164	-	1	-	1	-	2	3	12	37	92	169	289	417	462	333	147	51	18	2034
160	-	1	-	-	-	-	-	1	-	1	1	2	-	4	-	2	-	-	12
161	-	-	-	-	-	-	-	1	4	12	14	28	27	22	17	6	3	-	134
162.0-1	-	-	-	-	-	-	2	9	32	78	153	257	390	434	316	137	47	18	1873
162.2	-	-	-	-	-	2	-	1	-	1	1	2	-	2	-	2	1	-	12
164	-	-	-	1	-	-	1	-	1	-	-	-	-	-	-	-	-	-	3
170	-	-	-	-	-	-	-	-	1	-	1	1	1	1	-	-	-	-	5
177-179	1	-	-	2	3	15	2	6	4	6	16	42	83	137	144	125	75	41	702
177	-	-	-	-	-	-	-	-	1	2	15	40	80	137	142	122	72	41	652
178	1	-	-	2	3	15	2	6	2	3	1	1	1	-	-	2	-	-	39
179	-	-	-	-	-	-	-	-	1	1	-	1	2	-	2	1	3	-	11
180-181	3	1	-	-	-	1	2	3	9	22	29	47	81	80	67	45	14	9	413
180	3	1	-	-	-	1	1	1	7	14	17	25	38	19	16	11	5	4	163
181	-	-	-	-	-	-	1	2	2	8	12	22	43	61	51	34	9	5	250
190$^\alpha$	-	1	-	1	1	1	5	6	6	12	10	10	19	8	11	2	-	2	95
191$^\alpha$	-	-	-	-	2	1	1	2	5	1	2	9	17	15	11	14	9	5	94
192	5	-	-	-	-	-	-	1	-	-	2	1	1	5	-	1	-	-	16
193	8	4	3	8	10	7	5	12	8	12	10	17	13	18	-	3	3	2	143
194	-	-	2	-	4	4	4	5	1	3	2	1	6	4	1	3	1	-	41
195	-	1	1	1	-	-	1	-	-	2	1	1	1	2	2	-	-	-	13
196	-	-	-	4	1	8	3	1	1	2	-	6	3	4	1	1	1	-	36
197	2	-	-	2	3	3	2	-	1	5	2	3	2	4	-	2	1	3	35
199	-	-	-	-	-	1	3	1	6	5	9	18	19	32	23	12	15	7	151
200, 202	-	2	1	1	2	3	2	4	5	3	11	12	16	14	17	6	4	1	104
201	-	-	1	4	10	9	6	3	5	4	6	6	8	6	3	5	-	1	77
203	-	-	-	-	-	-	1	-	2	3	2	9	9	7	12	7	3	1	56
204	10	9	11	3	8	2	3	6	5	13	6	16	18	20	17	13	5	3	168
Not included above																			
Papilloma of urinary bladder	-	-	-	-	1	-	-	1	1	-	1	6	7	6	4	3	-	2	32
Basal-cell carcinoma of skin	-	-	-	2	2	4	9	14	23	39	55	59	106	96	86	69	28	16	608
Polycythaemia vera	-	-	-	-	-	-	1	1	-	3	3	1	1	3	-	-	-	-	13
Myelofibrosis	-	-	-	-	-	-	-	-	1	1	2	2	1	1	1	-	-	-	9

Tabulations by sex, site, age and morphological type should be performed regularly, if possible. However such analyses, to be of value, require large numbers of cases, particularly if meaningful numbers of the common types are to be tabulated. The monograph *Cancer in Sweden 1959-1965* (Swedish Cancer Registry, 1971) exemplifies this type of publication.

Age-specific rates can be calculated by calendar year, but average annual rates for periods of five years are less variable. Population denominators for each year, if available, are summed; otherwise, the denominator, preferably at the midpoint of the quinquennium, is multiplied by five. A suitable format for the reporting of site-, sex- and age-specific incidence rates is that used in *Cancer Incidence in Five Continents*, e.g., volume III (Waterhouse et al., 1976).

9.3.9 *Age-standardized incidence rates*

The age-specific incidence of cancer varies markedly with age. Hence, the crude rate for cancer at a specific site for, say males, in a population (total number of registrations at all ages divided by the total population) will be influenced by the age structure of males in the population. When the total population contains subpopulations which differ in age structure (e.g., ethnic groups, urban/rural areas), crude rates should not be used for comparison. It is best to compare the age-specific rates. For international comparisons involving many populations and large differences in age-structure, age-standardized rates are used to facilitate comparisons among populations. The effect of differences in age-structure on the comparison is removed by age-standardization.

A number of standard populations with differing age structure are used in age standardization. It is important to use populations which can also be used by others, and those given by Doll (1976) are strongly recommended. Doll (1976) discusses in detail the logic and techniques of age standardization.

It should be noted that the most valid basis of diagnosis (item 17) varies not only with organ but also with age. Age-standardized incidence rates cannot correct for such variation but are useful for comparisons of rates in populations with different age structures.

9.3.10 *Cumulative incidence rates*

A most useful summary measure for comparison of populations is the cumulative rate (Day, 1976). This approximates the cumulative risk, which is 'the risk an individual would have of developing the disease in question during a certain age period if no other causes of death were in operation. The age period over which the risk is accumulated has to be specified and would depend on the comparison being made. Thus, for childhood tumours one would take age 0-14; however, in general, risk over the whole life span, which can be taken as 0-74, would be the appropriate measure.' (Day, 1976).

The cumulative rate is the sum of the age-specific incidence rates for each year of age from birth to age 74.   Since age-specific incidence rates are usually computed for five-year age intervals, the cumulative rate is five times the sum of the age-specific incidence rates calculated over five-year age groups.   The first five years of life (age group 0-4) may be divided into age 0 (multiplied by 1) and age 1-4 (multiplied by 4).   The cumulative rate can be interpreted either as a directly age-standardized rate with the same population size in each age group, or as an approximation to the cumulated risk.   A corresponding measure for childhood cancer would sum the age-specific rates over each year of age from 0-14.   The cumulative rate is more conveniently expressed per hundred (per cent) than per hundred thousand (Day, 1976).

Figure 9.15 (from Day, 1976) compares the values of cumulative incidence rates with age-standardized rates.   In the absence of other causes of death, a male in Cali, Colombia, has a life-time risk of dying from lung cancer of approximately 1 in 47, compared with approximately 1 in 10 for a male in Birmingham, UK.   Although the differences between Cali and Birmingham are similar for age-standardized and cumulative rates, the absolute value of the latter has more intuitive appeal.

FIG. 9.15   COMPARISON OF CUMULATIVE INCIDENCE RATES WITH RATES AGE-STANDARDIZED TO A WORLD POPULATION AND TO AGES 35-64 (TRUNCATED RATE^a) (DAY, 1976)

Population	Incidence	Stomach	Lung	Breast	Cervix uteri	Leukaemia	Prostate	All sites	
		male	male	female	female	male	male	male	female
Cali, Colombia	Cumulative	7.34	2.14	3.08	8.35	0.38	2.71	29.11	29.78
	world pop.	57.5	17.5	27.3	75.6	5.2	23.2	(25.25)	(25.75)
	truncated	87.7	29.0	62.6	183.6	5.6	21.5		
Alameda County, US (Negro)	Cumulative	2.69	5.85	4.15	3.18	1.05	7.54	30.80	20.81
	world pop.	24.4	43.8	38.6	30.5	8.3	65.3	(26.51)	(18.78)
	truncated	33.0	88.9	75.0	75.4	8.9	55.6		
Birmingham, UK	Cumulative	3.13	9.73	5.58	1.39	0.52	1.85	30.11	21.69
	world pop.	25.2	73.3	51.1	13.6	5.3	18.4	(26.00)	(19.50)
	truncated	35.9	133.5	114.1	34.2	6.2	10.9		
Miyagi Prefecture, Japan	Cumulative	11.97	2.16	1.06	2.28	0.36	0.35	24.22	16.30
	world pop.	95.3	15.6	11.0	20.6	4.4	3.2	(21.51)	(15.04)
	truncated	164.1	22.6	27.5	52.8	4.7	2.0		

N.B. The figures for *all sites* that are given in parentheses are the exact cumulative risks.

^{a} From *Cancer Incidence in Five Continents*, Volume II

9.3.11 *Special reports*

From time to time, a cancer registry will wish to publish a more exhaustive analysis of its material.   The opportunity should be taken on this occasion to deal in detail with sources of information, departures from the ICD coding system and comments on findings of interest for each site.

Such studies may give detailed comparisons of geographical regions or populations-at-risk (e.g., in cumulative rates per hundred), survival studies, time trends in incidence, the number of cases seen each year and 4th-digit site tabulations.   Tabulations by histological diagnosis are important; the use of ICD-0 will be very helpful in this: for instance, the epidemiology of extranodal lymphatic malignancies, which has been obscured by their inclusion in categories 200 and 201 of the 7th, 8th and 9th revisions of the ICD can now be elucidated.

9.4 *Evaluating results*

9.4.1 *Incidence*

Whatever the chosen methods of presentation of incidence data, whether as age-specific or standardized rates or, in the absence of reliable population statistics, as relative frequency of sites, the resulting data must be scrutinized as to:

(a) Consistency of the number of cases in each calendar year: it is common that new registries initially show an increasing number of cases.   It is wise to defer reporting of rates until they are stable.   Sometimes numbers fall in the second or third years of operation, suggesting that prevalent as well as incident cases were initially being notified and registered.   A marked decrease in numbers may indicate a breakdown in reporting.   Random fluctuations in the number of cases may occur, especially for cancers at less common sites.

(b) Site distribution: any change in frequency by site (e.g., inconstant figures or disappearance of a particular tumour) must be investigated carefully before its validity is accepted.   Such a phenomenon may be due to a variety of factors, ranging from coding errors to interest by the medical profession in a recently described tumour (e.g., Burkitt's lymphoma, vaginal adenocarcinoma, mesothelioma).

(c) Diagnosis: two indices are generally used to indicate validity of diagnosis:

1. the percentage of microscopic confirmation.   This normally varies with anatomical location (high for accessible sites and for leukaemia) and with age (low in old people); and

2. the percentage of cases that remain registered on the basis of death certificate only.   This percentage will be relatively high in old people and in those who have malignant neoplasms which may have been diagnosed and treated on an outpatient basis only (e.g., prostatic carcinoma, chronic lymphatic leukaemia).   The registry tries to keep this percentage to a minimum by contacting the certifying physician for further information and by carefully checking any duplicates.

In addition, the percentage of all cases diagnosed as of undefined primary site may be worth investigation; a high percentage, arbitrarily set at 10%, might indicate inferior or swamped medical services or low utilization of available services.

(d) Demographic data: If for a considerable percentage of cases sex, age, region or residency status is unknown, incomplete notification and, possibly, lack of requests by registry staff for further information are likely.

9.4.2 *Completeness of coverage*

Under-reporting must be suspected if rates for all cancers (skin cancer preferably excluded) are considerably lower than those reported from other, similar areas. Under-reporting is also probable if histological confirmation nears 100%, since in this case, there must be cases of cancer in the community which have not been reported. For cases first notified from death certificates, a figure of over 15% has arbitrarily been selected as indicating under-reporting. A very low number (e.g., under 1%) of cases known only from death certificates might mean that not all of the certificates with a diagnosis of cancer have reached the registry. It is axiomatic that if the number of deaths from cancer exceeds the number registered, then registration is incomplete, unless the incidence of cancer at that site is declining at a very rapid rate. This and other aspects of the reliability of registration are further discussed by Muir & Waterhouse (1976).

9.4.3 *Interpretation of differences in incidence rates*

The methods used for comparison of rates either in consecutive periods within one country (trends) or for the same period among various countries are:

(a) presentation of groups of 5- or 10-year age-specific rates;
(b) cumulative rates; or
(c) age-standardized rates.

Differences within one registration area should be accepted as meaningful only if the indices described above (9.4.1 and 9.4.2) have not changed; only then are tests of statistical significance likely to be meaningful.

9.4.4 *Mortality*

Mortality data can be presented and interpreted in the same way as incidence data. Since a cancer registry utilizes the best available diagnosis, using all the information that has reached the registry and reporting it only after a time lapse of about two years, their mortality data based on information in the registry will probably differ from official mortality statistics, which are based on death certificate diagnoses only (Steinitz & Costin, 1971).

9.4.5 *Survival*

Survival analysis of the type discussed in section 9.2 is only justified when there is active follow-up, with positive confirmation of the living status at a specified time for all those not reported as dead.   For hospital registries, the acceptable lower limit is 95% effective follow-up.

Many population-based registries have to accept data as it is notified routinely (e.g., re-hospitalization, repeat biopsies, deaths). Even if these are complemented by information from the population register, survival analysis may still be held to be unreliable. Registries may try to present the *fatality* ratio as an indication of survival, i.e., the ratio of new cases to reported deaths from the same diagnosis occurring within a specified period.   In this case, incidence and mortality do not refer to identical cases but only to identical diagnoses, and the ratio is an indirect description of the general survival experience.

9.5 *Requests for use of cancer registry data*

All cancer registries must seek ways and means of being involved in teaching and medical research activities.   This is absolutely necessary for ensuring continuing cooperation with the medical community, for acquainting newer generations of medical students with its activities in order to be recognized as being worthy of research grants.   Furthermore, the more the data are used and analysed, the better the quality of the data, because errors and inconsistencies are thereby brought to light and can be corrected.

10. DATA PROCESSING

10. DATA PROCESSING

10.1 *Overview*

Three main types of data-processing installations are used by cancer registries - manual, mechanical and electronic. Their features are summarized in Table 10.1. Although in theory the same operations can be carried out with all types of installations, in practical terms their potential increases with increasing complexity. The major differences between the three types are in the recording material, and these are related to their physical properties.

Table 1. Features of major types of data-processing systems

Feature	Data-processing system		
	Manual	Mechanical	Electronic computer
Recording material	Card	80-column punch card	80-column punch card, magnetic tape, or disc
Recording device	Writing or typewriter	Card-punching machine	Machine for punching or direct data entry
Number of variables	Limited to one card	Many, on linked cards	No practical limit
Sorting	Manual	Card sorter (machine)	Sorting programme
Merging	Manual	Card collator (machine)	Merging programme
Editing	Manual	Visual check of printed lists	Editing programme
Up-dating of file: cancellation amendment addition	Removal of card Replacement of card Additional writing	Removal of card Replacement of card Additional punching	Up-dating programme
Capital investment	Small	Moderate (for machinery)	Large (for computer and programmes)
Running cost per tumour	High (labour costs)	Moderate	Low
Necessary skills	Simple	Relatively simple	Sophisticated
Visual access to data	Easy	Possible	Indirect
Total volume of data	1000-3000 tumours	3000 tumours upwards	Up to several million tumours

In a *manual* operation, the major manipulations of data are carried
out by hand, using either plain or printed cards - the latter with or
without holes on each border.   In a *mechanical punch card* operation
sorting and collating are performed mechanically on 80-column cards
with perforations which serve as the means of storing the data;   while
in an *electronic computer* operation the major manipulations are performed electronically on data stored on 80-column cards, magnetic tapes or
discs.

It is advisable to start a cancer registry with a manual operation,
preferably with simple cards, for a short trial period.   This offers
an opportunity to get acquainted with the flow of information, the
availability of desired data, the necessary checking procedures and, no
less important, the pitfalls of cancer registration.   This experience
is invaluable in subsequent use of electronic data processing.   In
view of the continuing electronics revolution, the latter possibility
must be considered in the long-term plans of all registries.

The design of a record system for electro-mechanical or electronic
data processing requires expert advice before equipment is leased or
purchased.   To protect confidentiality identifying data such as name
must not be seen by unauthorized persons.   If card punching or direct
data entry to computer tape is done commercially, data must first be
coded on special forms.   Modern computers can now protect confidentiality more effectively than traditional record systems.

10.2 *Manual systems*

10.2.1 *Simple cards*

The simplest type of manual system consists of data written on
cards, which can be hand-sorted and counted to generate tables (see
section 9.2 and Fig. 9.3).   Such a system is useful in very small
registries and, possibly, in the initial phases of larger registries.
The main advantages are ready availability and low cost;   no specialized
material is needed.

10.2.2 *Margin punch cards*

The most successful device developed for hand-processing moderately
large amounts of data is the margin punch card (Fig. 4.1).   These have
long been used by departments of pathology to facilitate location of
previous diagnostic reports and to tabulate and correlate specific
diagnoses.   However, before investing in such a system a registry is
strongly advised to investigate the availability of newer methods.

Margin punch cards contain a series of holes punched in a uniform
fashion around the margin of the card (see Figs 4.1 and 11.1).   Coded
information is recorded on the card by opening selected holes towards
the margin of the card, using a hand or electrically operated punching
device.   Margin punched cards have one great advantage over all other
punching systems, in that they can serve as a clinical abstract form,

with observations and remarks added in plain language, so that they have an 'individual' appearance. Cards that have been punched at a certain position are separated from those not punched by passing a long needle through the specified hole in an aligned deck of cards, lifting and shaking gently. Cards that have not been punched will be lifted with the needle, while those that have will be left behind. With the use of two or more needles, combinations of properties can be selected simultaneously.

Punching. Each digit is recorded in a coded fashion by punching over one or two of four holes, labelled 1, 2, 4 and 7. The digits 1, 2, 4 and 7 are coded by a single punch over the corresponding holes, while the remaining digits require two punches over holes whose labels sum to the digit: $8 = 7 + 1$, $6 = 4 + 2$, $5 = 4 + 1$, $3 = 2 + 1$. It may be important to have a punched code for zero (e.g., $7 + 4$, which could not otherwise be used for recording the digits 0 to 9), since otherwise positive information cannot be distinguished from a blank, that is, no punches in a given field. The latter is reserved for missing information which may become available later.

On the WHO card (Fig. 4.1), 1, 2 or 3 holes are punched for month (in items 6, 12, 13, 25), e.g., $7 + 2 + 1$ for October; $7 + 4$ for November and $7 + 4 + 1$ for December. No punch for month means 'no information'.

Sorting. Sorting of margin punched cards for a given item involves sequential passes of the needle through specified holes on the cards. Cards that remain on the needle are placed in front of cards that remain behind after each pass. For example, to sort on a single digit one makes four successive passes through the holes labelled 1, 2, 4, 7, in that order. However, at the end of this operation, if the $7 + 4$ code is used for zero, the cards punched zero will be at the end of the deck following the '9's' and must be moved to the front. To sort on a multiple-digit code number, one first sorts the units, then the tens, etc.

After the cards have been sorted on a given item (or items), tabulations of the numbers of cards with each possible code (or combination of codes) are made by hand-counting. However, it is necessary to 'read' each of the cards in succession to determine when a new code starts. Alternatively, the cards may be separated into groups with unique codes and then counted, which eliminates the necessity of reading the cards. It is convenient to have a system of containers set up for this purpose. Complete separation of cards into ten piles corresponding to each of the digits coded as above requires nine passes.

Other operations. The other operations in a margin punch card installation are generally of a strictly clerical nature: typing, filing, merging, etc. (see Fig. 10.1). A desk calculator should be available for checking totals of tabulations and for performing statistical calculations.

10.3 *Mechanical punch card system*

Small registries will not be able to afford to have such a system in the registry but may have free access to one in a hospital or university. Commercial processing is also possible but is much more expensive and poses problems of confidentiality (see section 3.4). The great advantage of such systems is that the processing of data is simple, and there is direct access to the data. However, only the data in one 80-column card can conveniently be processed at one time; thus, if registry data for a case are contained on two or more cards, a single, combined card containing selected variables must be made prior to analysis. This requires special unit record processing equipment. With the continuing development of user-oriented computer programmes, the former advantages pertaining to punch card systems for small operations no longer exist; however, for routine processing and for the production of reports a mechanical punch card system is still useful, provided the registry does not have to rent and maintain equipment.

Even when electronic computer processing is used, many registries maintain punch cards and use a sorter for preliminary counts and checks.

10.3.1 *Punch cards*

For punch card installations, the ubiquitous 80-column punch card serves as the physical medium for storing each record. The columns of the card each have 12 separate punching positions: Y, X, 0, 1, 2, 3, 4, 5, 6, 7, 8, 9. Columns are grouped together into fields, each field containing the code for one variable in the record, e.g., two columns for age. Fields are generally one of two types: numeric and alpha-numeric. Numeric fields have only one hole in each column, corresponding to a digit from 0 to 9; for example, a 4-column field for the registration number 8642, located in columns 3-6 of the card, would have an 8 punch in column 3, a 6 punch in column 4, a 4 punch in column 5 and a 2 punch in column 6. Alpha-numeric fields may contain punches for either digits or alphabetical characters; the latter are coded by two punches per column, one in the positions Y, X or 0 and the second in positions 1 to 9. Thus, the letter A is represented by the combination of Y and 1, while the letter P is X and 8. To extend the number of codes per single column, some registries have used single punches in the X or Y positions. This allows 12 codes per column instead of 10. Such alpha-numeric, single-column fields can be converted to numeric fields by computer, prior to further data processing.

Other multiple punch coding schemes may be devised. For example, limited numbers of three punch codes are used in the computer industry to represent special characters. Special *ad hoc* coding is sometimes devised to increase the amount of numeric information stored in each column. However, this practice leads to undue complications in processing, especially when converting to a standard type of computer-based system, and is not recommended.

10.3.2 *Coding and punching*

Data are coded on the notification form or abstract itself or on
special code sheets.   The coded data must be in the same order as the
corresponding fields (groups of columns) on the 80-column cards.   They
are punched on a key-punch machine which has a typewriter-type keyboard.
Typists can quickly learn to use a key punch for routine punching.
On many key punches, special programme cards automatically control
selection of field type, duplication of certain fields from the
preceding card, skipping of fields and spacing.   It is important that
the key-punch machine be equipped with a printer, which interprets
(prints) the contents of each column along the top of the card as it is
being punched.   Punching is verified on a card verifier, preferably by
another operator, using exactly the same coded data as was used on the
key puncher.   Recently, a machine has been developed on which both
punching and verification can be carried out.   Cards that have fields
that do not match after two attempts are notched, as an indication that
they should be re-punched.   Because verification takes as much time
as the original punching, it is sometimes incorporated into a quality
control system whereby only a random sample of cards in each batch is
fully verified.   If too many cards in the sample show errors, the
entire batch is completely verified.   The Puerto Rico Cancer Registry,
for example, accepts a 2% error rate in all fields, except primary site
and sex.   More than 2% of errors in a sample, or any errors at all in
site or sex, leads to verification of the entire year's punching.

10.3.3 *Sorting*

The sorter has an input or feed magazine, a sensing station and
13 or 14 receiving magazines.   The latter correspond to the 12 punching
positions plus blank and/or inadmissable punches.   The holes in each
column are read by a sensor, and cards are deposited automatically in
the appropriate receiving magazine.   Control features include selection
of the column on which the card is to be sorted and selection of the
field type (numeric *versus* alpha-numeric, or 1 to 9 *versus* Y, X, 0).
Sorting on a numeric field requires one pass through the machine for
each column (digit).   Sorting on alpha-numeric characters requires two
passes per column (character).   If cards are to be sorted on a multi-
column numeric field, the first pass is made for the column corresponding to units, the second for the column for tens, etc.   Alphabetical
name fields are sorted in reverse order, starting with the column
corresponding to the last letter in the name.

If the sorter is also to be used for making tabulations, it is
virtually mandatory that it be equipped with a card counter, preferably
one that counts each numerical punch in a given column plus the total
cards.   Card sorters vary widely in their speed.   Machines currently
being produced are capable of processing from 600 to 3000 or more cards
per minute, but high-speed sorters are rapidly being replaced by
computers.

10.3.4 *Merging, editing and tabulating*

A *collator* is used in merging and up-dating operations, for example, to merge or match two decks of pre-sorted cards on specified fields.

A reproducing *gang punch* is used for duplication of entire decks of cards; such duplication may be necessary to replace badly stored or worn card files, or if the registry maintains multiple arrangements of the tumour file, e.g., primary site, patient registration number (Table 7.1). The information contained in the duplicated deck of cards is listed at the top of each card by passing them through an *interpreter*.

Listing machines are convenient for checking the content of card files; programmable models even allow follow-up request letters and other materials to be written automatically from special card files set up for this purpose.

Finally, printed tabulations and arithmetical sums can be obtained from a pre-sorted card file by use of a *tabulator*, also known as an *accounting machine*. These versatile machines are 'programmed' by means of wired control panels which may be removed and stored for periodic processing. They operate on several card fields simultaneously, counting the number of cards in specified categories, accumulating the contents of specified fields in designated registers, printing subtotals and even listing the contents of each card as it passes through the machine. Such machines are useful in editing data, since selected variables can be juxtaposed in lists.

10.4 *Electronic computer systems*

The use of electronic computers in processing data has many advantages; however, in the past there have also been many problems, chiefly in relation to the greater interest of manufacturers in selling the machines than in developing user-oriented programmes which would simplify use of the computers.

Small, moderately priced computers are now being marketed, so that electronic computing will be more widely available in the future. Some new registries can thus start with computers after an initial pilot phase to test the data input system. Since this is a rapidly changing field, potential users are advised to obtain advice from a number of sources and manufacturers.

Processing with computers is in principle the same as that with other systems, as illustrated in Table 10.1. The main differences are in capacity, speed and the type of access to the data. Special programmes are needed for editing, merging, cancellation, etc.

Matching of new material coming into the registry is best done manually when it involves the use of names, as variables are much more readily and economically appreciated by eye than by computer.

The patient index file system described in section 7.3 may be used; alternatively, the patient index file can be stored in a computer and printed lists produced frequently for visual matching.   Such lists can be ordered alphabetically and by site.   In very large registries, matching by computer may be unavoidable and can be done by name, date of birth and other axes.   As described under item 4, the spelling of names (often abbreviated) may be standardized by use of a special coding system.   Many registries have used a phonetic system called Soundex.

An example of the content of three 80-column punch cards similar to those used in the Israel Cancer Registry is shown in Figure 10.1.

FIG. 10.1   DEMONSTRATION OF THE LINKAGE OF THREE 80-COLUMN PUNCH CARDS ADAPTED FROM THE ISRAEL CANCER REGISTRY

		Index card		Tumour card (one or more)		Institution card (one or more)	
		col.		col.		col.	
Linking items[a]	(A) Patient registration number	1-5	(A)	1-5	(A)	1-5	(A)
	(B) First name	6-10	(B)	6-10	(B)	6-10	(B)
	(C) Soundex (family name)	11-16	(C)	11-16	(C)	11-16	(C)
Other items		17-79	Family name Father's name Sex Year of birth Identity number Place of birth Residence Topography (ICD) Date of death Place of death etc.	17-79	Incidence date (D) Topography Morphology Stage at time of diagnosis Most valid basis of diag- nosis First treatment Habits Other diseases Key institution Follow-up etc.	17-79	(E) Institution Date of admission Date of discharge Investigations Treatment Transfer Discharge
Card identification Col. 80 and command			code		code		code
		New card	1	New card	4	New card	7
		Change, add or delete (except A,B,C)	2	Change, add or delete (except A,B,C,D)	5	Change (except A,B,C,E)	8
		Cancel total record	3	Cancel	6	Cancel	9
		Change A,B,C (total record transferred)	0	Change D: cancel + new card			

[a] Items A, B and C appear on each card.

The minimum linking items consist of the patient registration number (columns 1-5) and card type (column 80).   These are sufficient to sort a given set of cards into order by patient registration number and card type.   The addition of first name (columns 6-10) and an abbreviated family name (columns 11-16) assists checking of data and reduces errors, e.g., due to duplicate registration of the same patient.   This example reflects data processing which was available in the 1960s', and might be modified if redesigned today.

11. CANCER REGISTRATION IN DEVELOPING COUNTRIES

11. CANCER REGISTRATION IN DEVELOPING COUNTRIES

11.1 *Cancer as a health problem in relation to other diseases*[1]

Cancer is a health problem in all countries and continents, although its priority rating varies.   However, even in those developing countries where its priority is rated low, there is evidence to indicate that with improvements in the control of communicable diseases and in environmental sanitation and concomitant increase in life expectancy and thus in the average age of the population, the proportion of deaths attributable to cancer has been increasing and will increase in the future.   Thus, cancer ranks as the first or second cause of death in persons aged 15-74 in many countries of Latin America (Puffer & Griffith, 1967).

With increasing industrialization, urbanization and intensification of agriculture in the course of development, developing countries are liable to be exposed to further risks of cancer.   It is therefore of the utmost importance that developing countries pay increasing attention to their present cancer problems and prepare themselves to meet the challenge of the future, through setting up appropriate cancer control programmes and through purposeful research.   In doing so, they should benefit by the lessons learnt by the developed countries in the course of their industrialization.

There is insufficient realization that cancer control activities are multi-disciplinary and holistic in nature.   For far too long cancer treatment has remained a purely clinical, hospital-based activity.   It is necessary to extend the concept to include prevention, early recognition, adequate diagnosis and treatment and follow-up and rehabilitation.   To do this effectively a suitable information system is needed.

11.2 *Population covered and types of registration*

In many developing countries there are fewer specialized medical services and fewer physicians than in more affluent countries.   Cancer is diagnosed mainly in major hospitals serving large populations, but these rarely see all cases of cancer, or even a representative sample of all cases due to a number of types of selective biases.   The ease of recognition of a cancer influences which types of cancer are seen in major hospitals: cancers in superficial organs are likely to be seen

---

[1] Section 11.1 is taken from the report of a workshop on "The role of cancer research in developing countries", IARC, Lyon, March 1978.

more frequently, e.g., cancers of the skin, oral cavity, breast and penis may be proportionately over-represented.   Cultural factors may influence diagnosis of cancer of the uterine cervix.

Cancer registration is initially limited to major hospitals and is often based in pathology or radiotherapy departments.   Such registries are similar to population-based registries, although they are limited to hospital patients: there is no systematic follow-up;   no systematic recording of type of treatment;   and most of the registered cancer cases can be related to the population of a defined geographic area so that so-called minimum incidence or reporting rates can be computed (Muir et al., 1971).

With more widespread development of health services, more cancer cases will be diagnosed outside the main hospitals, and coverage will become more comprehensive.   All medical sources must be used and there should be no limitation with regard to the basis of diagnosis (item 17) provided that this is stated and defined.   Since the proportion of cases confirmed by histology may be low, any limitation based on its absence increases the risk of bias.

11.3 *Simple cancer registration*

Cancer registration must be adapted to available resources, and registration that is too ambitious is unlikely to succeed and to be maintained.   External assistance has often led to the setting-up of sophisticated systems copied from affluent countries, which cannot be continued when the assistance ceases.   Much can be achieved with simple cancer registration, and the emphasis should be on the quality of a limited amount of information.

It is wrong to assume that complicated techniques are essential in cancer registration: what matters is the quality of information, the coverage and the adequacy of the reference population.   These are the factors that lead to the best possible estimates of incidence and these can be achieved by relatively simple schemes.

11.4 *Tumour record for a simple system*

The minimal data necessary for any cancer registry are discussed in section 4.2.   These are incorporated in the model record shown in Figure 11.1, which includes birthplace, date of death and months of survival in addition to the minimal data in Figure 4.1.   A *pro forma* standard margin punch card is shown in Figure 11.1.   Such a card may of course be adapted to local needs.   The item numbers are the same as those given in Chapter 4.   Information for all items must be written in the central part of the tumour record whether or not margin punches are used for analysis.   Where a margin punch card is used for analysis, it is not necessary to code and punch the following: the cancer registry, personal identity number, names, and complete dates of birth, incidence and death.   Chapter 4 should be referred to in relation to each item in Figure 11.1.

FIG. 11.1 MODEL TUMOUR RECORD
AND MARGIN PUNCH CARD FOR SIMPLE CANCER REGISTRATION

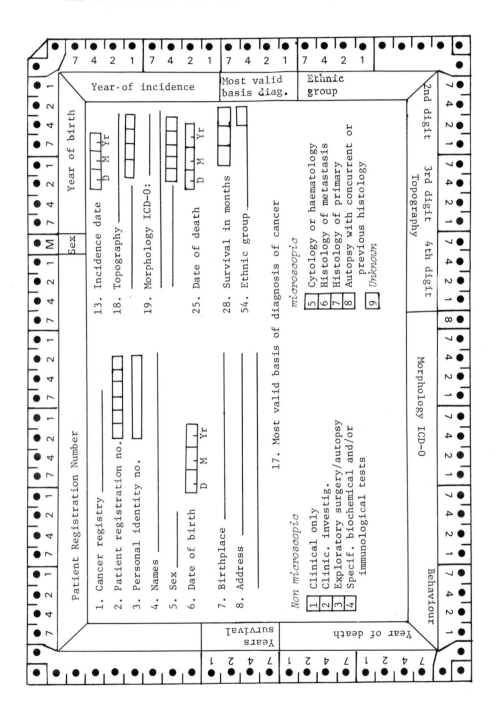

Cancer registry.   The name of the registry is recorded in words on the card but is not coded and punched for analysis by the registry (see Chap. 4, item 1).

Patient registration number.   Provision is made for punching the last two digits of the year, plus three digits.   The latter are less than the five illustrated in Chapter 4, item 2, since margin-punch cards will never be used for more than 999 patients per year.   This simple system can, of course, be expanded to any number of patient registrations per year, but more sophisticated data processing will be needed (see Chap. 10).

Personal identity number.   Many developing countries, e.g., Indonesia, have a system of national identity cards with unique personal numbers.   Use of these may be the only practical means of establishing the date of death since clinical follow-up is usually difficult and incomplete, and death certification may be unreliable.

Names.   All names must be recorded according to local practice (see Chap. 4, item 4).

Sex.   The sex is written in words.   For males, the hole is punched; for females it is left unpunched.   Females can thus be separated from males with a suitable long needle.   Alternatively, cards may be colour coded, e.g., males with white cards and females with coloured cards.

Date of birth.   Where full date of birth is not known, the year of birth corresponding to the approximate age is recorded.   Only year of birth is punched (see Chap. 4, item 6).

Place of birth.   Many developing countries have had large scale internal migrations from rural to urban areas.   Place of birth should be given in as much detail as possible, down to village (see Chap. 4, item 7).   If desired, place of birth may be coded and punched, using the spare holes in the margin of the card.   However, the three holes at each corner should be avoided if possible as corners tend to become bent with use.

Address.   This refers to the usual residence, and not to a temporary address (see Chap. 4, item 8).   As for place of birth, as much detail as possible should be recorded to avoid ambiguity.   In many countries the dialect spoken and distinct aspects of life style may be related to place of birth or to address, and in turn to differences in cancer risk.

As noted above, cancer registration is often restricted to large cities or the areas around them, since this is where the best medical facilities exist.   It is in the same places that jobs are available, attracting selected groups of the national population, mainly young males with or without their wives and children.   They may settle for weeks, months or years, perhaps even permanently.   Whether they are considered to be residents can only be defined in terms of duration;

the minimum time may be six or twelve months, for example. The
population figures provided by a census are heavily dependent on the
definition of residence, and cancer registries must use the same
criteria for cancer patients. This may imply laborious investigations of the residential history of persons with cancer, to which
physicians are unaccustomed. Nevertheless, the success of a cancer
registry – or, rather, the scientific validity of its data – will
depend upon the care with which an assistant clerk notes the residency
of patients. Errors in the accurate recording of residence may
result in dramatic overestimates of cancer incidence.

Demographers in census departments have considerable practical
knowledge in training persons who are not highly educated in obtaining
demographic data, such as residence, age, ethnic group, etc., and they
are often willing to run periodic courses to train hospital admission
clerks. Such a practice will ensure as much comparability as
possible between the numerator data from cancer cases and the denominator data from the census.

Incidence date. This item is defined in Chapter 4, item 13.
The year only is punched for analysis.

Topography. The anatomical site of the tumour must be recorded
on the card in words. In addition it should also be coded to a 4
digit code. The latter may be an ICD-9 code or an ICD-0 code, depending on local needs.

For cancer registration purposes, if the quality of the basic data
available to the cancer registry permits a detailed description of
topography and morphology for a sufficiently large proportion of cases
(say, 50 percent), it is recommended that the ICD-0 codes be used for
both topography and morphology.

If for other purposes, such as official reports, the registry is
required to report data according to the ICD-9, the written descriptions should be coded directly to ICD-9. Conversion from ICD-0 codes
to ICD-9 codes is difficult and is not recommended. In such circumstances, the ICD-9 code could also be written on the card in addition to
the ICD-0 codes.

For analysis by margin punch card, Figure 11.1 indicates that
only the 2nd, 3rd and 4th digits of the topography code need be
punched since the first digit is redundant for cancer data (it is not
used in analysis).

Morphology. This item should be recorded in words in as much
detail as possible. Provision is made for the ICD-0 coding of 5
digits, the 5th of which is a behaviour code which is used even if
other information on morphology is missing (see Chap. 8). The card
allows punching of the full 5 digit code. The first digit is an 8 or
9 – the hole is punched for an 8 and left unpunched for a 9.

Date of death and survival.   Direct follow-up of patients is
usually incomplete in developing countries.   Hence, date of death is
not available for many registered cancer patients, especially in
registries limited to hospital patients.   One of the most important
ways in which population-based registries in many developing countries
could meet the needs of clinicians would be by supplying information
on date of death, and thus on survival.   This is usually feasible
with comprehensive notification of deaths, although the identifying
information on a death certificate may be inadequate, e.g., incomplete
date of birth or address not adequately specific.   Where identity
cards are in use it may be possible to use the system to provide information on the occurrence of death (information on cause is not essential and may not be valid).

Where date of death is obtained, the complete date should be
written on the card.   Survival in months (item 28) is calculated and
recorded on the card.   Year of death and survival in years may be
punched and analysed when this information is available.   Up to 14
years of survival may be punched - for survival of 14 years and above
the code 14 may be used.

Ethnic group.   As much detail as available should be written on
the card (see Chap. 4, item 52 to 54).   A one digit field is shown
- this allows up to 14 codes to be punched.   The adjacent field may
be utilized also for larger classifications of ethnic group.

Most valid basis of diagnosis.   This item is precoded on the card,
and provision is made for punching on the margin.

Optional items.   Space is available on the card for punching a
limited number of optional items.   The choice will depend on local
needs.

11.5 *Input and output operations*

The procedures described in Chapters 7 and 9 are universal
and apply equally to developing countries.   Nevertheless some aspects
are more difficult, especially the detection of multiple registrations
of the same patient.   This is due to the frequent lack of precise
identifying information.   Since date of birth is often not available,
names, residence, ethnic group and site of cancer are used to detect
duplicates.   The search must be extended over several successive
years, since cancer cases with long survival may appear several times.
The high rates of cancers of the skin and of the uterine cervix
reported in some developing countries are in part due to repeated
inclusion of the same cases.   Such artificial inflation of incidence
rates may occur even with cancers for which a shorter survival has
been reported, and investigators should be aware of the danger.   Any
new case resembling a case already recorded should be suspected of
being a duplicate and all possible means of checking identity should
be used.   It is essential to use both a patient index file (section
7.3.2) and a tumour accession register (section 7.4.1) in all cancer
registries.

Manual data processing (section 10.2) can be used, at least initially. Simple printed cards based on Figure 11.1 can be used both as a written abstract of information and for hand sorting for tabulation of data (see section 9.2.2). Margin punch cards based on Figure 11.1 can also be printed, and, although more expensive, analysis is facilitated.

Initially, most registries produce relative frequency of cancer by sex and site. It is useful to keep lists of patient information as shown in Figure 11.2 which contain the minimal information described in section 4.2. Such lists can be general and for all sites, but other lists (at the three digit level) can be made separately for each cancer site. Using lists such as in Figure 11.2 it is relatively simple to count the number of male and female cases at each site (by ethnic group also if desired), and then calculate the relative frequency of cancer at each site. Similar analysis can also easily be done with margin punch (section 10.2) or simple cards (section 9.2.2).

It is easy to convert such manual systems to electro-mechanical or electronic data processing.

11.6 *Interpretation of results*

Any report of results should attempt to describe any bias which may be present, including the relative over-representation of certain sites. Sources of underestimation are numerous and can be evaluated on the basis of the number of hospitals, medical services and personnel serving the population-at-risk. A detailed description must always accompany the data published. Overestimates may result either from insufficient checking for duplicates, from the inclusion of prevalent cases, from the inclusion of non-residents or from an underestimation of the population-at-risk.

Conclusions can rarely be drawn from low incidence rates since there may be selective under-reporting. If sources of overestimation can reasonably be excluded, high rates suggest that the type of cancer being considered is in reality even more frequent, since these rates are likely to be minimum rates. Conclusions of this kind are of great value, since they may help discover the etiology.

11.7 *Conclusion*

Cancer registration is an arduous task in developing countries, due to shortages of medical facilities and personnel. The problems of identification of individuals, comprehensive case finding and definition of the reference population are most difficult to solve, and the risk of bias is always present.

It is wise to start simply. For some time results may be reported in the form of relative frequencies by sex (e.g., Menakanit et al., 1971) and ethnic group where relevant, rather than incidence rates,

FIG. 11.2 FORM FOR LISTING MINIMAL DATA

Registry ______________________________

City   Country

Date this page begun: ____________________

Patient Registration Number	Sex	Age	Place of birth	Residence	Ethnic group	Topography (ICD-O)	Morphology (ICD-O)	Most valid basis of diagnosis	Incidence date Mo Yr

even though external pressure may be exerted to do so.   Eventually, incidence rates will be reported with greater confidence.   At this stage, cancer registration in developing countries becomes much more rewarding; and this end justifies every effort to undertake the job, in spite of the difficulties.

POSTSCRIPT

In this monograph, we have tried to emphasize the need for cancer registration as part of an information system to help prevent and control cancer. We want to promote the setting up of new cancer registries in areas where there is not yet enough information, in order to learn more about malignancies and to initiate a concerted effort to improve the care of the cancer patient. For comparability, definitions and codes must be standardized; when other codes are used, they must be translatable to the agreed code.

We are aware that the proposed coding reflects current thinking about neoplasms, and future progress in understanding neoplastic diseases may lead to modifications. This has happened in the past; for instance, Hodgkin's disease was included among infectious diseases and was only later listed among malignant neoplasms.

The biggest developments in the future will be in the field of therapy, as new treatment procedures and schedules are tried out, and will thus mainly involve hospital registries.

REFERENCES

American Cancer Society (1964)   *The Hospital Cancer Registry, Definition, Purpose, Value, Operation and Cost*, New York, American Cancer Society, 142 p.

American College of Obstetricians and Gynecologists (1973) *Classification and Staging of Malignant Tumours of the Female Pelvis (Technical Bulletin, 23)*, Chicago

American College of Surgeons (1974a)   *Cancer Registry Manual*, Chicago, 64 p.

American College of Surgeons (1974b)   *Cancer Program Manual*, Chicago, 19 p.

American Joint Committee for Cancer Staging and End Results Reporting (1963)   *Reporting of Cancer Survival and End Results*, Chicago, American College of Surgeons

Armstrong, B., Stevens, N. & Doll, R. (1974)   Retrospective study of the association of use of *Rauwolfia* derivatives in English women. *Lancet, ii*, 672-675

Berkson, J. (1946)   Limitations of the application of fourfold table analysis to hospital data.   *Biom. Bull., 2*, 47-53

Bureau of Systems Development (1970)   *Name Search Technique, Project Search Special Report No. 1*, New York State Identification and Intelligence System, Albany, New York

Burnett, W.S. (1976)   *Introduction to New York State Cancer Registry.* In: Doll, R., Muir, C. & Waterhouse, J.A.H., eds, *Cancer Incidence in Five Continents*, Vol. III, Lyon, International Agency for Research on Cancer (*IARC Scientific Publications No. 15*), 584 p.

Carbone, P.P., Kaplan, H.S., Musshoff, K., Smithers, D.W. & Tubiana, M. (1971)   Report of the Committee on Hodgkin's Disease Staging Classification.   *Cancer Res., 31*, 1860-1861

College of American Pathologists (1965)   *Systematized Nomenclature of Pathology (SNOP)*, Chicago, 439 p.

Creech, J.L. (1974)   Angiosarcoma of the liver in the manufacture of polyvinyl chloride.   *J. occup. Med., 16*, 150-151

Davies, J.N.P. (1977)   *Spread and behaviour of cancer and staging.* In: Horton, J. & Hill, G.J., *Clinical Oncology*, Philadelphia, London, Toronto, W.B. Saunders Company, pp. 35-48

Day, N. (1976)   *A new measure of age standardized incidence, the cumulative rate.*   In: Waterhouse, J.W., Muir, C.S., Correa, P. & Powell, J., eds, *Cancer Incidence in Five Continents*, Vol. III, Lyon, International Agency for Research on Cancer (*IARC Scientific Publications No. 15*), pp. 443-445

De Jong, U.W., Day, N.E., Muir, C.S., Barclay, T.H.C., Bras, G., Foster, F.H., Jussawalla, D.J., Kurihara, M., Linder, G., Martinez, I., Payne, P.M., Pedersen, E., Ringertz, N. & Shanmugaratnam, T. (1972)   The distribution of cancer within the large bowel.   *Int. J. Cancer, 10*, 463-477

DOE (Department of Employment) (1972)   *Classification of Occupations and Directory of Occupational Titles*, Vol. 1, London, Her Majesty's Stationery Office, 206 p.

Doll, R. (1967)   *Prevention of Cancer. Pointers from Epidemiology*, London, Tonbridge, Whitefriars Press Ltd., 143 p.

Doll, R. (1972)   Cancer in five continents.   *Proc. R. Soc. Med., 65*, 49-55

Doll, R. (1976)   *Comparison between registries. Age standardized rates.*   In: Waterhouse, J.W., Muir, C., Correa, P. & Powell, J., eds, *Cancer Incidence in Five Continents*, Vol. III, Lyon, International Agency for Research on Cancer (*IARC Scientific Publications No. 15*), pp. 453-459

Dukes, C.E. & Bussey, H.J.R. (1958)   The spread of rectal cancer and its effect on prognosis.   *Brit. J. Cancer, 12*, 309-320

Finnish Cancer Registry (1976)   *Cancer Incidence in Finland 1973*, Helsinki, Cancer Society of Finland, 32 p.

Hakama, M. & Pukkala, E. (1977)   Selective screening for cervical cancer. Experience of the Finnish mass screening system.   *Br. J. prev. soc. Med., 31*, 238-244

Hamperl, H., ed. (1969)   *Illustrated Nomenclature of Cancer*, Berlin, New York, Springer

Harmer, M.H. (1972)   *TNM Classification of Malignant Tumours of Breast, Larynx, Stomach, Cervix uteri, Corpus uteri*, Geneva, UICC

Herbst, A.L., Robboy, S.J., Scully, R.E. & Paskanzer, D.C. (1974)   Clear-cell adenocarcinoma of the vagina and cervix in girls: an analysis of 170 registry cases.   *Am. J. Obstet. Gynecol., 119*, 713-724

Heyman, J. (1937)   *Annual Report on the Results of Radiotherapy in Cancer of the Uterine Cervix*, Geneva, League of Nations Health Organization

Higginson, J. & Oettlé, A.G. (1960)   Cancer incidence in the Banta and 'Cape Colored' races of South Africa. Report of a cancer survey in the Transvaal (1953-55).   *J. nat. Cancer Inst., 24*, 589-671

ILO (International Labour Organisation) (1968) *International Standard Classification of Occupations (ISCO)*, revised edition, Geneva

Ing, R, Ho, J.H.C. & Petrakis, N.L. (1977) Unilateral breast-feeding and breast cancer. *Lancet, ii*, 124-127

INSERM (Institut National de la Santé et de la Recherche Médicale Section Cancer) (1971) *Code Histologique des Tumeurs Humaines*, Paris, 138 p.

Jick, H. (1975) Reserpine and breast cancer. A perspective. *J. Am. med. Assoc., 233*, 396-397

Johannesson, G., Geirsson, G. & Day, N. (1978) The effect of mass-screening in Iceland 1965-74 on incidence and mortality of cervical carcinoma. *Int. J. Cancer, 21*, 432-437

Jussawalla, D.J. & Jain, D.K. (1976) *Cancer Incidence in Greater Bombay, 1970-1972*, Parel, Bombay, The Indian Cancer Society, 105 p.

Key, C.R. (1976) *Introduction to New Mexico Cancer Registry*. In: Waterhouse, J.W., Muir, C., Correa, P. & Powell, J., eds, *Cancer Incidence in Five Continents*, Vol. III, Lyon, International Agency for Research on Cancer (*IARC Scientific Publications No. 15*), pp. 443-445

Knowelden, J., Mork, T. & Phillips, A.J., eds (1970) *The Registry in Cancer Control*, Geneva, Union Internationale contre le Cancer (*UICC Technical Report Series No. 5*), 42 p.

Koszarowski, T., Kolodziejska, H., Gadomska, H., Staszewski, J., Wieczorkiewicz, A., Wronkowski, Z., Warda, B. & Karewicz, K. (1972) *Cancer Registry Report in Selected Areas of Poland, 1965-1972. Organisation of Cancer Control in Poland*, Warsaw, Polish Medical Publishers

Laszlo, J., Cox, E. & Angle, C. (1976) Special article on tumor registries. The hospital tumor registry. Present status and future prospects. *Cancer, 38*, 395-402

Menakanit, W., Muir, C.S. & Jain, D.K. (1971) Cancer in Chiang Mai, North Thailand. A relative frequency study. *Brit. J. Cancer, 25*, 225-236

Miller, A.B., ed. (1975) *Manual for Cancer Records Officers*, Toronto, National Cancer Institute of Canada

Modan, B., Baiolatz, D., Mart, H., Steinitz, R. & Levin, G. (1974) Radiation-induced head and neck tumours. *Lancet, i*, 277-279

Muir, C.S. & Waterhouse, J.A.H. (1976)   *Reliability of registration.*
    In: Waterhouse, J., Muir, C., Correa, P. & Powell, J., eds,
    Cancer Incidence in Five Continents, Vol. III, Lyon, International
    Agency for Research on Cancer (*IARC Scientific Publications No. 15*),
    pp. 45-51

Muir, C.S., Shanmugaratnam, K. & Tan, K.K. (1971)   Incidence rates
    for microscopically diagnosed cancer in the Singapore population
    1960-1964. *Singapore med. J., 12*, 323-332

Muir, C.S., MacLennan, R., Waterhouse, J.A.H. & Magnus, K. (1976)
    *Feasibility of monitoring populations to detect environmental
    carcinogens.*   In: Rosenfeld, C. & Davis, W., eds, *INSERM
    Symposia Series Vol. 52, IARC Scientific Publications No. 13,*
    pp. 279-294

NCI (National Cancer Institute) (1974)   *Selected Sections of 1967 End
    Results Group Code Manual Supplementing SEER Code Summary,*
    Bethesda, Md., 99 p.

NCI (National Cancer Institute) (1975a)   *Extent of Disease, Codes
    and Coding Instructions. Cancer Surveillance Epidemiology and End
    Results Reporting,* Bethesda, Md., 78 p.

NCI (National Cancer Institute) (1975b)   *Third National Cancer
    Survey: Incidence Data,* Bethesda, Md., US Department of Health,
    Education and Welfare (*DHEW Publication No. NIH 75-787),* 454 p.

Payne, P.M. (1973)   *Cancer Registration,* Belmont, Surrey, South
    Metropolitan Cancer Registry, 61 p.

Pedersen, E., Høgetveit, A.C. & Andersen, A. (1973)   Cancer of
    respiratory organs among workers at a nickel refinery in Norway.
    Int. J. Cancer, 12, 32-41

Percy, C.L., Berg, J.W. & Thomas, L.B., eds (1968)   *Manual of Tumor
    Nomenclature and Coding (MOTNAC),* New York, American Cancer
    Society, Inc., 74 p.

Puffer, R.R. & Griffith, G.W. (1967)   *Patterns of Urban Mortality.
    Report of the Inter-American Investigation of Mortality,*
    Washington, DC, Pan American Health Organization (*Scientific
    Publication No. 151),* 353 p.

Ringel, A. (1970)   *The Cancer Registry,* Rockville, Md., Bureau of
    Health Planning and Resources Development (HRA/DHEW), 45 p.

Shambaugh, E.M., ed. (1975)   *Self Instructional Manual for Tumor
    Registrars,* Bethesda, Md., US Department of Health, Education and
    Welfare, Public Health Service, National Institutes of Health
    (*DHEW Publication No. NIH 75-917),* 107 p.

Shanmugaratnam, K. & Wee, A. (1973) *'Dialect Group' variations in cancer incidence among Chinese in Singapore.* In: Doll, R. & Vodopija, I., eds, *Host Environment Interactions in the Etiology of Cancer in Man*, Lyon, International Agency for Research on Cancer (*IARC Scientific Publications No. 7*) pp. 67-82

Staszewski, J., Muir, C.S., Slomska, J. & Jain, D.K. (1970) Sources of demographic data in migrant groups for epidemiological studies of chronic diseases. *J. chron. Dis., 23*, 351-373

Steinitz, R. & Costin, C. (1971) Cancer mortality. Vital statistics *versus* cancer registry. *Isr. J. med. Sci., 7*, 1405-1412

Swedish Cancer Registry (1971) *Cancer Incidence in Sweden 1959-1965*, Stockholm, National Board of Health and Welfare, 197 p.

Tuyns, A.J. (1970) *Techniques of registration.* In: Doll, R., Muir, C. & Waterhouse, J.A.H., eds, *Cancer Incidence in Five Continents*, Vol. II, Berlin, Heidelberg, New York, Springer, 388 p.

UICC (International Union Against Cancer) (1962) *TNM Classification of Malignant Tumors*, Geneva

UICC (International Union Against Cancer) (1974) *TNM General Rules*, Geneva

United Nations (1968) *International Standard Industrial Classification of all Economic Activities (ISIC)*, New York

US Senate (1971) *Report of the National Panel of Consultants on the Conquest of Cancer*, Washington DC, US Government Printing Office (*Document No. 92-9*), 376 p.

Waterhouse, J., Muir, C.S., Correa, P. & Powell, J., eds (1976) *Cancer Incidence in Five Continents*, Vol. III, Lyon, International Agency for Research on Cancer (*IARC Scientific Publications No. 15*), 584 p.

WHO (World Health Organization) (1967-1978) *International Histopathological Classification of Tumors*, Series No. 1-20, Geneva

WHO (World Health Organization) (1973) *Application of the International Classification of Diseases to Dentistry and Stomatology (ICD-DA)*, Geneva, 114 p.

WHO (World Health Organization) (1975) *Official Record. Resolution of the World Health Assembly*, Geneva

WHO (World Health Organization) (1976a) *WHO Handbook for Standardized Cancer Registries*, Geneva (*WHO Offset Publication No. 25*), 94 p.

WHO (World Health Organization) (1976b) *International Classification of Diseases for Oncology (ICD-0)*, Geneva, 131 p.

WHO (World Health Organization) (1977) *Manual of the International Statistical Classification of Diseases, Injuries and Causes of Deaths (Based on the Recommendations of the Ninth Revision)*, Geneva, 773 p.

Wynder, E.L., Lemon, F.R. & Bross, I.J. (1959)   Cancer and coronary
    artery disease among Seventh-day Adventists.   *Cancer, 12,*
    1016-1028

APPENDIX

APPENDIX

1. United Nations Standard Country Code[1,2]

A numerical code designed for international use is given in
Annex 1 of this Appendix.   Each item of the code identifies a country
or territory of the world.   The basic numerical code consists of a
three-digit number which serves to identify each country or territory
uniquely.   These numbers have been obtained by arranging the countries
in alphabetical order, using their names in the English language, and
assigning a number following this order.   Intervals have been provided
in the numerical sequence to allow for future development and extension
of the list.   The countries included, and the form of the country
names used, are as specified in *Country Nomenclature for Statistical
Use, Rev. 7* (document of the Statistical Office of the United Nations),
updated to July 1969.

Basic unit of classification

The entities which have been coded in Annex 1 relate to the geographical area of the countries and territories.   These codes can
also be for nationality where appropriate, e.g., 250 France can also
indicate French nationality or 504 Morocco - Moroccan.

It is expected that, although this classification of countries and
territories is complete, there may be specialized entities which a
user of this scheme will need to identify.   Therefore, to meet this
requirement the codes from 900 to 999 have not been allocated, thus
reserving them for the user's own purposes.   In any transmission of
data using this coding scheme, a simple check for codes with a leading
9 would eliminate any non-standard code.

---

[1] Text adapted from Department of Economic and Social Affairs, Statistical Office of the United Nations, Statistical Papers, Series M
No. 49, United Nations, New York, 1970.

[2] The designations employed and the presentation of the material in
this publication do not imply the expression of any opinion whatso-
ever on the part of the Secretariat of the World Health Organization
concerning the legal status of any country, territory, city, or area
or of its activities, or concerning the delimitation of its frontiers
or boundaries.

ANNEX 1

United Nations Numerical Country Code
Three-digit code

000	Total	090	British Solomon Islands
004	Afghanistan	092	British Virgin Islands
008	Albania	096	Brunei
012	Algeria	100	Bulgaria
016	American Samoa	104	Burma
020	Andorra	108	Burundi
024	Angola	112	Byelorussian Soviet Socialist Republic
028	Antigua	116	Cambodia
032	Argentina	120	Cameroon
036	Australia	124	Canada
040	Austria	128	Canton and Enderbury Islands
044	Bahamas	132	Cape Verde Islands
048	Bahrain	136	Cayman Islands
052	Barbados	140	Central African Republic
056	Belgium	144	Ceylon
058	Belize	148	Chad
060	Bermuda	152	Chile
064	Bhutan	156	China (mainland)
068	Bolivia	158	China (Taiwan)
072	Botswana	162	Christmas Island (Aust.)
076	Brazil	166	Cocos (Keeling) Islands
080	British Antarctic Territory	170	Colombia
084	British Honduras	174	Comoro Islands
086	British Indian Ocean Territory	178	Congo (Brazzaville)

180	Congo (Democratic Republic of)	296	Gilbert and Ellice Islands
184	Cook Islands	300	Greece
188	Costa Rica	304	Greenland
192	Cuba	308	Grenada
196	Cyprus	312	Guadeloupe
200	Czechoslovakia	316	Guam
204	Dahomey	320	Guatemala
208	Denmark	324	Guinea
212	Dominica	326	Guinea-Bissau
214	Dominican Republic	328	Guyana
218	Ecuador	332	Haiti
222	El Salvador	336	Holy See
226	Equatorial Guinea	340	Honduras
230	Ethiopia	344	Hong Kong
234	Faeroe Islands	348	Hungary
238	Falkland Islands (Malvinas)	352	Iceland
242	Fiji	356	India
246	Finland	360	Indonesia
250	France	364	Iran
254	French Guiana	368	Iraq
258	French Polynesia	372	Ireland
260	French Southern and Antarctic Territories	376	Israel
		380	Italy
262	French Territory of the Afars and the Issas	384	Ivory Coast
		388	Jamaica
266	Gabon	392	Japan
270	Gambia	396	Johnston Island
274	Gaza Strip (Palestine)	400	Jordan
278	German Democratic Republic	404	Kenya
280	Germany, Federal Republic of	408	Korea, Democratic People's Republic of
282	German Democratic Republic, Berlin		
		410	Korea, Republic of
284	Germany, West Berlin	414	Kuwait
288	Ghana	418	Laos
292	Gibraltar		

422	Lebanon		548	New Hebrides
426	Lesotho		554	New Zealand
430	Liberia		558	Nicaragua
434	Libya		562	Niger
438	Liechtenstein		566	Nigeria
442	Luxembourg		570	Niue Island
446	Macau		574	Norfolk Island
450	Madagascar		578	Norway
454	Malawi		582	Pacific Islands (Trust Territory)
458	Malaysia		586	Pakistan
462	Maldives		590	Panama, excluding Canal Zone
466	Mali		592	Panama Canal Zone
470	Malta		596	Papua (now Papua New Guinea)
474	Martinique		600	Paraguay
478	Mauritania		604	Peru
480	Mauritius		608	Philippines
484	Mexico		612	Pitcairn Island
488	Midway Islands		616	Poland
492	Monaco		620	Portugal
496	Mongolia		624	Portuguese Guinea
500	Montserrat		626	Portuguese Timor
504	Morocco		630	Puerto Rico
508	Mozambique		634	Qatar
512	Muscat and Oman		638	Reunion
516	Namibia		642	Romania
520	Nauru		646	Rwanda
524	Nepal		650	Ryukyu Islands
528	Netherlands		654	St Helena
532	Netherlands Antilles		658	St Kitts-Nevis-Anguilla
536	Neutral Zone		662	St Lucia
540	New Caledonia		666	St Pierre and Miquelon
544	New Guinea (now Papua New Guinea)		670	St Vincent

674	San Marino	810	Union of Soviet Socialist Republics
678	Sao Tomé and Principe	818	United Arab Republic
682	Saudi Arabia	826	United Kingdom
686	Senegal	830	United Republic of Cameroon
690	Seychelles	834	United Republic of Tanzania
694	Sierra Leone	840	United States
698	Sikkim	850	United States Virgin Islands
702	Singapore	854	Upper Volta
706	Somalia	858	Uruguay
710	South Africa	862	Venezuela
716	Southern Rhodesia		Vietnam
720	Southern Yemen	866	Former Dem. Republic of Viet-Nam
724	Spain	868	Former Republic of South Viet-Nam
728	Spanish North Africa	872	Wake Island
732	Spanish Sahara	876	Wallis and Futuna Islands
736	Sudan	882	Western Samoa
740	Surinam	886	Yemen
744	Svalbard and Jan Mayen Islands	890	Yugoslavia
748	Swaziland	894	Zambia
752	Sweden	896	Areas not elsewhere specified
756	Switzerland	898	Not specified
760	Syria	900+	Special Codes for areas etc. required by user
764	Thailand		
768	Togo		
772	Tokelau Islands		
776	Tonga		
780	Trinidad and Tobago		
784	Trucial Oman		
788	Tunisia		
792	Turkey		
796	Turks and Caicos Islands		
800	Uganda		
804	Ukrainian Soviet Socialist Republic		

2. Editing for Consistency of Data Items[1]

Editing for consistency of data items can take place either before or after coding. The use of "intelligent" data entry terminals to edit data as they are keyed is becoming increasingly popular. This process allows the entry terminal to check data for legitimate codes and for consistency between fields as the data are entered. This has the additional advantage of allowing discrepancies to be checked prior to their being added to the permanent data base. The editing and consistency checking may also be done by the computer itself after all data have been entered. In addition the computer can also be used to check for consistency between incoming data and data previously reported to the central registry. Where discrepancies are noted, an error list can be created or algorithms can be established which will allow previously submitted data to be updated.

Since one of the most important functions of a central registry is the consolidation of information from a variety of sources for a given patient, every effort must be expended to ensure that the aggregated data are internally consistent. The following is devoted to a discussion of consistency checks between data items both within a single record and among multiple records submitted to the United States SEER Program. In brief the SEER Program in a consortium of 11 population-based central registries which report data in coded format to the U.S. National Cancer Institute on an annual basis. Since the NCI receives data in a coded format only, all errors uncovered must be referred to the individual registries for resolution. For each independent primary cancer one data record is submitted to the NCI. However, for persons having more than one independent primary cancer, the patient identification number is the same for each data record submitted; hence it is possible to check for consistency between records as well.

Below are listed 14 of the current inter-record edits which are currently being utilized. These edits should be useful to any registry since they pertain to data elements which most registries would ordinarily collect. In addition to the edits listed two new edits are being initiated to check for consistency between marital status and age at diagnosis (children under the age of 15 should be single) and between age at diagnosis and cancer site and type (certain malignancies do not occur in young children, retinoblastoma occurs exclusively in children).

---

[1] Adapted from J.L. Young, The role of a central cancer registry with emphasis on quality control. Presented at the IACR Meeting, Buenos Aires, Argentina, 4 October 1978. This Appendix illustrates one aspect of quality control in cancer registration. It is given as an example of what is done in one system.

SEER Inter-Field Edits

   (Field A in conjunction with Field B)

Field A Item Name[1]	Field B Item Name[1]	Editing Criteria
Type of reporting source (item 80)	Follow-up status (item 24)	If this is an autopsy or death certificate only case, then follow-up status must be dead
Type of reporting source (item 80)	Cause of death (item 26)	If this is an autopsy only or death certificate only case, then cause of death must be specified
Year of birth (item 6)	Age at incidence date (item 11)	Age must = calc. age or (calc. age - 1) where CALC. AGE = (1900 + incid. yr) - (X + birth yr). IF THIS CONDITION: Incid. yr = or > birth yr THEN CALC AGE = (1) 100 or greater if the person was born in the 1800's and 1800 is used for "X" in the calc age formula. However, then the Age field can only be 98; OR (2) the results of the calc age formula using 1900 for "X".

---

[1] Adapted to conform as far as feasible to item names in Chap. 4.

Field A Item Name	Field B Item Name	Editing Criteria

		IF THIS CONDITION:
		
		  Incid. yr < birth yr
		
		THEN CALC. AGE =
		
		  The results of the calc. age formula using 1800 for "X" because with this condition a person could only have been born in the 1800's.
		
		The results of this edit might uncover an error in the Incid. yr and not in the Age or Birth yr.

Year of Birth (item 6)	Incidence date (item 13)	Year of date of incidence must be = or > year of birth
Sex (item 5)	Primary site (item 18)	Site codes in the range 1740-1749 and 1790-1849 are invalid for males. Site code 1759 and codes in the range 1850-1879 are invalid for females.
Incidence date (item 13)	Date cancer directed therapy started	Incidence date must be = or < date therapy
Incidence date (item 13)	Date of last follow-up or death	Inc. date must be = or < date follow-up
Primary site (item 18)	Histologic type (item 19)	This edit is defined in the Site/Histology Validation Edit description.
Primary site (item 18)	Extent of Disease (items 21, 23, 58, 59)	This edit is performed according to the EOD code allowable for each site.
Histologic type (item 19)	Most valid basis of diagnosis (item 17)	If behaviour code is *in situ* then there must be a positive histology.

Field A Item Name	Field B Item Name	Editing Criteria
Histologic type (item 19)	Extent of disease (items 21, 23, 58, 59	If behaviour code is *in situ*, then extent of disease must be *in situ*.
Primary site (item 18)	Laterality (item 64)	The following ICD-O sites must have a valid laterality code

The following ICD-O sites:

1420 Parotid gland
1421 Submaxillary gland
1460 Tonsil
1462 Tonsillar pillars
1601 Eustachian tube, Middle ear
1602 Maxillary sinus
1604 Frontal sinus
1623 Lung, upper lobe
1624 Middle lobe
1625 Lung, lower lobe
1628 Lung
1629 Lung, NOS
1630-1639 Pleura
1740-1749 Female breast
1759 Male breast
1830 Ovary
1832 Fallopian tube
1860 Undesc. testis
1869 Testis
1875 Epididymis
1876 Spermatic cord
1878 Other male genital sites
1890 Kidney parenchyma
1892 Ureter
1900-1909 Eye
1940 Suprarenal gland
1941 Parathyroid gland
1945 Carotid body

Field A Item Name	Field B Item Name	Editing Criteria
Date cancer directed therapy started	First course of cancer directed therapy (items 65-69)	Date of therapy must contain a valid date if first course of therapy indicates therapy was performed

Field A Item Name	Field B Item Name	Editing Criteria
Follow-up status (item 24)	Cause of death (item 26)	If follow-up status = alive, then cause of death must = 0000; if follow-up status = dead, then cause of death must not = 0000.

SEER Site/Histology Validation Edit

When both the site and the histologic type (including behaviour code) are found to be valid, a site/type combination edit will be performed. This edit will not be performed if there is the code x in position y, indicating no histology.   The site/histology combination is edited in one of two ways:

1. *Site/Type Edit 1 - Histology (5 digits): Site*

The Morphology Section of the ICD-0 notes certain histologies that have specific sites assigned to them.   Those histologies that are SEER reportable are designated on the SEER Site-Specific Histology List.   This list is the reference for the first site/type edit.   The information is also included on the SEER Histology List.   Nonmelanotic skin sites are not included because they are not reportable.   Only the site-specific code of the first (preferred) term of each histology code in ICD-0 is used.

The first site/type edit involves checking the four digit histology plus the bahaviour code to see if it is site specific.   If so, the site is edited to see if it is the proper site.   If it is not the assigned site, a diagnostic message is generated.

2. *Site/Type Edit 2 - Site: Histology (3 digits)*

Cases which do not fall into the site specific histology category will go on to the second site/type edit which checks for allowable three digit histology codes for each site.   The Site/Histology Validation List designates each site and the three digit histology codes that are considered valid for each site.   This list frequently specifies ranges of site codes but only valid site codes within the range are applicable. Histology codes have had to be repeated in some cases in order to allow for computer processing of the data directly from the list.   The histology terms on the Site/Histology Validation List are not necessarily the first terms as specified in the ICD-0.   A diagnostic message will be generated for those cases for which the three digit histology code is not specified as valid for the site code.

In addition to the above edits, the following combinations are invalid:

1. An unknown site (1999) with a histology that has an
   in situ behaviour code.

2. Ill-defined sites (1950-1958) with histologies in
   the 872_/ - 879_/ range.

SEER Inter-Record Edits

Whenever a patient has more than one record on file, the following fields will be edited to ensure proper consistency between records:

Place of birth (item 7)
Must be equal on all records.

Year of birth (item 6)
Must be equal on all records.

Race (item 54)
Must be equal on all records.

Sex (item 5)
Must be equal on all records.

Sequence number

(1) When there is more than one record for a patient, no record may contain a zero in the sequence.

(2) There can be only one record with a "1" or a "2" in the sequence number.

(3) There cannot be a record with a "9" in the sequence number if there is another record(s) with a "1", "2" or "3" in the sequence number.

Date of follow-up
Must be equal on all records.

Follow-up status (item 24)

(1) If there is coded as being alive in any one record, the other records must contain the same code.

(2) If the code indicates that the patient is dead, the other records must contain the same code.

Site/Histology (items 18, 19)
Currently this edit will list for review all cases that have the same site code and three digit histology and are not paired organ sites.

Site/Type Edit 1 - Histology (5 digits): Site

SEER (ICD-0) Histology Validation List

Assigned site	Histology
	814-838 Adenocarcinomas
	8140/2 Adenocarcinoma-*in situ*
	8140/3 Adenocarcinoma, NOS
	8141/3 Scirrhous adenocarcinoma
151_[1]	8142/3 Linitis plastica
	8143/3 Superficial spreading adenoca.
151_	8144/3 Adenocarcinoma, intestinal type
151_	8145/3 Carcinoma, diffuse type
157_	8150/3 Islet cell carcinoma
157_	8151/3 Insulinoma, malignant
157_	8152/3 Glucagonoma, malignant
	8153/3 Gastrinoma, malignant
157_	8154/3 Mixed isl.cell & exocrine adenoca.
155_	8160/3 Cholangiocarcinoma
155_	8161/3 Bile duct cystadenocarcinoma
155_	8170/3 Hepatocellular carcinoma, NOS
155_	8180/3 Comb. hepatocel. carc. & cholangiocarc.
	8190/3 Trabecular adenocarcinoma
	8200/3 Adenoid cystic carcinoma, NOS
	8201/3 Cribriform carcinoma
	8210/3 Adenoca. in adenomatous polyp
	8211/3 Tubular adenocarcinoma
153_	8220/3 Adenoca. in adenoma. polyposis coli
	8230/3 Solid carcinoma, NOS
	8231/3 Carcinoma simplex
	8240/3 Carcinoid tumor, malignant
	8241/3 Carcinoid tumor, argentaffin, mal.
	8242/3 Carcin. tumor, non-argent., mal.
	8243/3 Mucocarcinoid tumor, malignant
	8244/3 Composite carcinoid
162_	8250/3 Bronchiolo-alveolar adenocarcinoma
	8251/3 Alveolar adenocarcinoma
	8260/3 Papillary adenocarcinoma, NOS
	8261/3 Adenocarcinoma in villous adenoma
	8262/3 Villous adenocarcinoma
1943	8270/3 Chromophobe carcinoma
1943	8280/3 Acidophil carcinoma
1943	8281/3 Mixed acidophil-basophil carcinoma
	8290/3 Oxyphilic adenocarcinoma

[1] The symbol _ equals any valid last, i.e., 4th digit.

Assigned site	Histology
1943	8300/3 Basophil carcinoma
	8310/3 Clear cell adenocarcinoma, NOS
1890	8312/3 Renal cell carcinoma
	8320/3 Granular cell carcinoma
1941	8322/3 Water-clear cell adenocarcinoma
	8323/3 Mixed cell adenocarcinoma
1939	8330/3 Follicular adenocarcinoma, NOS
1939	8331/3 Follicular adenoca. well diff.
1939	8332/3 Follicular adenoca. trabecular
1939	8340/3 Papillary & follicular adenoca.
1939	8350/3 Nonencapsulated sclerosing carc.
1940	8370/3 Adrenal cortical carcinoma
	8380/3 Endometrioid carcinoma
1830	8381/3 Endometrioid adenofibroma, mal.

SEER (ICD-O) Site-Specific Histology List

Assigned site	Histology
162_	8042/3 Oat cell carcinoma
180_	8076/2 Sq. cell carc.-*in situ*
180_	8076/3 Sq. cell carc., micro-invasive
187_	8080/2 Queyrat's erythroplasia
173_	8081/2 Bowen's disease
151_	8142/3 Linitis plastica
151_	8144/3 Adenocarcinoma, intestinal type
151_	8145/3 Carcinoma, diffuse type
157_	8150/3 Islet cell carcinoma
157_	8151/3 Insulinoma, malignant
157_	8152/3 Glucagonoma, malignant
157_	8154/3 Mixed isl.cell & exocrine adenoca.
155_	8160/3 Cholangiocarcinoma
155_	8161/3 Bile duct cystadenocarcinoma
155_	8170/3 Hepatocellular carcinoma, NOS
155_	8180/3 Comb. hepatocel. carc. & cholangiocarc.
153_	8220/3 Adenoca. in adenoma. polyposis coli
162_	8250/3 Bronchiolo-alveolar adenocarcinoma
1943	8270/3 Chromophobe carcinoma
1943	8280/3 Acidophil carcinoma
1943	8281/3 Mixed acidophil-basophil carcinoma
1943	8300/3 Basophil carcinoma
1890	8312/3 Renal cell carcinoma
1941	8322/3 Water-clear cell adenocarcinoma
1939	8330/3 Follicular adenocarcinoma, NOS
1939	8331/3 Follicular adenoca. well diff.
1939	8332/3 Follicular adenoca. trabecular
1939	8340/3 Papillary & follicular adenoca.
1939	8350/3 Nonencapsulated sclerosing carc.
1940	8370/3 Adrenal cortical carcinoma
1830	8381/3 Endometrioid adenofibroma, mal.
173_	8390/3 Skin appendage carcinoma
173_	8400/3 Sweat gland adenocarcinoma
173_	8410/3 Sebaceous adenocarcinoma
173_	8420/3 Ceruminous adenocarcinoma
1830	8441/3 Serous cystadenocarcinoma, NOS
1830	8450/3 Papillary cystadenocarcinoma, NOS
1830	8460/3 Papillary serous cystadenocarcinoma
1830	8461/3 Serous surface papillary carcinoma
1830	8470/3 Mucinous cystadenocarcinoma, NOS
1830	8471/3 Papillary mucinous cystadenoca.

Assigned site		Histology
174_	1759	8500/3 Infiltrating duct carcinoma
174⁻	1759	8501/2 Comedocarcinoma, non-infiltrating
174⁻	1759	8501/3 Comedocarcinoma, NOS
	174_	8502/3 Juvenile carcinoma of the breast
	1939̄	8511/3 Medullary carc. with amyloid stroma
	174_	8512/3 Medullary carc. with lymph. stroma
	174⁻	8520/2 Lobular carcinoma-*in situ*
	174⁻	8520/3 Lobular carcinoma, NOS
	174⁻	8530/3 Inflammatory carcinoma
	174⁻	8540/3 Paget's disease, mammary
	174⁻	8541/3 P. dis. & infil. duct carc., breast
	164̄0	8580/3 Thymoma, malignant
	1830	8600/3 Theca cell carcinoma

Site/Type Edit 2 - Site: Histology (3 digits)

SEER (ICD-O) Site/Histology Validation List

LIP	140.0 to 140.9	Neoplasm, malignant	800
		Carcinoma, NOS	801
		Carcinoma	802
		Spindle cell carcinoma	803
		Papillary carcinoma, NOS	805
		Squamous cell carcinoma, NOS	807
		Intraepidermal squamous cell carcinoma	808
		Adenocarcinoma, NOS	814
		Adenoid cystic carcinoma	820
		Papillary adenocarcinoma	826
		Sweat gland adenocarcinoma	840
		Mucoepidermoid neoplasm	843
		Papillary cystadenocarcinoma	845
		Mucinous adenocarcinoma	848
		Malignant melanoma	872
		Amelanotic melanoma	873
		Lentigo, malignant	874
		Spindle cell melanoma	877
		Blue nevus, malignant	878
		Fascial fibrosarcoma	881
		Fibrosarcoma, NOS	881
		Liposarcoma	885
		Embryonal	891
		Mixed tumor, malignant	894
		Carcinosarcoma	898
		Hemangiosarcoma	912
		Malignant lymphoma, NOS	959
		Lymphosarcoma, NOS	961
		Lymphocytic lymphosarcoma	962
		Lymphoblastic lymphosarcoma	963
		Reticulum cell sarcoma	964
		Plasma cell myeloma	973
TONGUE	141.0 to 141.9	Neoplasm, malignant	800
		Carcinoma, NOS	801
		Carcinoma	802
		Papillary carcinoma, NOS	805
		Squamous cell carcinoma, NOS	807
		Intraepidermal squamous cell carcinoma	808
		Transitional cell carcinoma NOS	812

TONGUE	141.0 to 141.9	Adenocarcinoma	814
		Adenoid cystic carcinoma	820
		Mucoepidermoid neoplasm	843
		Adenosquamous carcinoma	856
		Malignant melanoma	872
		Sarcoma, NOS	880
		Rhabdomyosarcoma, NOS	890
		Embryonal rhabdomyosarcoma	891
		Mixed tumor, malignant	894
		Hemangioendothelioma	913
		Kaposi's sarcoma	914

3. Topographical Terms with different Code Numbers in MOTNAC and ICD-0/ICD-9

Term	Code number	
	MOTNAC	ICD-0/ICD-9
Lingual tonsil	1465	141.6
Intestine, NOS	1539	159.0
Abdomen, NOS	1588	195.2
Mediastinum	1631	164.9
Intrathoracic site	1639	195.1
Heart	1715	164.1
Skin of scrotum	1735	187.7
Uterus, NOS	1829	179.9
Urachus	1898	188.7
Peripheral nerve	1924	171._
Sympathetic nervous system	1926	171._
Parasympathetic nervous system	1927	171._
Thymus	1942	164.0

For further information on conversion, contact:

Mrs Constance Percy
Landow Building Room B506
National Cancer Institute
7910 Woodmont Avenue
Bethesda, Maryland 20014
U.S.A.

INDEX

INDEX

PUBLICATIONS OF THE INTERNATIONAL AGENCY FOR RESEARCH ON CANCER

SCIENTIFIC PUBLICATIONS SERIES

IARC MONOGRAPHS ON THE EVALUATION OF THE CARCINOGENIC RISK OF CHEMICALS TO MAN

WHO/IARC publications may be obtained, direct or through booksellers, from:

ALGERIA : Société Nationale d'Edition et de Diffusion, 3 bd Zirout Youcef, ALGIERS

ARGENTINA : Carlos Hirsch SRL, Florida 165, Galerías Güemes, Escritorio 453/465, BUENOS AIRES

AUSTRALIA : *Mail Order Sales :* Australian Government Publishing Service Bookshops, P.O. Box 84, CANBERRA A.C.T. 2600 ; *or over the counter from* Australian Government Publications and Inquiry Centres *at :* 113–115 London Circuit, CANBERRA CITY A.C.T. 2600 ; Shop 42, The Valley Centre, BRISBANE, Queensland 4000 ; 347 Swanston Street, MELBOURNE VIC 3000 ; 309 Pitt Street, SYDNEY N.S.W. 2000 ; Mt Newman House, 200 St. George's Terrace, PERTH WA 6000 ; Industry House, 12 Pirie Street, ADELAIDE SA 5000 ; 156–162 Macquarie Street, HOBART TAS 7000 — Hunter Publications, 58A Gipps Street, COLLINGWOOD VIC 3066

AUSTRIA : Gerold & Co., Graben 31, 1011 VIENNA I

BANGLADESH : The WHO Programme Coordinator, G.P.O. Box 250, DACCA 5 — The Association of Voluntary Agencies, P.O. Box 5045, DACCA 5

BELGIUM : Office international de Librairie, 30 avenue Marnix, 1050 BRUSSELS — *Subscriptions to World Health only :* Jean de Lannoy, 202 avenue du Roi, 1060 BRUSSELS

BRAZIL : Biblioteca Regional de Medicina OMS/OPS, Unidade de Venda de Publicações, Caixa Postal 20.381, Vila Clementino, 04023 São PAULO, S.P.

BURMA : *see* India, WHO Regional Office

CANADA : *Single and bulk copies of individual publications (not subscriptions) :* Canadian Public Health Association, 1335 Carling Avenue, Suite 210, OTTAWA, Ont. K1Z 8N8. *Subscriptions : Subscription orders, accompanied by cheque made out to the* Royal Bank of Canada, OTTAWA, Account World Health Organization, *should be sent to the* World Health Organization, P.O. Box 1800, Postal Station B, OTTAWA, Ont. K1P 5R5. *Correspondence concerning subscriptions should be addressed to the* World Health Organization, Distribution and Sales, 1211 GENEVA 27, Switzerland.

CHINA : China National Publications Import Corporation, P.O. Box 88, PEKING

COLOMBIA : Distrilibros Ltd, Pío Alfonso García, Carrera 4a, Nos 36–119, CARTAGENA

CZECHOSLOVAKIA : Artia, Ve Smeckach 30, 111 27 PRAGUE 1

DENMARK : Ejnar Munksgaard, Ltd, Nørregade 6, 1164 COPENHAGEN K

ECUADOR : Librería Científica S.A., P.O. Box 362, Luque 223, GUAYAQUIL

EGYPT : Nabaa El Fikr Bookshop, 55 Saad Zaghloul Street, ALEXANDRIA

EL SALVADOR : Librería Estudiantil, Edificio Comercial B No 3, Avenida Libertad, SAN SALVADOR

FIJI : The WHO Programme Coordinator, P.O. Box 113, SUVA

FINLAND : Akateeminen Kirjakauppa, Keskustatu 2, 00101 HELSINKI 10

FRANCE : Librairie Arnette, 2 rue Casimir-Delavigne, 75006 PARIS

GERMAN DEMOCRATIC REPUBLIC : Buchhaus Leipzig, Postfach 140, 701 LEIPZIG

GERMANY, FEDERAL REPUBLIC OF : Govi-Verlag GmbH, Ginnheimerstrasse 20, Postfach 5360, 6236 ESCHBORN — W. E. Saarbach, Postfach 101610, Follerstrasse 2, 5 COLOGNE 1 — Alex. Horn, Spiegelgasse 9, Postfach 3340, 6200 WIESBADEN

GREECE : G. C. Eleftheroudakis S.A., Librairie internationale, rue Nikis 4, ATHENS (T. 126)

HAITI : Max Bouchereau, Librairie "A la Caravelle", Boîte postale 111-B, PORT-AU-PRINCE

HONG KONG : Hong Kong Government Information Services, Beaconsfield House, 6th Floor, Queen's Road, Central, VICTORIA

HUNGARY : Kultura, P.O.B. 149, BUDAPEST 62 — Akadémiai Könyvesbolt, Váci utca 22, BUDAPEST V

ICELAND : Snaebjörn Jonsson & Co., P.O. Box 1131, Hafnarstraeti 9, REYKJAVIK

INDIA : WHO Regional Office for South-East Asia, World Health House, Indraprastha Estate, Ring Road, NEW DELHI 110002 — Oxford Book & Stationery Co., Scindia House, NEW DELHI 110000 ; 17 Park Street, CALCUTTA 700016 (*Sub-Agent*)

INDONESIA : M/s Kalman Book Service Ltd, Jln. Cikini Raya No. 63, P.O. Box 3105/Jkt., JAKARTA

IRAN : Iranian Amalgamated Distribution Agency, 151 Khiaban Soraya, TEHERAN

IRAQ : Ministry of Information, National House for Publishing, Distributing and Advertising, BAGHDAD

IRELAND : The Stationery Office, DUBLIN 4

ISRAEL : Heiliger & Co., 3 Nathan Strauss Street, JERUSALEM

ITALY : Edizioni Minerva Medica, Corso Bramante 83–85, 10126 TURIN ; Via Lamarmora 3, 20100 MILAN

JAPAN : Maruzen Co. Ltd, P.O. Box 5050, TOKYO International 100–31

KOREA, REPUBLIC OF : The WHO Programme Coordinator, Central P.O. Box 540, SEOUL

KUWAIT : The Kuwait Bookshops Co. Ltd, Thunayan Al-Ghanem Bldg, P.O. Box 2942, KUWAIT

LAO PEOPLE'S DEMOCRATIC REPUBLIC : The WHO Programme Coordinator, P.O. Box 343, VIENTIANE

LEBANON : The Levant Distributors Co. S.A.R.L., Box 1181, Makdassi Street, Hanna Bldg, BEIRUT

LUXEMBOURG : Librairie du Centre, 49 bd Royal, LUXEMBOURG

MALAYSIA : The WHO Programme Coordinator, Room 1004, Fitzpatrick Building, Jalan Raja Chulan, KUALA LUMPUR 05–02 — Jubilee (Book) Store Ltd, 97 Jalan Tuanku Abdul Rahman, P.O. Box 629, KUALA LUMPUR 01–08 — Parry's Book Center, K. L. Hilton Hotel, Jln. Treacher, P.O. Box 960, KUALA LUMPUR

MEXICO : La Prensa Médica Mexicana, Ediciones Científicas, Paseo de las Facultades 26, Apt. Postal 20–413, MEXICO CITY 20, D.F.

MONGOLIA : *see* India, WHO Regional Office

MOROCCO : Editions La Porte, 281 avenue Mohammed V, RABAT

MOZAMBIQUE : INLD, Caixa Postal 4030, MAPUTO

NEPAL : *see* India, WHO Regional Office

NETHERLANDS : N. V. Martinus Nijhoff's Boekhandel en Uitgevers Maatschappij, Lange Voorhout 9, THE HAGUE 2000

NEW ZEALAND : Government Printing Office, Mulgrave Street, Private Bag, WELLINGTON 1, *Government Bookshops at :* Rutland Street, P.O. Box 5344, AUCKLAND ; 130 Oxford Terrace, P.O. Box 1721, CHRISTCHURCH ; Alma Street, P.O. Box 857, HAMILTON ; Princes Street, P.O. Box 1104, DUNEDIN — R. Hill & Son, Ltd, Ideal House, Cnr Gillies Avenue & Eden St., Newmarket, AUCKLAND 1

NIGERIA : University Bookshop Nigeria Ltd, University of Ibadan, IBADAN — G. O. Odatuwa Publishers & Booksellers Co., 9 Hausa Road, SAPELE, BENDEL STATE

NORWAY : Johan Grundt Tanum Bokhandel, Karl Johansgt. 43, 1010 OSLO 1

PAKISTAN : Mirza Book Agency, 65 Shahrah–E–Quaid–E–Azam, P.O. Box 729, LAHORE 3

PAPUA NEW GUINEA : WHO Programme Coordinator, P.O. Box 5896, BOROKO

PHILIPPINES : World Health Organization, Regional Office for the Western Pacific, P.O. Box 2932, MANILA — The Modern Book Company Inc., P.O. Box 632, 926 Rizal Avenue, MANILA

POLAND : Składnica Ksiegarska, ul Mazowiecka 9, 00052 WARSAW (*except periodicals*) — BKWZ Ruch, ul Wronia 23, 00840 WARSAW (*periodicals only*)

PORTUGAL : Livraria Rodrigues, 186 Rua do Ouro, LISBON 2

SIERRA LEONE : Njala University College Bookshop (University of Sierra Leone), Private Mail Bag, FREETOWN

SINGAPORE : The WHO Programme Coordinator, 144 Moulmein Road, G.P.O. Box 3457, SINGAPORE 1 — Select Books (Pte) Ltd, 215 Tanglin Shopping Centre, 2/F, 19 Tanglin Road, SINGAPORE 10

SOUTH AFRICA : Van Schaik's Bookstore (Pty) Ltd, P.O. Box 724, 268 Church Street, PRETORIA 0001

SPAIN : Comercial Atheneum S.A., Consejo de Ciento 130–136, BARCELONA 15 ; General Moscardó 29, MADRID 20 — Librería Díaz de Santos, Lagasca 95, MADRID 6 ; Balmes 417 y 419, BARCELONA 6

SRI LANKA : *see* India, WHO Regional Office

SWEDEN : Aktiebolaget C. E. Fritzes Kungl. Hovbokhandel, Regeringsgatan 12, 103 27 STOCKHOLM

SWITZERLAND : Medizinischer Verlag Hans Huber, Länggass Strasse 76, 3012 BERNE 9

SYRIAN ARAB REPUBLIC : M. Farras Kekhia, P.O. Box No. 5221, ALEPPO

THAILAND : *see* India, WHO Regional Office

TUNISIA : Société Tunisienne de Diffusion, 5 avenue de Carthage, TUNIS

TURKEY : Haset Kitapevi, 469 Istiklal Caddesi, Beyoglu, ISTANBUL

UNITED KINGDOM : H. M. Stationery Office : 49 High Holborn, LONDON WC1V 6HB ; 13a Castle Street, EDINBURGH EH2 3AR ; 41 The Hayes, CARDIFF CF1 1JW ; 80 Chichester Street, BELFAST BT1 4JY ; Brazennose Street, MANCHESTER M60 8AS ; 258 Broad Street, BIRMINGHAM B1 2HE ; Southey House, Wine Street, BRISTOL BS1 2BQ. *All mail orders should be sent to* P.O. Box 569, LONDON SE1 9NH

UNITED STATES OF AMERICA : *Single and bulk copies of individual publications (not subscriptions) :* WHO Publications Centre USA, 49 Sheridan Avenue, ALBANY, NY 12210. *Subscriptions : Subscription orders, accompanied by check made out to the* Chemical Bank, New York, Account World Health Organization, *should be sent to the* World Health Organization, P.O. Box 5284, Church Street Station, NEW YORK, NY 10249. *Correspondence concerning subscriptions should be addressed to the* World Health Organization, Distribution and Sales, 1211 GENEVA 27, Switzerland. *Publications are also available from the* United Nations Bookshop, NEW YORK, NY 10017 (*retail only*), *and single and bulk copies of individual* International Agency for Research on Cancer *publications (not subscriptions) may also be ordered from the* Franklin Institute Press, Benjamin Franklin Parkway, Philadelphia, PA 19103

USSR : *For readers in the USSR requiring Russian editions :* Komsomolskij prospekt 18, Medicinskaja Kniga, MOSCOW — *For readers outside the USSR requiring Russian editions :* Kuzneckij most 18, Meždunarodnaja Kniga, MOSCOW G-200

VENEZUELA : Editorial Interamericana de Venezuela C.A., Apartado 50785, CARACAS 105 — Librería del Este, Apartado 60337, CARACAS 106

YUGOSLAVIA : Jugoslovenska Knjiga, Terazije 27/II, 11000 BELGRADE

ZAIRE : Librairie universitaire, avenue de la Paix Nº 167, B.P. 1682, KINSHASA I

Special terms for developing countries are obtainable on application to the WHO Programme Coordinators or WHO Regional Offices listed above or to the World Health Organization, Distribution and Sales Service, 1211 Geneva 27, Switzerland. Orders from countries where sales agents have not yet been appointed may also be sent to the Geneva address, but must be paid for in pounds sterling, US dollars, or Swiss francs.

Price: Sw. fr. 40.—   US $ 25.00   Prices are subject to change without notice.   IARC/2/78